GUIDE TO

FASHION

ENTREPRENEURSHIP

THE **PLAN**, THE **PRODUCT**, THE **PROCESS**

Fairchild
Books

GUIDE TO
FASHION
ENTREPRENEURSHIP
THE **PLAN**, THE **PRODUCT**, THE **PROCESS**

MELISSA G. CARR
Dominican University
River Forest, Illinois

LISA HOPKINS NEWELL
Columbia College Chicago
Chicago, Illinois

Dominican University
River Forest, Illinois

FAIRCHILD BOOKS / NEW YORK

Fairchild Books
An imprint of Bloomsbury Publishing Inc.

1385 Broadway
New York
NY 10018
USA

50 Bedford Square
London
WC1B 3DP
UK

www.fairchildbooks.com

First published 2014

© Bloomsbury Publishing Inc., 2014

Library of Congress Cataloging-in-Publication Data
A catalog record for this book is available from the Library of Congress
2013954133

ISBN: PB: 978-1-60901-493-3

Typeset by Precision Graphic Services, Inc.
Cover Design by Simon Levy Associates
Text design by Alicia Freile, Tango Media
Printed and bound in China

Table of Contents

Extended Table of Contents

Preface

In this age of progressive entrepreneurism, *Guide to Fashion Entrepreneurship: The Plan, the Product, the Process* is a comprehensive step-by-step entrepreneurial action plan that examines how fashion industry product concepts are created, branded, marketed, channeled, and merchandised to the consumer. Fashion entrepreneurship is a magnanimous and multifaceted journey that's often steeped in ambition, authenticity, ingenuity, and an unyielding passion to audaciously create from one's own vantage point. It is often perceived as complex, personal, imperfect, and experimental; however, it holds a powerful dynamism that can shift a perspective, ignite a movement, or inspire a mood that builds an emerging brand into a lifestyle-driven, profitable business. Fashion business students, fashion design students, and aspiring fashion industry professionals are empowered with tools to successfully identify market opportunities, execute product differentiation, and market a new brand or brand extension in the multichannel retail environment.

Organization

The step-by-step chapter format unveils a comprehensive action plan. The text is divided into four sequential parts—The Plan, The Product, The Partner, and The Process. Each chapter progressively examines how the various fashion industry segments are planned and developed. The text delves into the interrelationship of allied industries with perspectives on consumer and market research, brand development, product development, sourcing, multichannel distribution, marketing and business plans, and strategic growth.

Part I. THE PLAN

The Plan (Chapters 1, 2, and 3) sets the foundation of the text by exploring the creative entrepreneur. Entrepreneurs are vital contributors in all segments of the fashion industry. Increasingly, many professionals are choosing entrepreneurship to express their creative voice. The text explains how creating a business and developing the business's short-term purpose and long-term goals are important tools to create powerful brand statements that reflect the epicenter of the company's positioning. By analyzing and conducting market research, a company can better identify which consumer groups will purchase its product or service. As an entrepreneur it is imperative to conduct consumer research that effectively establishes the brand's target market. This key piece of information can help drive the plan for product development and brand extensions. To cut through the clutter of product saturation, entrepreneurs utilize branding as an effective way to differentiate their products and to establish credibility with the consumer. One must carefully orchestrate interplay between inspired creativity and analytical rigor. Creating a brand perception requires intrusion—a remapping of a consumer's brand preference.

Part II. THE PRODUCT

The Product (Chapters 4, 5, 6, and 7) sets the platform for successful entrepreneurs to develop new products and product extensions that embody the company's mission, vision, and brand positioning. New products are often the acute response to market opportunities. The text expounds upon the necessity for the target consumer to remain at the crux of an entrepreneur's passion to create products that are relevant and timely for the brand. The text posits, if new products are on the cusp of the market trend or market sensitive, will consumers flee their existing brand preference for new options? Furthermore, the text sets the foundation for strategic sourcing and the steps involved in the production process with domestic contractors or offshore contractors. An emphasis is placed on the strategic and operational elements of establishing and maintaining domestic supply chains. Entrepreneurs can have a viable product, but unless it is priced to yield a profit the outcome can be detrimental to the company. Lastly, the text expounds upon developing a solid pricing strategy as critical for an entrepreneur to start and stay in business. Having a comprehensive understanding of the pricing components will enable an entrepreneur to set margins that yield profitability. Establishing the cost, the wholesale price, and manufacturer suggested retail price are fundamental for market penetration.

Part III. THE PARTNER

The Partner (Chapters 8, 9, 10, and 11) examines the entrepreneur's distribution strategy. Entrepreneurs must have astute business acumen in the industry sector of their product. As with most endeavors, the success or failure of a new product launch is often directly tied to the planning process. Distribution encompasses all the physical activities necessary to make a product or service available to the target customers when and where they need it. The distribution strategies and channels that an entrepreneur chooses should match the characteristics of their product or service. Strategies are a curious mixture of fact and insight, knowledge, experience, and creativity. In today's complex multinational organizations, strategy development draws on the skills of management from across the company and in all functional areas. The text discusses the go-to-market distribution strategy. For optimal market exposure, multichannel distribution is often used to establish and sustain high sales performance. Understanding what the buyer is seeking and how to get the product in front of them will assist in launching a successful brand in stores and online. The text taps into the World Wide Web. Online distribution explores the analytics, online sales applications, and ways to persuasively market product to induce sales through search engine optimization. Furthermore, this part of the textbook explores social media and blogging as avenues to get started in the online world.

Part IV. THE PROCESS

The Process (Chapter 12, 13, 14, and 15) ensures the entrepreneur's overall readiness. An entrepreneur can readily engage the marketing environment with a well-defined plan. A marketing plan introduces the company, identifies the goals, explores the marketing strategies and tactics, and finishes with a budget and defined timeline for execution. The marketing plan must reinforce the branding strategy and distribution plan. In totality, it is the communication conduit. Entrepreneurs also need a business plan as a fundamental guide to drive their business. A well-devised business plan informs an entrepreneur's decision-making ability at the crux of an opportunity or challenge. The text examines the basics of establishing a business entity and how to set up basic accounting practices. It explores the fundamentals of labeling requirements for products and what components of a product can be protected—from brand name to tagline. *Strategic Growth* explores the dynamic of timing—knowing when to expand or exit the business. Entrepreneurs also will learn about exit strategies that yield accelerated growth for the brand.

Text Features

Guide to Fashion Entrepreneurship: The Plan, the Product, the Process follows the assumption and perspective of a multifaceted entrepreneur who will independently execute task or work with a small team. Each chapter has engaging features that reinforce entrepreneurial concepts into a plan of action tailored to identify market trends, develop innovative concepts, and develop product assortment plans, sourcing strategies, distribution plans, sales projections, and promotional plans.

- *Examples* are featured throughout the text. For continuity and elaboration, the authors have intentionally utilized specific companies such as the technical athletic apparel company **lululemon athletica,** and the holistic beauty company **dirt (Erthe Beaute LLC)** to reinforce the progressive unfolding of various entrepreneurial concepts.
- *Create-A-Minute Tip* boxes are reflective sidebar captions to highlight and reiterate points in the chapters. This character sketch is highlighted in each chapter. Her notes are informative, conscientious inquiries and tips that reinforce key points to know and refer to.
- *Case Studies* exemplify relevant industry matters that relate to the content of each chapter.
- *Activities* are application simulations to culminate into an entrepreneurial action plan.
- *Key Concepts, Summary, Trade Terms,* and *Online Resources* appear in each chapter.
- The *Glossary* contains defined industry terms that are bolded in the text and listed as "Trade Terms" at the end of each chapter.
- **Instructor's Resources/Instructor's Guide with Test Bank** provides suggestions for planning the course and using the text in the classroom, supplemental assignments, and sample exams with multiple choice and True/False questions.
- *PowerPoint® presentation* provides a framework for lecture and discussions.

Acknowledgments

We wish to thank former executive editor Olga Kontzias, for embracing our prospectus. Our sincerest appreciation to Julie Vitale, who generously elevated our manuscript with her insights and editing contribution that steered it to completion. We express gratitude to our fellow fashion entrepreneurs who inspired this work, and the peer reviewers who ensured it was relevant (Joseph Hancock, Drexel University; Derek W. Cockle, LIM College; Scarlett Wesley, University of Kentucky; Mary Mhango, Marshall University; Diane Ellis, Meredith College; Soo H. Kim, Savannah College of Art and Design; Dhona Spacinsky, Academy of Couture Art; Luanne K. Mayorga, College of Dupage; Leo Z. Archambault, Mount Ida College). With the highest regard, we wish to thank the myriad of editors, art directors, and associates at Fairchild Books and Bloomsbury Publishing, including: Joseph Miranda, Development Manager; Amanda Breccia, Acquisitions Editor; Edie Weinberg, Art Development Editor; Eleanor Rose, Designer; Charlotte Frost, Production Editor; and Priscilla McGeehon, Publisher, Fairchild Books. We thank you for welcoming us to join your esteemed enclave of authors.

Melissa G. Carr

As with any worthwhile pursuit, this book would not be possible without the support and encouragement of my fellow colleagues at Dominican and throughout the fashion community. In particular I would like to thank Tracy Jennings for all her time and wisdom. Also, a note of gratitude to my students at Dominican University who give me inspiration and joy in what I do.

Writing this book has been a collaborative effort and a joint enterprise. The tireless commitment of my co-author, Lisa Hopkins Newell, to this project and to thoughtful communication and feedback have made the many months leading up to the publishing of this book an enriching experience I will treasure. May her collegiality continue to inspire her students.

This book is dedicated to my husband, Bob Carr. Thank you for always standing by my side as I pursue various ventures. You continue to be my inspiration and motivation. I know I can always count on you to make me laugh along with our dear friends Craig, Vera, and Tony when it is much needed. Ava, your confidence, beauty, and strength are what give me the courage to purse my dreams. Ryan, your energy, determination, smile, and laugh are contagious and give me the strength to continue when I most needed it. To my mother and father, Frank and Sonia Fernandez, who supported me throughout this process and as well as my career. Thank you for all the wisdom, love, and support you've given me. You are my #1 fans and for that I am eternally grateful.

Lisa Hopkins Newell

The proficiency to convert twenty-six alphabetical letters into words that connect, communicate, challenge, convey, and possibly change a mind is a gift that I thank God for bestowing. This endeavor is dedicated to my incredible family. Thank you for blessing me with your spiritual insight, love, and support. You are my think tank, safe space, and village who unceasingly enrich my life journey.

To my beautiful daughters, Madison Ilise and Kirstin Alivia, thank you for relentlessly allowing me to pursue a plethora of projects and creative endeavors amongst motherhood. Madi, your confidence, grace, and intelligence will enable you to walk on water—no life vest needed. Kiri, your radiance, creative genius, and photographic eye is a heavenly gift—no one sees what you can, keep "shooting" to the top. My parents, Georgette and Allen Hopkins, thank you for planting an invincible seed through your entrepreneurial hustle that's created a generational harvest. Sharon Hopkins Jones, thank you for being my right, rational, and "inappropriate" mind at all times. Mark A. Hopkins, thank you for wisdom, piercing logic, and your incessant laugh. Élan Jones, your cross-country running has taught me that pace is everything. Landon Jones, your thespian talent confirms your impeccable character. To my friends and the "lovelies," thank you for supporting the essence of my being with your friendship.

Professional collaboration is only as brilliant as its parts. To my co-author, Melissa G. Carr, thank you for unyielding commitment, drive, and foresight to bring this project to fruition. It's been a pleasure to blend our thoughts, words, and energy into published work. To Dianne Erpenbach, thank you for launching my career in academia. Thank you to Debbie Elmore, who inspired and ignited my "powerhouse" drive in the fashion industry. Thank you to Cheryl Mayberry McKissack for your life-coach dynamism and for launching my publishing career. To my entrepreneurial partners—Audria Green, Ginger Pasch, Grace Marsh, and Annabel Carrillo—and my host of interns, thank you for digging dirt with me.

To my Columbia College Chicago and Dominican University colleagues, you're the best. To Dana Connell, thank you for your mentorship and candy breaks. To Jerry Svec, I appreciate your tutelage in Fashion Product—you are brilliant. To Ken Walters, thank you for pushing the Merchandising course to new heights. To my students—past, present, and future—you inspire me as a lifelong learner in the laboratory of life. To my fashion mentees and creative protégés—your difference is your absolute genius. Love Only.

Cover Image Credits

Top left: Giuseppe Zanotti shoes, courtesy of Fairchild Fashion Media
Top right: Vera Wang, courtesy of Fairchild Fashion Media
Center right: Maiyet gold ring, courtesy of Fairchild Fashion Media
Bottom left: Kelly Wearstler with model, courtesy of Fairchild Fashion Media
Bottom center: Louis Vuitton handbag, courtesy of Fairchild Fashion Media
Bottom right: Jason Wu, courtesy of Fairchild Fashion Media

PART I
THE PLAN

Fashion entrepreneurs are the human catalysts that undergird, shift, and propel the revered world of fashion. Beneath the surface of every successful globally recognized designer eponymous brand or manufacturer is an entrepreneur or team of entrepreneurs who realized a void, found a niche, and devised a plan to execute their creative strokes of genius. Success must be planned, orchestrated, and manipulated from the onset. Creating a brand and launching a product is one of the most defining moments in a fashion entrepreneur's career. The elation and anticipation of product readiness, reaction, and results quickly can turn into anxiety if one lacks foresight and preparedness.

As with most endeavors, the success or failure of a new product launch often is directly tied to the planning process. Textile producers, retailers, consumers, media, and a multitude of other primary, secondary, retail, and auxiliary-level industry segments rely upon our ability to converge ingenuity and tangibility in a way that gains loyalty with the consumer at large. We are the trigger for what is new and next in an industry that demands innovation at every price point. Fashion entrepreneurs are the creative conduit for products and services that fulfill needs and stimulate wants, but the overarching goal is to yield sales and profit. In this ever-evolving industry, we sit at the helm of creativity yet at the feet of our consumers. This power surge and struggle only can be harnessed into harmony with a solid plan of action that we have explored in the opening chapters—THE PLAN.

1

Entrepreneur Endeavors

Entrepreneurs are vital contributors in all segments of the fashion industry. Increasingly, many professionals are choosing entrepreneurship to express their creative voice. An ever-changing economy has sparked a renewed interest in developing and creating products and services. Product diversification has become steadily embraced by consumers. This grants an opportunity for the creative expression of entrepreneurs in the marketplace. As a burgeoning entrepreneur with a new venture, identifying one's strengths and weaknesses as a founder and manager is critical for success. Furthermore, developing the business's short-term purpose and long-term goals are important tools in creating powerful statements that reflect the epicenter of the company's positioning.

The Entrepreneur

The success of the fashion industry depends on the creative force of entrepreneurs. An **artisan entrepreneur** is a person with significant technical skills and limited business knowledge who starts a business.[1] An **opportunistic entrepreneur** is a person with superior managerial skills and technical knowledge who starts a business.[2] Each can excel with the right business tools and the ability to identify a viable niche.

An entrepreneur must overcome the consumers' tendency to remain loyal to brands they trust rather than purchase new or unknown brands. An entrepreneur must offer the customer a consistent experience every time the product is purchased. The brand must make a connection with the customer. This can be done through varied points of communication, for example trunk shows, in-store product demonstration, and social media. Granting the customer an experience will encourage brand loyalty. Hanky Panky is an intimate apparel brand that has a loyal customer due to its sizing strategy of one-size fits all. Their comfortable fit product promise has become synonymous with their brand name. Figure 1.1.

KEY CONCEPTS

+ Explore the role of an entrepreneur.

+ Identify the characteristics of a successful fashion entrepreneur.

+ Understand the construct and foundation of a fashion business entity.

An Entrepreneurial Profile

During an economic downturn, there is often a rise in entrepreneurship due to the instability of the workplace. Many believe that it is easier to start their own businesses than to find a career in their field. As a result, entrepreneurs must have vigor for their new venture and the stamina and determination to find the niche in which to create and market a product. There are pleasures and pitfalls to entrepreneurship. It allows flexibility and freedom, but you must learn to master your fate. Table 1.1 displays the advantages and disadvantages of business start-ups.

Emerging entrepreneurs need to know their business and personal strengths and how to use them to create a successful company. Equally important is identifying your weaknesses to avoid hindering the business plan process (Figure 1.2).

TABLE 1.1 ADVANTAGES AND DISADVANTAGES OF BEING AN ENTREPRENEUR

ADVANTAGES	DISADVANTAGES
Flexibility	Financial investment
Creativity	Unpredictable work schedule
Independence	Salary fluctuation
Control	Multi-tasking roles
Great earning potential	Time investment

Figure 1.2 Rewards of an entrepreneur.

Traits of a Thriving Entrepreneur

Entrepreneurs who thrive in the fashion industry often have a vast number of common characteristics, as shown in Figure 1.3. These shared characteristics can help guide them along the path in creating a successful brand. Traits that aren't an innate facet of an entrepreneur's skill set can be learned or achieved by setting goals and working in the industry. Experience is the ultimate teacher. It provides tangible insight for future application. In the fashion industry, experience is highly recommended because it allows the entrepreneur to learn the trade tools while being in the business.

Passion

There is an inner drive that pushes entreprenuers to reach their fullest potential. It reflects their commitment to their creativity. Entrepreneurs are privileged to wholeheartedly put their efforts into building a branded business. They must live the brand and believe in the product in order to create and build a business around it, and this requires passion. Entrepreneurship is reciprocal—what is put into a business is what will be gained from it. Passion will help one achieve desired goals and will be reflected in the success of the business.

Figure 1.3 A successful entrepreneur exhibits positive traits to create a winning brand.

Determination

An entrepreneur must be fully vested in building something from nothing. A company's success will stem from an unyielding commitment of time, resources, and finances. Entrepreneurs might become discouraged when obstacles present themselves. But giving up on any part of the business means the entrepreneur must regroup and realign to avoid the unraveling of the business. Being fearlessly determined is required to overcome the obstacles of starting a new business.

Ethics and Integrity

A branded business must always maintain the highest standards of integrity to be respected in the industry. Entrepreneurs set the trajectory of their start-up with an ethical foundation. They prefer to work with suppliers and contractors who have a code of conduct that adheres to the ethical standards and working conditions. Entrepreneurs must protect their brand's and their company's integrity to avoid negative affiliations that will tarnish their image. Entrepreneurs must position their brand to create an overall positive impact. An effective way to generate a positive aura is by incorporating social responsibility partnerships for awareness and environmentally friendly tactics within the organization at large. Both efforts make a positive difference in society and reveal the goodwill of the company.

Vision

Many entrepreneurs have an instinctive vision. However, to make the business come to life, the vision must be in writing. Business plans provide direction for the day-to-day operations. Successful entrepreneurs do not conduct business blindly, without setting any goals. The entrepreneur's vision becomes the road map of the business and will help them stay on track to meet the initial short-term goals.

Autonomy

Entrepreneurs are often considered a "one-person team." They indulge in cross-functional responsibilities that require them to maintain a multifaceted role at all times. During start-up, the lack of financial resources often forces the entrepreneur into complete autonomy. Hiring staff can be costly, so one must be self-disciplined and self-directed to create a branded business until resources allow for growth. Utilizing interns can often ease the workload.

Adaptability

One of the greatest traits that an entrepreneur must have is adaptability. During the start-up phase, the entrepreneur might encounter challenges that warrant changes. Everyone involved must be willing to improve, refine, and sometimes modify the product or the positioning to meet the market demand. Things can change rapidly and without warning, so being adaptable is a requirement.

Competitiveness

Entrepreneurs must be able to effortlessly market and sell their brand. Although marketing, social media, and point-of-purchase materials will reinforce a brand's positioning, entrepreneurs must stay focused to keep their business's or brand's niche identity. Stay brand focused. In business, one is always competing with other brands to be placed to the market. Having a competitive spirit is key to success.

Motivation

It is important to be self-motivated. Entrepreneurs must seek new opportunities to create a profitable brand. Creating a positive mental mantra will help hurdle the obstacles. Many entrepreneurs carve out a segment of time each day to assess their success as form of product viability and personal renewal. Often they read social media to affirm consumer interest.

Every entrepreneur will hit unexpected obstacles, however they must be able to convert them into challenges that yield new opportunities. Successful entrepreneurs often recognize they must be a primary contributor to their company's development. They tend not to sit, wait, and hope the business will fall into place. They remain motivated by pushing the brand forward—it's what keeps the entrepreneur striving for success the industry.

Money Management

Entrepreneurs must have fiscal responsibility. The livelihood of the business can depend on how finances are managed. By spending without planning, one will often yield unnecessary expenditures and losses. Entrepreneurs must closely monitor all usage of funds—from cost of goods to labor and overhead, funds must be allocated and budgeted by category.

Time Management

One must be prepared to commit long hours to the start-up phase of a business. Being organized will help ensure effective time management that will help the business run smoothly. Avoid distractions and remain focused. Creating a calendar or daily to-do list will help achieve goals and keep the business on track.

Pitfalls

The perfect entrepreneur does not exist. Everyone has flaws and characteristics that need improvement. It is important to have an understanding of what shortcomings an entrepreneur may have to better oneself and be successful. Understanding the pitfalls of being an entrepreneur will help in avoiding these common traps:

- Lack of consistent and ongoing market research
- Being unaware of new developments in their specific business sector
- Staying affixed in old modalities of technology and branding techniques
- Not changing with the consumer lifestyle trends, wants, or needs each season
- Being inflexible: resisting change or being so controlling that it inhibits growth
- Lack of financial wherewithal or budgetary adherence
- Resisting group thinking due to personal gratification of being right

Inflexibility/Fixation

Entrepreneurs must have a nimble mind-set. They must be willing to challenge the status quo in their segment of business while also recognizing what is valuable about established practices. Many entrepreneurs think that the solution to starting a branded business is seeking the oddities; however, staying within the boundaries also can be beneficial to harnessing creativity in an established sector.

Lack of Planning

Entrepreneurs must create a plan of action. This business plan will provide a clear, distinct guideline to launch a thriving brand. An entrepreneur who does not plan risks failure due to all the uncertainty that comes along with starting a brand. It is important to know what the next objective is to achieve the intended goal.

Poor Communication

Entrepreneurs can have the best idea in their mind, but lack of communication skills could prevent the idea from coming to a realization. Communication and negotiation are vital when conducting business. Poor communication can result in lack of interest, lack of funding, and lack of business.

Lack of Humility

Confidence is instrumental to a flourishing entrepreneur, but posturing as if one is all knowing can tarnish the brand image. There is a fine line between humility and lack thereof. The difference is arrogance versus confidence. Entrepreneurs often think that if their brand is featured in media, then they have achieved success, but this does not guarantee a profit. The entrepreneur should remain focused on consumers' needs, not just personal achievement. Utilize constructive criticism to the company's advantage. It is important to seek knowledge for the betterment of the company.

Lack of Financial Resources

Entrepreneurs can overspend when creating a brand. Credit cards and loans are often perceived without consideration of repayment. The "spend now and worry later" approach can hinder and stifle business and sometimes dissolve the brand. Take time to understand the financial repercussions when building a brand, and do not expedite the process to grow if there is a lack of financial resources.

Lack of Discipline

Lack of discipline generates fear, laziness, and procrastination. Setting objectives and goals with the focus and diligence to accomplish them is paramount to the task. Remember that only two-thirds of small businesses last beyond the first two years, so it is important to avoid these pitfalls.

Personal Assessment

Creating a product and running a business can become overwhelming for a small business entrepreneur. There are many sacrifices and challenges that present themselves on the entrepreneurial journey. Having traits of a successful entrepreneur will help in the development of the business. **Personal assessment** is a fundamental process in beginning to understand whether entrepreneurship is a wise choice. Having a great idea or product is a critical foundation; however, realizing the overarching demand to create a viable business requires self-reflection. Leadership and negotiation skills, time management, and financial knowledge can be acquired, but commitment must be the entrepreneur's driving force. The first year commitment of time, energy, and resources must be paramount to personal preferences. Many entrepreneurs make the hard choice between personal preferences and business demand. It is a measure of short-term sacrifice for long-term gain.

A company's image can be enhanced by being socially responsible and showing good faith to its customers. The company can give back to the community with time or money or make sure that all products are being ethically made.

Table 1.2 is an example of a self-assessment questionnaire that can be used to discover personal traits that may determine your success as an entrepreneur. The assessment tool should be read from the left column. Circle the one response that best fits the statement, using the following scale: 4 = Always, 3 = Usually, 2 = Sometimes, and 1 = Never. When the survey is completed, transfer the circled numbers into the box labeled *Personal Character Assessment Summary*. Each row should then be totaled, and the results will show both strengths and weaknesses. The highest total for any row is 16, and the lowest is 4. If a low score was attained in any of the categories, then consider finding ways to improve that skill set. Some ways to build those skill sets are:

- *Research:* Often research and books are used to strengthen personal skill sets that are in progress. There are many self-help and how-to books on the market that can assist with building business savvy techniques and basic negotiation skills.
- *Courses and Seminars:* Taking courses at a college or university to refresh basic industry practice or attending business seminars relevant to the industry can often assist an entrepreneur in overcoming perceived deficits.
- *Mentor:* Find another entrepreneur to act as a mentor. A mentor can be a previous professor, a friend, a family member, a person that one meets at an industry event, or a previous employer. It is imperative that a mentor has experience within the industry sector. A mentor must be objective and insightful, not overbearing and controlling. By shadowing a mentor, a burgeoning entrepreneur can learn and filter skills that will assist in becoming a successful entrepreneur.

Once the branded business is up and running, the entrepreneur can employ or contract staff to add value and further grow the business. An entrepreneur may not be strong in all facets of a business, but a successful entrepreneur knows how to build on existing skills.

Defining the Concept

Once the traits and skill sets of an entrepreneur have been examined, it's time to conceptualize the intended product. The concept needs to be different, or better, than current product in the marketplace. The product is an entrepreneur's most valuable asset. Establishing a niche within the marketplace allows the entrepreneur to provide products to a market that other businesses have overlooked. If the product is viable, it should have

TABLE 1.2 **COMPLETING YOUR SELF-ASSESSMENT**

	PERSONAL CHARACTERISTICS QUESTIONS	ALWAYS	USUALLY	SOMETIMES	NEVER
1	I hate being in a position of having to do things; I prefer to act before I am forced to.	4	3	2	1
2	I keep looking for different things I can do.	4	3	2	1
3	If I am faced with a problem, I try to solve it.	4	3	2	1
4	I find out for myself what I need to know.	4	3	2	1
5	When I am working on something, I often check its quality to make sure it is good.	4	3	2	1
6	I treat family, friends, and my own convenience as less important than getting a job done.	4	3	2	1
7	I like to find ways of doing things less expensively than before.	4	3	2	1
8	I think logically about what I am doing and what I am going to do.	4	3	2	1
9	If there are several choices, I think carefully about each one of them before taking action.	4	3	2	1
10	I believe I can overcome obstacles.	4	3	2	1
11	When someone disagrees with me, I try to deal with the disagreement instead of pretending it doesn't exist.	4	3	2	1
12	I am good at convincing people to buy things.	4	3	2	1
13	I learn useful facts from people "in the know."	4	3	2	1
14	If I see a problem coming, I do something about it now rather than waiting for it to happen.	4	3	2	1
15	I try to view my problems as opportunities.	4	3	2	1
16	When things are difficult, I find it very hard to give up.	4	3	2	1
17	When I am going to do something, I first ask questions to find out how to do it.	4	3	2	1
18	My work is better than other people's.	4	3	2	1
19	I am willing to work hard long hours to do what I said I would.	4	3	2	1
20	I try to minimize the time it takes to do things.	4	3	2	1
21	I try to foresee possible obstacles when I am making plans.	4	3	2	1
22	I find ways around problems that other people failed to find before.	4	3	2	1
23	I know I can do what I set out to do.	4	3	2	1
24	I try to confront differences of opinion openly, not to pretend they don't exist.	4	3	2	1
25	If I want somebody to do something, I can persuade him or her to do it.	4	3	2	1
26	I try to build networks of contacts in order to find out what I need to know.	4	3	2	1
27	I can see for myself what actions need to be taken; I do not depend on others to tell me.	4	3	2	1
28	When I run into obstacles, I see it as a chance to learn something new.	4	3	2	1
29	I do not ignore difficulties; I try to overcome them.	4	3	2	1
30	I make extensive, systematic inquiries about how to do things.	4	3	2	1
31	I want to produce the best product of its type.	4	3	2	1
32	I will do almost anything to finish a task on time.	4	3	2	1
33	I look for ways of working more quickly.	4	3	2	1
34	I do not plan on the assumption that all will go well. I anticipate problems and I plan for them.	4	3	2	1

(continues)

TABLE 1.2 **COMPLETING YOUR SELF-ASSESSMENT** *(continued)*

	PERSONAL CHARACTERISTICS QUESTIONS	ALWAYS	USUALLY	SOMETIMES	NEVER
35	I find innovative solutions to problems.	4	3	2	1
36	When I start a task, I am confident I can complete it.	4	3	2	1
37	I do not like to ignore interpersonal problems. I would rather admit to them and try to solve them.	4	3	2	1
38	When I need people to do a task for me, I can get them to do it.	4	3	2	1
39	I try to develop friendships because they are a fundamental resource for success.	4	3	2	1
40	I do not like to wait until I must take action. I act before I have to.	4	3	2	1
41	If an opportunity arises, I act on it immediately.	4	3	2	1
42	If one solution doesn't work, I try to find another.	4	3	2	1
43	If a problem needs to be analyzed, I analyze it myself.	4	3	2	1
44	I want whatever I do to be of higher quality than anyone else's is.	4	3	2	1
45	If a job has to be completed, I am prepared to sacrifice my personal convenience in order to do it.	4	3	2	1
46	I try to reduce costs.	4	3	2	1
47	I try to plan how I will get over difficulties before I actually meet them.	4	3	2	1
48	I develop new ideas.	4	3	2	1
49	If I meet a challenge, I can overcome it.	4	3	2	1
50	If I am having a problem with somebody else, I like to face up to it openly with that person.	4	3	2	1
51	I can persuade people to do things for me.	4	3	2	1
52	I look at my friends as part of my strength for the future.	4	3	2	1

PERSONAL CHARACTER ASSESSMENT SUMMARY

ANSWER VALUES					TOTAL	CATEGORY
1.	14.	27.	40.	=		Initiative
2.	15.	28.	41.	=		Sees and acts on opportunities
3.	16.	29.	42.	=		Persistence
4.	17.	30.	43.	=		Information seeking
5.	18.	31.	44.	=		Concern for high-quality work
6.	19.	32.	45.	=		Commitment to work contract
7.	20.	33.	46.	=		Efficiency orientation
8.	21.	34.	47.	=		Systematic planning
9.	22.	35.	48.	=		Problem solving
10.	23.	36.	49.	=		Self-confidence
11.	24.	37.	50.	=		Assertiveness
12.	25.	38.	51.	=		Persuasion
13.	26.	39.	52.	=		Use of influence strategies

Source: Women's Enterprise Centre, http://www.womensenterprise.ca/sites/default/files/files/self_assessmentweb.pdf

Figure 1.4 lululemon has developed a strong niche product and understands its target customer. The lululemon flagship store in Kitsilano, Vancouver. *Source: Christopher Morris/Corbis.*

customers who are reachable, whose numbers are growing rapidly, and whom established vendors are not currently serving.

Niche development is a focused, targetable product or service that can be created for the intended market. Figure 1.4 shows an example of lululemon athletica, a niche brand. The company has created yoga and running attire while keeping its core customers lifestyle in mind. A niche tends to be narrowly defined and offer a unique benefit (Box 1.1). The product can be tailored through the eyes of a specific target market. A product is only as good as its brand; therefore, elements need to be incorporated—such as logos, color schemes, and marketing messages—to appeal to a specific audience. Chapter 3 further explores brand personification.

To select a niche, start by asking the following questions:

- What is the void in the marketplace?
- What are the current trends of the proposed product/service segment?
- Who is the intended target market, and how large is this market segment?
- How will the target customer benefit from the product/service?
- What other brands may pose direct and indirect competition?

BOX 1.1 Niche Product

lululemon athletica attire is an example of a niche product because of the special qualities of its athletic wear and its distinct consumer profile.

- Great quality that is expected with every piece
- Created with durable, high-performance fabric
  - Unique fabric, "Luon," that is trademarked
  - Comfortable high-performance and fashionable pieces

- Extremely strong brand identity
  - Recognized worldwide
- Marketing strategy
  - Connections with communities and neighborhoods

After you find a promising niche, you can then establish whether or not you will be at ease with the anticipated income from it. See Box 1.2 and Figure 1.5, profile of designer Miriam Carlson.

Mission and Vision

Vision statements and mission statements are the inspirational words that clearly and concisely communicate the direction and goals of the company. They give meaning and direction to all facets of the business. By generating a clear mission statement and vision statement, a company can powerfully communicate its intentions. See Box 1.3, the mission and vision statement for a body scrub line, called *dirt*.

Mission Statement

The mission statement is the backbone of the business and should be developed to give a sense of direction for the branded business. A **mission statement** defines the business and its reason for its existence. This mission does not need to be clever, but it should state what the company is all about. The statement should be concise and not superfluous. The future customer should be able to read it and have an understanding of who the company is and for what it stands. It should be a reflection of every aspect of the business. The statement can explain the brand, pricing, quality, service, position in the marketplace, and growth potential. A mission statement is not set in stone and can change as the company develops.

Creating the mission statement:

1. Identify the company's niche.
2. Describe what the focus and accomplishments will be.
3. Integrate socially meaningful and measurable criteria.
4. Refine the words to create a concise and precise statement of the mission.

Vision Statement

The **vision statement** further defines the company's purpose while communicating the value of the brand. It provides direction and describes outcomes that are five to ten years away. In addition, it explains how the company is expected to behave and inspires the company to give its best. The vision statement should be used as the entrepreneur's way of staying

BOX 1.2 Designer Profile: Miriam Carlson

What is your company name?

miriam cecilia.

What is your niche and how did you find your niche?

Each season, designer Miriam Carlson begins with an artistic statement by designing a small concept collection that embodies that season's inspiration. Carlson then extracts elements from the miriam cecilia concept collection and translates them into wearable, affordable, and striking pieces for the miriam cecilia ready-to-wear line that is sold and distributed to boutiques.

The concept line consists of hand-tacked intricate draping and natural elements, such as the incorporation of the mineral mica. Each concept piece is a one-of-a-kind item and allows the custom clients to see what is possible for their own orders.

The ready-to-wear line is designed and produced seasonally. Each year consists of a spring/summer collection and an autumn/winter collection. miriam cecilia aims to embody classic elegance, current trends, nature-infused inspiration, distinctive draping, high quality, and locally manufactured items.

What is your mission and vision for your company?

miriam cecilia is a women's apparel company that offers cocktail and evening dresses, separates that can be mixed and matched, and jewelry. miriam cecilia operates both a custom line and a wholesale line, which can be found at local boutiques. miriam cecilia products are different because they are inspired by spontaneous moments found in nature and the transitional function between vast landscapes and the bustling city. Organically hand-draped detailing and volume-packed manipulation of fabrics is translated into sleek silhouettes that effortlessly take the miriam cecilia client from day to evening.

The new miriam cecilia studio/showroom located in the Lincoln Park neighborhood of Chicago, IL, has provided the brand an established brick-and-mortar presence, which has led to direct walk-by customers.

Figure 1.5 Miriam Carlson, a Chicago-based designer, has a collection entitled "miriam cecilia." *Source: Miriam Carlson.*

By creating a presence in a community that fits the miriam cecilia demographic, sales have increased through made-to-order pieces and custom clients. Carlson plans to continue to grow the public interface with the Chicago customers.

What are your company's values and what do you stand for as a company?

miriam cecilia believes in creating garments that are well made, well constructed, and will stand the test of time. Consumers are becoming much more aware of where they are spending their money. They want to know that the garments they are purchasing are an investment. The target customer of miriam cecilia is much more concerned about the quality and the life span of the garment and is willing to pay a higher price for these benefits. miriam cecilia makes it a point to produce locally in Chicago and work with local professionals for all aspects of the business. miriam cecilia's customers appreciate and find importance in locally made garments and find peace in knowing that the garment was made in a responsible way.

Who is your customer?

Our customer is a woman ranging in age from 25 to 45, living in an urban setting of 200,000+. She is a business professional with a creative edge. Our customer is embarking on new adventures in her life. She is taking in everything around her and embracing the journey. Whether it is a first date, a proposal, a wedding, a trip, or a business cocktail party, she looks to the dynamic designs of miriam cecilia.

What differentiates your product from the competition?

miriam cecilia garments are versatile, which saves clients money. miriam cecilia offers statement pieces that can transition from day to evening with minimal accessorizing. miriam cecilia garments feature a blend of the trends of the season as well as feminine detailing and timeless silhouettes that can be worn from season to season.

BOX 1.3 A Mission and Vision Statement for a Beauty Company

Our "groundbreaking" mission is to create beauty products with natural ingredients that nourish the body, exhilarate the senses, and harmonize the spirit.

Our "groundbreaking" vision is to unearth the topical landscape of the beauty industry with luxurious products that inspire and arouse wholeness that comes from within.

We support grassroots and national organizations that reinforce our mantra that "natural beauty" stems from the root and blossoms into view. Like a seed planted into the soul, it is a gift that flourishes from the inside out.

"A gift is a precious stone in the eyes of him that have it; wherever so it turns, it prospers."

Proverbs 17:8

Source: Courtesy of Erthe Beaute, LLC.

motivated to reach business goals. Investors should look at a vision statement and have an understanding of what the long-term goals of the company are and whether there is a shared vision to invest in the company. Creating the vision statement:

1. **Identify the mission.** The mission statement should be created before the vision statement can be started.
2. **Describe the long-term goals of the company.** The goals need to be clear and concise. The more concrete the vision statement is, the more likely that others will believe in what the brand is trying to accomplish in the next couple of years.
3. **Follow through on the vision statement.** A vision statement must not be a blanket statement, but one in which others can see what the brand is trying to accomplish. The company as a whole needs to align itself with the vision statement. Anyone who reads the vision statement must be able to see that every facet of the business supports the vision statement.

A vision statement and mission statement are not interchangeable, but both statements should complement each other.

Social Responsibility

The mission statement helps define the company and needs to express where it stands socially. **Social responsibility** is important because business entities that take an active role in supporting their communities help to expand their company's image. The goal of social responsibility is to ensure that the company sustains and promotes ethical standards while pursuing profits at the same time.

A growing number of companies are investing money in corporate social responsibility programs to create goodwill for their company and brand portfolio. Kate Spade has teamed up with Women for Women International (WFWI) in an effort called Hand in Hand, which will assist in providing job opportunities in war-torn Afghanistan. Afghan women will team up with Kate Spade to create 5,000 products annually in 2012 to start and will expand that to 15,000 pieces by 2013. Figure 1.6 shows various products from Kate Spade and its partnership with WFWI.

Figure 1.6 The 2012 line from Kate Spade's partnership Women for Women International included handmade scarves, mittens, necklaces, and other accessories. The partnership provided sustainable employment opportunities for Afghan women, so that they are able to contribute to the economic growth and stability of their country. *Source: Fairchild Fashion Media.*

Corporate responsibility can also help to offset negative impressions consumers may have about a company or product. A study found in *Journal of Service Research* stated that a "company's reputation for corporate social responsibility had a greater effect on consumers' willingness to overlook negative information about the company than the company's reputation for being customer-oriented."[3] Jean-Paul Agon, L'Oréal chairman and chief executive officer (see Case Study 1.1), explains how today's consumers are more aware of what companies are doing to be socially responsible in our society. L'Oréal has an annual worldwide Citizen Day, as shown in Figure 1.7, during which company personnel are encouraged volunteer their time in the community According to L'Oréal chairman and CEO, Jean-Paul Agon,

> Citizen Day is a day where every L'Oréal employee can take action and act as spokesperson for the Group's commitment to the community. It's a day of sharing when, working together, we can have a positive impact on the world around us. A company's goal should not only be to create wealth but also to create value for the public and for society as a whole.

CASE STUDY 1.1   **The Importance of Social Responsibility**

The entrepreneur has an important role in achieving social responsibility within the brand. According to Jean-Paul Agon, L'Oréal chairman and CEO, today's beauty consumers are different than they were years ago. "The consumer has become universal, digital, and socially responsible. [C]onsumers are increasingly responsible citizens. Expectations about large companies are becoming more demanding, with people believing [firms] should invest more in sustainability, share [their] prosperity and create value for society as a whole," he explained. "We have to share our prosperity and our development with the communities around us." The focus is not only on larger companies, but on all companies and how their brands are giving back to society. L'Oréal has an event called Citizen Day, where they give back to the community.

Source: Jennifer Weil. 2012. "Jean-Paul Agon Masters a New Universe." WWD, June 1. http://www.wwd.com/beauty-industry-news/retailing/jean-paul-agon-masters-a-new-universe-5935423

Figure 1.7 L'Oréal has an annual worldwide Citizen Day, during which the company's personnel volunteer their time in the community. *Source: iStockPhoto.*

An entrepreneur can find many ways to take an active role in being socially responsible:

- A simple way to execute social responsibility is by choosing a nonprofit organization to advocate and bring awareness to their cause through participation or contribution of money, products, or time.
- In terms of production, companies must thoroughly research to ensure the manufacturer used for production does violate labor laws or qualify as a sweatshop. The company must advocate against using child labor.
- Supporting production in the United States will also boost the American economy.
- Energy efficiency will avoid waste, such as trying to eliminate raw materials that are not used in the final product, using products that are toxin free, and reducing the amount of packaging.

Tip 1.2 **Create-a-minute!**

Using a **DBA** (doing business as) allows for the ease of developing multiple brands and maximizes the company's growth opportunity. Multiple brands can be developed once the existing brand is successful.

Summary

Understanding the role of an entrepreneur is important when starting a business and creating a brand. A business can be overwhelming to begin, but the right tools can lead an entrepreneur on her way. When beginning the venture of creating a company, it is important to identify traits of a successful entrepreneur. Identifying the niche will help in developing a strong mission and vision statement for the company that will guide the entrepreneur through the entrepreneurial process and help with understanding and identifying where the company wants to stand with regard to social responsibility.

Online Resources

Start a Fashion Business

Start a Fashion Business offers tips and advice for starting and running a fashion business.
http://www.startafashionbusiness.co.uk/quiz-can-you-run-fashion-business.html

Entrepreneur.com

Entrepreneur offers information on entrepreneurship.
http://www.entrepreneurship.org/en/resource-center/conducting-a-swot-analysis.aspx

Score

Score is a nonprofit association whose members individually mentor aspiring entrepreneurs and small-business owners, offers training, workshops, and resources.
www.score.org

Activity 1.1 Mission and Vision Statement

Start by writing a brief mission statement and vision statement for your brand. The mission is the purpose of the company. The vision is the long-term goals of the company. Both should identify the philosophy of your business.

Activity 1.2 Social Responsibility Plan

Create a Social Responsibility plan. Give an overview on the company's commitment to social responsibility. Offer three ideas on how the company can be socially responsible in the industry. Social Responsibility is the obligation of the company to make decisions and take actions that will enhance the welfare and interests of society as well as the brand.

Notes

1. Longenecker, Justin G., J. William Petty, Leslie E. Palich, and Carlos W. Moore. 2008. *Small Business Management: Launching & Growing Entrepreneurial Ventures*. Mason, Ohio: Cengage Learning.

2. Ibid.

3. *Small Business Encyclopedia: Entrepreneur.com*. "Mission Statement." http://www.entrepreneur.com/encyclopedia/mission-statement. Accessed Dec. 21, 2011.

4. L'Oréal.com. "Citizen Day 2013: Over 4,500 employees mobilize in France." *L'Oréal*. Accessed 20 Jan 2014. http://www.loreal.com/Article.aspx?topcode=CorpTopic_MEDIAS_Actualites_CitizenDay.

TRADE TERMS

artisanship entrepreneur

opportunistic entrepreneur

personal assessment

niche development

mission statement

vision statement

social responsibility

DBA

Bibliography

Eisingerich, Andreas B., and Gunjan Bhardwaj. 2011. "Does Social Responsibility Help Protect a Company's Reputation?" *MIT Sloan Management Review—The New Business of Innovation,* March 23. Accessed Dec. 21, 2011. http://sloanreview.mit.edu/the-magazine/2011-spring/52313/does-social-responsibility-help-protect-a-companys-reputation/.

Entrepreneur.com. "Social Responsibility Definition." *Small Business Encyclopedia: Entrepreneur.com.* Accessed May 1, 2012. http://www.entrepreneur.com/encyclopedia/term/82646.html.

Mindtools.com. "Mission Statements and Vision Statements—Leadership Techniques from MindTools.com." *Mind Tools—Management Training, Leadership Training and Career Training.* Accessed Dec. 21, 2011. http://www.mindtools.com/pages/article/newLDR_90.htm.

Silverstein, Barry. 2010. "Can Luxury Brands Sustain Themselves by Becoming Sustainable?" *Brand Channel,* Nov. 16. Accessed Jan. 31, 2012. http://www.brandchannel.com/home/post/2010/11/16/Luxury-Brands-Get-Sustainable.aspx.

Srivathsan, G.K. 2011. "6 Questions to Ask Before Selecting a Niche." *Technshare,* May 7. Accessed April 21, 2012. http://www.technshare.com/selecting-niche/.

Women's Enterprise Centre. 2011. "Personal Characteristics Assessment.pdf." *Women's Enterprise.com,* July 15. Accessed April 24, 2012. http://www.womensenterprise.ca/resourcelibrary/Business%20Planning.

2

A Moving Target

Customers can be likened to a moving target. Their demands, motivations, lifestyle, and product choices are constantly evolving. By analyzing and conducting market research, a company can better identify which consumer groups will purchase its product or service. As an entrepreneur, it is imperative to conduct consumer research that effectively establishes the brand's target market. The primary guidelines to research consumers are basic market segmentation variables—demographic, geographic, psychographic, and behavioral (Figure 2.1). The vantage point of the entrepreneur is as the producer of goods. Identifying the brand's core and fringe customers will be the first step to maximizing sales and growing business. This key piece of information can help drive the plan for product development and brand extensions.

Market Research

Most often, entrepreneurs have an innovative product or service in mind prior to starting their business. A primary step for an entrepreneur is to develop the target market by conducting market research. This is essential because the best ideas can fail if there is not a desire for the product in the marketplace. **Market research** is the process of gathering, analyzing, and interpreting information about a market, a product, or service to be offered for sale in that market. Market research also considers the past, present, and potential customers for the product or service. It reviews the characteristics, spending habits, location, and consumer needs, the overall industry, and particular brand competitors.[1]

The first step in market research is to acquire key information:

• What are the current trends in the product segment? Trends can be researched in trade publications, magazines, newspapers, and online websites such as Women's Wear Daily (WWD) and Worth Global Style Network (WGSN).

Figure 2.1 Who is your customer? Estée Lauder. *Source: Kevin Mazur/Getty Images Entertainment /Getty Images.*

- What are dominant/competitive brands in the market segment? It is imperative to shop the competition in retail stores and online.
- What is the range of prices in the product segment? Online price comparison, as well as targeting stores that carry similar products, will inform the entrepreneur of the retail price category in which to position the brand.
- What are the best geographic locations to market the product? By researching the varied geographic markets, the entrepreneur will find the most viable markets for brand placement.
- What are the best sales outlets for product be sold? It is important to sell the brand in retail stores or with online partners where the product is most desired by the consumer.

Researchers should conduct both quantitative and qualitative research for the brand. **Quantitative research** looks for ways to quantify information using numbers. **Qualitative research** looks to identify information by analyzing information. When conducting these two types of research, primary and secondary research methods should be used. **Primary research** is when the research being conducted is done firsthand. Primary research can be done by:

- Conducting a focus group to garner feedback from potential consumers. Utilize a questionnaire or survey to sequester feedback. Figure 2.2 provides a sample questionnaire for a jewelry line. A questionnaire can help pinpoint further insight to what the target customer is seeking. Figure 2.3 illustrates the body care company *dirt* that used focus groups for market research. Interviewing potential retailer buyers can be an effective way to garner feedback (see additional information in Chapter 10). When forming a focus group, an entrepreneur should:
  - Seek information by having a specific purpose for the session. The intention should be to garner a cross-sectional perspective in a group setting. A list of questions should be formed to answer those specifics that the entrepreneur is seeking. Some sample questions are as follows:
    - What are the current/dominant industry trends?
    - If samples are shown, what are the product's perceived strengths and weaknesses?
    - What or who would be a potential competitor and what do members of the focus group like about those competitors?
    - How frequently would they use your product? How much would they spend?
    - What features are missing or would they like to see in the product?
  - Set a time and let them know how long the session will run. Provide snacks and drinks during the session. Record the session or have someone else take notes.
  - Friends or family may not always be the best people to have in the focus group, since they may have personal bias toward the entrepreneur. The group must be subjective and representative of the target population. Post ads in local papers, place fliers throughout town. Many times an incentive will most likely ensure that the target market will attend. An incentive could be a monetary gift, or a gift certificate for a local restaurant or retailer.

PRIMARY RESEARCH QUESTIONNAIRE FOR A JEWELRY LINE

1. **In the last 12 months how frequently did you purchase jewelry?**
   a. Once a month
   b. Once every 6 months
   c. Once a year
   d. Only on special occasions

2. **What kind of jewelry did you purchase?**
   a. Fine
   b. Costume
   c. Bridge
   d. Ethnic

3. **What type of women's jewelry did you purchase?** *(Please check all that apply)*
   a. Ring
   b. Necklace
   c. Bracelet
   d. Earring
   e. Brooch
   f. Bridal Jewelry
   g. Charms
   h. Watch
   i. Other Women's Fine Jewelry
   j. None of the above

4. **What is the material or composition of the last women's jewelry item purchased?** *(Please check all that apply)*
   Metals:
   a. Fine gold jewelry (e.g., 14k and above, not gold plate)
   b. Fine platinum jewelry
   c. Fine sterling silver jewelry
   d. Gold plate, gold filled or vermeil
   e. Other, not known
   f. None of the above

   Gemstones: *(Please check all that apply—If "none," please indicate "none of the above")*
   a. Diamond jewelry
   b. Pearl jewelry
   c. Other precious gemstone jewelry (such as emeralds, sapphires, rubies, etc.)
   d. Semi-precious gemstone jewelry (such as opals, topaz, amethyst, etc.)
   e. Other/Not Known
   f. No Gemstones/None of the above

5. **How much did you spend on your last jewelry item purchased?** *(For multiple items purchased most recently, please report the most expensive single item purchased)*
   a. Under $50
   b. $51–$100
   c. $101–$249
   d. $250–$499
   e. $500–$999
   f. $1,000–$2,499
   g. $2,500–$4,999
   h. $5,000–$9,999
   i. $10,000–$24,999
   j. $25,000 or more

6. **What were the primary reasons why you bought the last jewelry item?** *(Check up to three reasons)*
   a. Price/Value Relationship
   b. Style and Design
   c. Favorite Gemstone or Color of Gemstone
   d. Excellent Quality
   e. Favorite Metal or Color of Metal
   f. Matches a Particular Outfit
   g. For a Special Occasion
   h. Perfect Gift
   i. Discounted Price
   j. Favorite Brand or Designer
   k. Replace a Worn Out/Lost Item
   l. Custom Design
   m. Other Reasons not mentioned above

7. **How satisfied were you with your most recent jewelry item purchased?**
   a. Very Satisfied
   b. Somewhat Satisfied
   c. Neither Satisfied or Dissatisfied
   d. Somewhat Dissatisfied
   e. Very Dissatisfied

8. **In what kind of store did you purchase your last jewelry item?**
   a. Department Store, such as Sears, JCPenney, Neiman Marcus, Bloomingdales, etc.
   b. Specialty Fashion Shop or Boutique, such as Gap, Banana Republic, Limited, Chicos, etc.
   c. Independently or Locally Owned Jewelry Store
   d. Chain Jewelry Store, such as Zales, Kay's, Bailey Banks & Biddle, Tiffany's, etc.
   e. Duty-free store
   f. Other Specialty Luxury Shop or Boutique
   g. Warehouse Club, Outlet Store, and/or Discount Store
   h. Through Internet, Mail Order or TV Shopping
   i. Other Types of Stores Not Listed Above
   j. None of the above

9. **When choosing a store to shop for jewelry, how important are these factors, using a scale where a = Very Important to e = Not Important**
   a. Very Important
   b. Somewhat Important
   c. Neither Important/Unimportant
   d. Somewhat Unimportant
   e. Not Important

10. **In the coming year, do you expect to spend more than, less than, or the same buying jewelry?**
    a. More than
    b. About the same
    c. Less than

11. **Which of the following group would you consider yourself a part of?**
    a. Very Price Conscious
    b. Price Conscious
    c. Not at all Price Conscious

Figure 2.2 Primary Research Questionnaire for a Jewelry Line. *Source: Courtesy of Unity Marketing Online. http://www.unitymarketingonline.com/reports2/jewelry/pdf/jewelry2004surveyquestionnairedraft.pdf*

Figure 2.3 *d*irt market research consisted of idea generation, planning, and product development and utilized focus groups to tweak the final body scrub production. *Source: Erthe Beaute, LLC.*

- The day of the focus group, be prepared to ask questions. The questions should be phrased in a manner that will not just give a yes or no answer. Record the session and make sure that members are given a chance to give their answers. Let each member know that they will be recorded, and have them sign a consent form.
- After the session, make sure to sit down and add any notes or ideas that pop into one's mind. Use this information to decide if there is a need for the product.
- Shopping the market. Go into the retail environment. Investigating competitors and noncompetitors will give you an idea of best-selling brands and products and slow sellers in the marketplace. Customers' buying habits can be viewed and analyzed.
- Attending trade shows that cater to the market segment of the product or associations such as the Apparel Industry Board, Inc. (AIBI), that conduct webinars and events on topics that could assist in research. The AIBI offers classes in costing products, legalities of business, contractors, the many ways of selling, and public relations and marketing.

Secondary research is information gathered from other resources. A variety of free information can be found in material generated by government departments The U.S. Small Business Administration (SBA) is an excellent tool to use when starting a business. They are a U.S.-based agency that provides support and assistance to entrepreneurs and small business. SBA offers assistance with entrepreneurial development (education, information, technical assistance, and training), accessing capital, government contracts, disaster assistance, and advocacy for small business. Another potential source is an organization such as SCORE, a nonprofit association that educates entrepreneurs and helps small businesses start, grow, and succeed nationwide. SCORE is a resource partner with the U.S. SBA. SCORE offers a mentoring program, in-person and online workshops—such as how to start your own business—and templates and tools. The U.S. Census Bureau conducts surveys and censuses each year and offers decennial censuses, the American Community Survey, the Puerto Rico Community Survey, the Economic Census, and a Population Estimates Program. Civic organizations, such as the Chamber of Commerce and Rotary Club, commercial development organizations, and local banks can offer valuable information.

Industry trade publications and online sites are another great source for secondary information (Figure 2.4). Trade publications can be magazines, newspapers, or wire services that are geared toward specific industries. *Cosmetic World,* shown in Figure 2.5, is one example of a trade publication that focuses on the women's fashion industry, its manufacturers, and retailers. Trade publications are an excellent source of material on current trends and forecasts. Case Study 2.1 explains what is happening in the beauty industry in regards to brand loyalty and brand recognition (Figure 2.6).

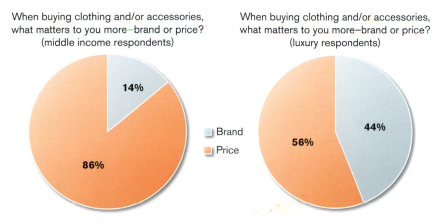

When buying clothing and/or accessories, what matters to you more—brand or price? (middle income respondents)

When buying clothing and/or accessories, what matters to you more—brand or price? (luxury respondents)

14%
86%
44%
56%

Brand
Price

Figure 2.4 Secondary research can be done through examining trade publication surveys. *Source:* WWD, *Fairchild Archive.*

Figure 2.5 Secondary research can be done through trade publications. *Source:* WWD, *Fairchild Archives.*

IBISWorld.com is an online database that gives an industry profile, as shown in Figure 2.7. Each profile gives general statistics and includes analysis of industries in the United States. Data like this can cost an entrepreneur a starting rate of $825 for a single report, so finding online sites that provide the information instead are good resources.

A combination of quantitative and qualitative research can give the entrepreneur a thorough understanding of what is currently being offered by others and what may be missing in the marketplace. Information that is gathered using primary and secondary research can often assist in the product development process, which is determining the needs and expectations of the target customer. Secondary research should be examined first, since it is information that is already out there. Secondary data will then assist in answering any questions that the entrepreneur is looking for and give a better understanding of what information is needed to create the brand. Researching the market will assist in developing the brand. The process is imperative to the success of the brand's development, design, and marketing. Primary and secondary research help navigate the risks involved in bringing a new product or brand to the marketplace.

Defining the Customer

Successful entrepreneurs identify their target market by conducting market research to decipher and develop a niche for their products. A **target market** is who the consumer will be for a product or service. Determining the target market will keep the entrepreneur focused on a single group of consumers when developing the product or service.

Market Segmentation

Market segmentation is a subset of a market made up of people or organizations with one or more characteristics that cause them to

Figure 2.6 Emerging makeup brand Ardency Inn was created by LVMH alumni Gilles Kortzagadarian and Stephane Siboni. It's aimed at music and beauty fans. The collection offers highly pigmented, buildable color cosmetics. *Source: 911 Pictures.*

Figure 2.7 Industry information can be found on IBISWorld. *Source: IBISWorld.*

demand similar products and/or services based on qualities of those products, such as price or function.[2] The purpose of market segmentation is to identify what subset of people will potentially buy the product. Unless the product will appeal to all consumers, it is important to take a look at the potential market and examine each variable.

Segmentation Variables

The market can be examined through geographic, demographic, psychographic, affirmative and cognitive, and behavioral segmentation, all of which are known as **segmentation variables.** Moreover, market

Tip 2.1 **Create-a-minute!**

Targeting the core customer can be difficult if one does not understand where their needs and wants lie.

BOX 2.1 Sample of a Customer Profile

Segmentation Types/Bases	Illustrative Categories
Geographic Segmentation	
Region	North, south, east, west
City Size	Up to 100,000, 100,001+
Population Density	Urban, suburban, rural
Climate	Hot, temperate, cold
Demographic Segmentation	
Age	Up to 12, 13–19, 20–39, 40–59, 60+
Gender	Female, male
Household Size	1, 2, 3, 4 or more persons
Income	Up to $25,000, $25,001–$50,000, over $50,001
Occupation	Professional, blue-collar, retired, unemployed
Education	High school or less, some college, college graduate
Sociocultural Segmentation	
Culture	Up to 12, 13–19, 20–39, 40–59, 60+
Subculture	
Religion	Baptist, Catholic, Jewish, Muslim
National origin	Italian, French, Greek
Race	Hispanic, African American, Asian
Social class	Upper class, middle-class, working-class, lower-class
Marital status	Single, married, divorced, widowed
Psychographics	Achievers, strivers, strugglers
Behavioral Segmentation	
Brand loyalty	None, divided, undivided loyalty
Store loyalty	None, divided, undivided loyalty
User rate	Light, medium, heavy
User status	Nonuser, ex-user, current user, potential user

segments can also be divided into subcategories in which supplementary variables are added to subsets of the market segment to further narrow down the target market. Box 2.1 shows an example of a customer profile.

Geographic segmentation is the means of dividing the market into groups according to a specific region. This type of segmentation considers where a consumer lives. Retailers will often gather information such as zip codes or telephone numbers to ascertain where customers are located. This information will often provide insight to growth opportunity. Geographic segmentation deems that people who live in the same area may share similar needs and wants compared to people who live in other parts of the country. This is due to the fact that there are similarities in demographic and psychographic characteristics of residents. Some examples of geographic variables are:

- *Region:* by continent, state, county, city, suburb, or neighborhood.
- *Size of metropolitan area:* segmented according to size of the population.
- *Population density:* whether the area is considered urban, suburban, or rural.
- *Climate:* various weather patterns are common to certain parts of a region.

Demographic segmentation is dividing the market based on the demographics, such as gender, age, household size, income, occupation, and other variables. The U.S. Census Bureau is the largest collector of personal demographic information in the United States. Their goal is to provide data regarding population and housing as well as American economic and demographic indicators. Demographics assist in determining the appropriate market to sell the product. The preferred consumer may be a hip young urban woman in a major city, so the information garnered from the demographics research will give a starting base.

Box 2.2 shows all six generations of consumers. It is important to have a thorough understanding of the age group that is being targeted. Every consumer within an age segment may not fit within the analysis of a particular generation; however, one can generalize consumer behavior. Each generation has its own buying habits and needs. As an entrepreneur, it is important to make sure that the product or service is meeting the needs or addressing a potential want of the targeted consumer.

It is also important to understand how economic recessions impact each generation. Generation Y, which is entering the workforce now, encountered a grave impact due to unforeseen employment variables that inevitably yielded fewer jobs. Generation X is the next most affected generation due to loss of employment. Figure 2.8 is an example of a Generation Z member, Harper Seven Beckham.

Psychographic segmentation groups consumers according to their lifestyles by looking at attributes relating to activities, interest, personality, values, attitudes, or interests. There are various consulting groups that analyze a company; a prominent one is VALS, which consults and offers consumer research service. This describes many psychographics. According to VALS, it examines customers' profiles and understands how to best target them through:

- Providing a fresh perspective by "getting into the heads" of the customers.
- Identifying the best targets—retain the most profitable customers or attract new consumers.
- Creating richly textured consumer profiles or personas of psychological traits, attitudes, behaviors, lifestyles, and demographics.
- Increasing communication effectiveness by identifying the target's distinct communication styles, content preferences, and media channel use.
- Innovating new products and services for specific consumer targets.
- Locating geographic concentrations of the target.

Figure 2.8 Harper Seven Beckham, Generation Z. *Source: Christopher Peterson/Corbis.*

BOX 2.2 Consumer Groups

GI Generation: (born before 1925)
This group is considered to have loyal behavior to consumer goods. The GI Generation has insignificant buying power but has a very strong influence over the buying power of the other generations. They are extremely price-sensitive.

Fashion brand personality market: Betty White, Lauren Bacall

The Silent Generation: (born 1925–1944)
The Silent Generation has insignificant buying power but has a very strong influence over the buying power of the other generations. They have money to spend and are underserved by the fashion industry. This group prefers actual relationships, then virtual buying experiences.

Fashion brand personality examples: Diana Ross, Barbara Streisand, Jack Nicholson

The Boomers: (born 1945–1964)
This group prefers to seek service along with products. They are the biggest consumers of products to make you look and feel young, targeted directly at their need for youth, aspiration for thinness, trepidation about aging, and overall liveliness. The Boomers have a high amount of discretionary income.

Fashion brand personality market: Demi Moore, Barack and Michelle Obama

Gen X: (born 1965–1984)
As Gen X ages, they will have more discretionary income and become the new targets for marketing and advertising. This group will look for relationships with the organizations that are marketing their products.

Fashion brand personality market: Jennifer Lopez, Kim Kardashian, Justin Timberlake

Millennials, or Gen Y: (born 1985–2004)
This group is bright, educated, and has a social conscience. Products they purchase will come from socially conscious companies. Gen Y was born during the technology boom.

Fashion brand personality market: Kylie Jenner, Selena Gomez, Harry Styles

Gen Z: (born 2005–present)
This group is the most tech-savvy of all generations and is being born during the Apple "i" boom. Currently, this group is the most influential because, that they have the most power. The group cares about their peers and about fun.

Fashion brand personality market: Suri Cruise, Shiloh Jolie-Pitt, Kingston Rossdale

Source: Adapted from Emily Brooks. 2012. "Understanding All 6 Generations Of Consumers." *Edibles Advocate Alliance (TM)*, Jan. 13. http://www.ediblesadvocatealliance.org/local-food---agriculture-business-blog/bid/38451/Effective-Marketing-Understanding-All-6-Generations-Of-Consumers.

Figure 2.9 shows an example of a psychographic profile and Box 2.3 is a sample of a VALS type.

Social-cultural segmentation examines a social group and its culture. The segment is broken down into subgroups to analyze sociological or cultural variables, such as social class, stage in the family life cycle, religion, race, national origin, social class, values, beliefs, or customs.

Behavioral segmentation classifies customers by comparable purchasing intentions and behavior. Each consumer group expects different benefits from the product that they are purchasing, so it is important to understand their motives and buying behavior. Behavioral segments can group consumers in terms of:

User Rate
Some markets can be segmented into light, medium, and heavy use of a product. Erthe Beaute LLC, the parent company of *dirt*, a natural body scrub, targets its repertoire to users who are concerned about using body

BOX 2.3 VALS Experiencers vs. Innovators

Your primary VALS type is Experiencer, and your secondary type is Innovator.

The primary VALS type represents your dominant approach to life. The secondary classification represents a particular emphasis you give to your dominant approach.

Experiencers are motivated by self-expression. Young, enthusiastic, and impulsive consumers, Experiencers quickly become enthusiastic about new possibilities but are equally quick to cool. They seek variety and excitement, savoring the new, the offbeat, and the risky. Their energy finds an outlet in exercise, sports, outdoor recreation, and social interaction.

Experiencers are avid consumers and spend a comparatively high proportion of their income on fashion, entertainment, and socializing. Their purchases reflect the emphasis that they place on looking good and having "cool" stuff.

Favorite Things:
- VW
- *Rolling Stone*
- Red Bull
- To be entertained

Innovators are successful, sophisticated, take-charge people with high self-esteem. Because they have such abundant resources, they exhibit all three primary motivations in varying degrees. They are change leaders and are the most receptive to new ideas and technologies. Innovators are very active consumers, and their purchases reflect cultivated tastes for upscale niche products and services.

Image is important to Innovators, not as evidence of status or power but as an expression of their taste, independence, and personality. Innovators are among the established and emerging leaders in business and government, yet they continue to seek challenges. Their lives are characterized by variety. Their possessions and recreation reflect a cultivated taste for the finer things in life.

Favorite Things:
- BMW
- *Wired*
- Sparkling water
- A rewarding experience

Strategic Business Insights. "VALS." *Strategic Business Insights.* Accessed Jan. 13, 2012. http://www.strategicbusinessinsights.com/vals/.

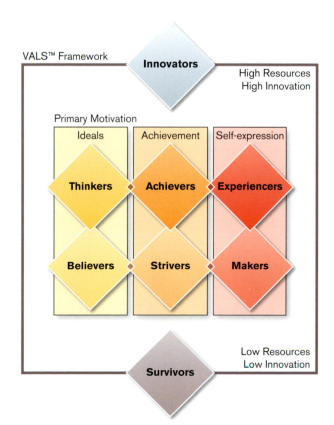

Figure 2.9 Innovators/Survivors. An example of an Innovator vs. a Survivor, according to the VALS Framework. The VALS system is subdivided into eight market segments based upon resources and primary motivation in the U.S. market.

products that contain synthetics and chemicals. Their customers desire natural products to exfoliate and nourish their skin. The brand has tapped into a market segment that recognizes that using the product twice a week yields maximum product results.

Brand and Retail Loyalty

Loyal consumers are those who buy one brand or shop at a specific retailer for its consumer goods. Retailers view these consumers as valuable core customers. Coach is known for their superior quality handbags and has a loyal consumer base. As of October 2012, Coach had more than 3.7 million Facebook fans, 339,144 Twitter followers, and many successful blogging campaigns. "Coach consumers have a specific emotional connection with the brand. Part of the company's everyday mission is to cultivate consumer relationships by strengthening this emotional connection." [3]

User Status

It is important to understand whether the target market is a nonuser, ex-user, current user, or potential user of a product category. In the last couple of years, men have become current users of shapewear, for example. Prior to that, companies were discovering there was a potential market for this product when the beauty industry identified the men's personal care segment. Figure 2.10 shows the brand Spanx, which now offers shapewear for men. Spanx was started in 2000 by Sara Blakely in Atlanta. The brand started out as shapewear for women and expanded to

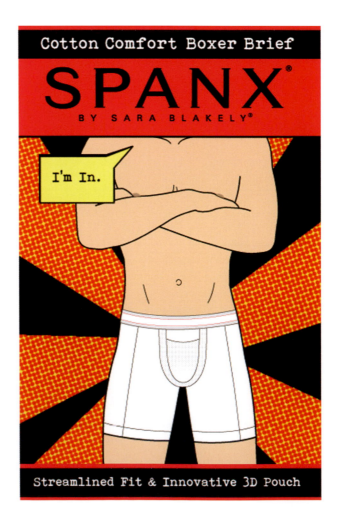

Figure 2.10 Spanx has a menswear collection of products. *Source: Spanx by Sara Blakely/ AP Photo.*

men in 2010. The brand has found success and began opening a chain of boutiques in 2012 that sell garments for both men and women.

Segmentation and target market development are paramount. Research will help define your company's target market by identifying which consumers will be most receptive to the new product or service and what segment will yield the most profitability. Figure 2.11 is an ad for NYDJ (Not Your Daughter's Jeans), a denim company started in 2005 that found a market with women over 40 who still wanted fashionable jeans that fit their body shape. These jeans have 4 percent Lycra compared to the average 2 percent in the denim industry, and it sculpts the women's bottom half as well as gives the appearance of a lifted derriere.

Figure 2.11 NYDJ brand targets fashionable women over the age of forty. Actress Kelly Rutherford poses with her mother, Harriet Edwards. *Source: Christopher Peterson/Splash News/Corbis.*

Consumer Behavior

Needs Versus Wants
The U.S. population is continually changing.

> Emerging economies such as those of China, India, Brazil, South Africa, and others represent the fastest-growing middle-class consumer markets in the world. Nearly one billion potential customers are beginning to earn enough discretionary income to afford quality brands and quality consumer experiences. At the same time, many of these markets are just now seeing widespread penetration of the Internet and social networks—in societies where upwards of 60 percent of the population is under the age of 30.[4]

Discretionary income is the income that is left over after spending on personal necessities, such as food, shelter, and clothing. Understanding the target market and their discretionary income will assist in developing and marketing the brand.

The first step is to identify whether a product is a want or a need for the consumer. Entrepreneurs need to answer this question. Most often a consumer is motivated by a want and will quickly profess it as a need. Abraham Maslow's Hierarchy of Needs is a pyramid that reviews the desires of each level of human growth (Figure 2.12). For many customers, there is a need to fill each level. There is a product that can fulfill each level of the hierarchy. Understanding Maslow's hierarchy can help better identify target customers and what drives their behaviors.

It is important to understand where the product falls on Maslow's Hierarchy of Needs, as well as where the consumer is at that point in time. As a determinant of market research, the entrepreneur should steer the product or service to appeal to the consumer, regardless. This will help improve engagement of the targeted consumer. Furthermore, an entrepreneur must be sensitive to the target consumer not being a decision maker in the purchasing arena. The influencers can be family members, friends, communities, and the media. A recent media-influenced consumer trend is summed up by the term "masstige."

Masstige
Masstige is a term introduced by Michael Silverstein, a leader of the Boston Consulting Group's global Consumer Practice, and Neil Fiske, former president, CEO, and director of Eddie Bauer Holdings, Inc, derived from the words "mass" and "prestige." The term is used for

Self-Actualization
Personal growth and fulfillment

Self-Esteem
Achievement, Status, Responsibility, Reputation

Love and Belonging
Family, Affection, Relationships, Work groups

Security
Health, Family, Job, Property

Physiological
Food, Water, Air, Sex, Sleep

Figure 2.12 Maslow's Hierarchy of Needs.

Tip 2.2 **Create-a-minute!**

A consumer-shopping trend is to purchase high and low product, so each market area ranging from luxury to budget should be analyzed.

products aimed at providing "luxury to the masses."[7] Masstige has become an opportunity for entrepreneurs to further define their target markets.

Market indulgence has evolved into three major types:

a. *Accessible super-premium products:* products from a luxury-item manufacturer that are priced at the high end of their category but can be afforded by the middle-class market. For example, Mercedes-Benz, a high-end car manufacturer, offers the Maybach for its typical consumer at $300,000 but also offers a C-class coupe starting at $26,000, a sticker price closer to the middle-class car buyer's budget. The C-class would be considered an accessible premium product.

b. *Old luxury brand extensions:* a brand diffusion tends to be a lower price line that is inspired by the brand's higher priced collection so that that the mass market can afford it. For example, Marc Jacobs offers a basic pump for $645 versus a Marc by Marc Jacobs's basic pump that sells for $190.

c. *Mass prestige or masstige brands:* these are neither at the top of their price category nor at the lower end. Masstige is right in between mass and class. For example, La Mer moisturizing lotion is $220, Olay's is $6.99, and Origins lotion is $46. The Origins price point is an appealing, affordable alternative for the customer who is seeking a premium alternative in lieu of a conventional product. An entrepreneur can tap into this market by using a distinctive packaging that will compete with more prestige brands. Custom-designed primary and secondary containers can give a more exclusive look to a product.

In tandem with masstige, consumers have started to seek quality products in spite of their price. It is considered fashionable for a single consumer to shop and purchase products from luxury to budget. Consumers are mixing their product preferences with brands that range from Missoni to Target house brands. Designers are aggressively tending to this trend: Missoni sells its products in Saks Fifth Avenue but it collaborated with Target to create an exclusive, less-expensive limited-edition, collection. A consumer will purchase leggings at Forever 21 for $19.99, yet will purchase a pair of Christian Louboutin shoes at $800. Consumers are no longer fixed into a price category but will cross the boundaries for basic or extravagant products that reflect quality at an affordable price. Figure 2.13 shows singer Nicki Minaj wearing a Forever 21 color-block dress accessorized with a Chanel handbag.

With this newly adopted trend, a company can position its products as a prestige product at a very affordable price point. The Coach brand encapsulates this with their affordable luxury image—an affordable price for a quality product. Coach has successfully broadened its consumer base without compromising the image.

As an entrepreneur, it is important to understand today's consumer. Not surprisingly, the industry is finding that fashion is no longer one price fits all. Consumers of all spectrums of the fashion industry are cross-shopping. People who shop at Neiman Marcus are also hitting shops such as Forever 21 for statement pieces. Similarly, customers who shop at H&M are also shopping at Barneys. Ed Jay, senior vice president of American Express Business Insights, says that consumers are either shopping high or low. "High-end brands are holding ground among consumers, while spending at value-oriented stores has also been pretty stable. It's a tough place for mid-tier right now," he said, referring to retailers like the Gap, Chico's, and Ann Taylor." [5]

Competitive Edge

It is important to understand how to build an infrastructure that attracts consumers to the product in lieu of the competition. An entrepreneur must define the brand's competitive edge. **Competitive edge** is defined as having an advantage over competitors. A company needs to define its product's point of difference or uniqueness/distinct characteristics. This will assist in defining the product's edge.

Figure 2.13 Nicki Minaj wearing a Forever 21 dress and a Chanel handbag. *Source: Corbis.*

Consider the luxury brand Hermès and their Birkin handbag. The handbag ranges from entry retail price of $9000 to $150,000. The main reason that this brand and style bag has a competitive edge is due to the quantity/scarcity, quality craftsmanship, exclusivity, and increase in value over time. There are a limited number of bags that are produced. The bag takes time to produce, and quality materials are used. A genuine Birkin bag is handcrafted by a skilled craftsperson, who is trained by the Hermès company for up to five years, and a bag can take up to forty-eight hours to produce. The bag has a waitlist of more than two years and can only be found brand new at a Hermès boutique. The Birkin bag also is said to be the only fashion bag that increases in value over time, often being referred to as an "investment." [6]

Analyze the perceived competition to discover how your product is different. Review other brands that have parallel products. This will help determine your product's competitive edge.

When conducting competitive research, it is important to review primary and secondary elements. Aspects of a competitor that should be looked at are:

- *Company websites:* Many will provide the mission and history of the product.
- *Retail partnerships:* These can tell you about the brand and its customer. Ask a salesperson about the brands they carry, which brands are their best sellers, and why.
- *Customer opinion:* Ask customers who purchase the competitor's products what they like and don't like about the brand.
- *Marketing:* Follow competitors' marketing to see what message they are trying to give.
- *The product itself:* Purchase the product and use it or wear it, depending on the product type. How do garments wear, and how are they cared

for? What are the ingredients of a given beauty product? Does it do what it says it will?

- *Public relations:* Sign up for the competitor's distribution list to continually get information about what they are doing.

After analyzing the research information, your company can identify a niche in the market and focus on the following tasks.

- **Be a trendsetter and redefine a product or service.** It is important to be creative and redefine status quo. Take an existing product and add a twist of ingenuity. Make it relevant with enhancements.
- **Cater to an overlooked, underserved slice of the market.** If the competition is going after a certain market, then take a look at who else is out there. Consumers have unique needs, and those are the customers who oftentimes might be neglected.
- **Personalizing the customer's experience.** A consumer can find almost any product but may not always get a positive buying experience. There are many ways to provide a pleasant experience. The Internet has become one of the fastest-growing places where consumers are shopping. Personalizing one's experience online can give you that competitive edge.

Business SWOT Analysis

Entrepreneurs must identify their product and where it is positioned against its competition. This will enable a firm understanding of the company viability and vulnerability to support its development. A **SWOT analysis** stands for strengths, weaknesses, opportunities, and threats. See Figure 2.14 for an example of a SWOT analysis. A SWOT analysis enables an entrepreneur to see a snapshot of the current environment

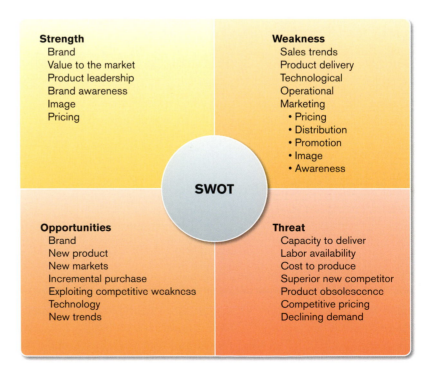

Figure 2.14 An example of a SWOT analysis for dirt.

and whether or not the brand will survive. It is a good framework for developing a product by answering earnestly on the strategy, position, and direction of the brand. The SWOT analysis should be used as a starting point and to view the overall picture of the brand. When creating a SWOT analysis, one should look at the following:

- *Strengths* are what give the company a competitive advantage. Examples: the uniqueness of the company, the value to the market, product leadership, brand awareness, image, sharp pricing.
- *Weaknesses* are areas where the brand may be vulnerable in the marketplace. It is important to identify weaknesses to be able to improve the business. Examples: sales trends, product delivery, lack of technology, marketing.
- *Opportunities* are ways the business could expand within the market. Examples: expand the company, create a new product, venture into a new market, increase purchases, exploit the competitor's weakness, advancement in technology, and explore new trends.
- *Threats* are external issues that can create problems for the company. Examples: capacity to deliver, labor availability, increasing cost in goods to produce, entry of strong competitor, superior new product entering the market, product obsolescence, competitive pricing, change in customer buying.

All four aspects should be analyzed so that a brand can leverage its strengths, fix its weakness, take advantage of its opportunities, and avoid any threats. A SWOT analysis should be continually reviewed due to the ever-changing nature of the business. In time, one area in the SWOT analysis may fit into a different category. For example, if an opportunity is ignored, it can become a threat if a rival decides to use it.

Summary

A product is created with a customer in mind. When seeking information about the target customer it is important to conduct consumer research to review the market segment variables—geographic, demographic, psychographic, affirmative and cognitive, and behavioral segmentation. Maslow's Hierarchy of Needs will provide an understanding of what consumers' basic needs are and what drives customer behaviors. Understanding this will help to position the product as a need or a want. The information gathered about potential customers will assist in driving the direction of the brand.

Online Resources

Bizstats
Bizstats is an online platform for small business information.
www.bizstats.com

Strategic Business Insights
VALS is a product of the division of Strategic Business Insights consulting that helps producers understand consumer behavior.
www.strategicbusinessinsights.com/vals

Helium
Helium is a site that features information from writers that are able to share their knowledge.
www.helium.com

TRADE TERMS

market research

quantitative research

qualitative research

primary research

secondary research

target market

market segmentation

segmentation variables

geographic segmentation

demographic segmentation

psychographic segmentation

social-cultural segmentation

behavioral segmentation

discretionary income

masstige

competitive edge

SWOT analysis

Activity 2.1 Customer Profile

Develop a customer profile. Create a muse board showcasing your core customer. The guidelines in Box 2.1 should be filled out to describe the core customer. Write a one-page narrative describing the consumer. Cite a minimum of three customer profile sources: data, anecdotal, interviews, or professional publications.

Activity 2.2 Competitive Edge

Competitive edge is the ability of the company to produce goods and services more effectively than competitors do, thereby outperforming them. Relating to your mission, describe your competitive edge. Fill out Table 2.1 and analyze your company's competitors.

Activity 2.3 SWOT Analysis

Create a SWOT analysis for the company. Use Figure 2.14 as a guide to fill out the analysis. Use the trade publications listed in Table 2.2 to find industry information

Notes

1. "Market Research." *Small Business Encyclopedia: Entrepreneur.com.* Accessed Dec. 21, 2011. http://www.entrepreneur.com/encyclopedia/term/82436.html.

2. "Market Segmentation." *NetMBA.* Internet Center for Management and Business Administration, Inc. Accessed Oct. 3, 2012. www.netmba.com/marketing/market/segmentation.

3. Saibus Research. "Coach Is Still an Undervalued Blue Chip Firm." *SeekingAlpha.com.* Accessed Oct. 9, 2012. http://seekingalpha.com/article/1495872-coach-is-still-an-undervalued-blue-chip-firm

4. Dover, Mike, and Rob Salkowitz. 2011. "Co-Creating Your Brand with Young World Consumer-Entrepreneurs." *IVEY Business Journal,* Jan. Accessed Oct. 9, 2012. www.iveybusinessjournal.com/topics/strategy/co-creating-your-brand-with-young-world-consumer-entrepreneurs.

TABLE 2.1 **COMPETITOR ANALYSIS**

YOUR BRAND	BRAND 1	BRAND 2	BRAND 3	BRAND 4
Product Placement				
Strength				
Weakness				
Annual Sales				
Product Line				
Quality				
Price Structure				
Marketing Activity				
Target Customer				
Expanding or Shrinking				
Competitive Edge				

This table is an example of competitor analysis that can be filled out to compare the strength and weakness of the brand's competition.
Source: Shari Waters, "What's Your Competitive Edge? Learn How To Conduct Competitive Analysis." *About.com Retailing.* Accessed Dec. 21, 2011. http://retail.about.com/od/competition/a/comp_edge.htm.

5. Dickler, Jessica. 2012. "Consumers: We Want Gucci or Target. Forget the Gap."
CNN Money, Mar. 9. Accessed Oct. 9, 2012. http://money.cnn.com/2011/03/09/pf/
consumers_prefer_luxury/index.htm.

6. Li, Chris. 2008. "Hermès Bags and Hermès Birkin: The Epitome of Luxury." *Articles
Base,* July 10. Accessed March 26, 2009. http://www.articlesbase.com/fashion-articles/
hermes-bags-and-hermes-birkin-the-epitome-of-luxury-478568.html

7. Silverstein, Michael, Neil Friske, and John Butman. 2003. *Trading Up: The New
American Luxury.*

TABLE 2.2 **RETAIL TRADE PUBLICATIONS**

NAME OF PUBLICATION	USEFUL FOR	HOW TO ACCESS IT
About Retail	This website provides information about the retail industry.	www.retailindustry.about.com
Bizstats	Access to financial ratios, business statistics, and benchmarks.	www.bizstats.com
CosmeticWorld	A website with industry news on the beauty industry.	www.cosmeticworld.com
ESRI	Leading source of geo-demographic data used for store location. The specific web page on the ESRI site allows a person to enter a zip code and get a description of the geo-demographic profile of the zip code.	www.esri.com/data/community_data/community-tapestry/index.html
Hoovers	A division of D&B that provides financial information about firms.	premium.hoovers.com/subscribe/ind/factsheet.xhtml?HICID=1518
Internet Retailer	A website on market trends, technology, competitive practices, and the e-commerce industry.	www.internetretailer.com
Modern Jeweler	Monthly magazine for jewelry retailers. Looks at trends in jewelry, gems, and watches.	www.modernjeweler.com
New York Times	Website on entrepreneurship and small businesses.	www.nytimes.com/business/smallbusiness/
NRF SmartBrief	Daily e-mail newsletter highlighting links to the top retail headlines.	www.nrf.com/RetailHeadlines
Retail Bulletin	The Retail Bulletin is an online information source aimed at meeting retailers' need for quick, accurate and up-to-date news about the industry.	www.theretailbulletin.com
Retail Customer Experience	Magazine and email newsletter focusing on the customer experience in stores and on websites. Website for publication has slide shows and research reports.	www.retailcustomerexperience.com
Retailing Today	Published biweekly, providing news, trends, and research for decision makers in the 150 largest retailers.	www.retailingtoday.com
RetailWire	An online discussion forum reporting key dynamics and issues affecting the retailing industry.	www.retailwire.com
Stores	Monthly magazine published by the National Retail Federation (NRF). Aimed at retail executives in department and specialty stores, it emphasizes broad trends in customer behavior, management practices, and technology.	www.stores.org
Supply Chain Brain	*Global Logistics & Supply Chain Strategies* offering case studies, executive interviews, and features providing information on the latest technology, services and processes needed to maximize supply chain efficiency.	www.glscs.com
WGSN	A website with trend forecasting information, business information, and news about the fashion industry.	www.wgsn.com
WWD	Daily newspaper reports fashion and industry news on women's and children's ready-to-wear, sportswear, innerwear, accessories, and cosmetics.	www.wwd.com

Source: "Retail Trade Publication." *Warrington College of Business Administration: David F. Miller Center for Retailing Education and Research.* University of Florida. http://warrington.ufl.edu/centers/retailcenter/docs/TeachRetail_RetailTradePublications.pdf

Bibliography

American Marketing Association. "Dictionary." Accessed April 21, 2012. http://www.marketingpower.com/_layouts/Dictionary.aspx.

Berry, A.W. 2009. "Marketing: Understanding Segmentation Variables." June 29. Accessed Jan. 13, 2012. http://www.insidebusiness360.com/index.php/marketing-using-market-segmentation-variables-18624/

Entrepreneur.com. s.v. "Secondary Market Research." Accessed Dec. 21, 2011. http://www.entrepreneur.com/encyclopedia/term/82616.html.

Entrepreneurship.org. "Conducting a SWOT Analysis." Accessed Dec. 21, 2011. http://www.entrepreneurship.org/en/resource-center/conducting-a-swot-analysis.aspx.

Fleming, Jamie. "How to Start a Focus Group." *eHow.* Accessed Oct. 1, 2012. http://www.ehow.com/how_5127517_start-focus-group.html.

Horyn, Cathy. 2012. "The Fine Line." *New York Times,* Jan. 25. http://www.nytimes.com/2012/01/26/fashion/haute-couture-the-fine-line.html

Nykiel, Donald A. 2003. *Marketing Your Business.* Binghamton, New York: The Haworth Press, Inc.

Olivarez, Brittany. 2011. "Selling Psychology: Wants vs. Needs." *Helping Psychology,* Jan. 18. Accessed Jan. 13, 2012. http://helpingpsychology.com/selling-psychology-wants-vs-needs.

Peck, Krista. 2012. "Your Brand and Maslow's Hierarchy of Needs." *Insode FMM,* Dec. 14. http://insidefmm.com/2012/12/why-customers-buy-customer-behavior/

Silverstein, Michael J., Neil Fiske, and John Butman. 2008. *Trading Up: Why Consumers Want New Luxury Goods—and How Companies Create Them.* New York: Penguin Group.

Spaeder, Karen E. "How to Research Your Business Idea." *Entrepreneur.com.* Accessed Dec. 21, 2011. http://www.entrepreneur.com/article/70518.

Spors, Kelly K. 2011. "Three Ways to Find an Edge in a Crowded Market." *Entrepreneur.com,* July 7. Accessed Dec. 21, 2011. http://www.entrepreneur.com/article/219945.

Textilesindepth.com. "Types of Fashion: Different Types of Fashion, Types of Fashion Styles, Types of Fashion Design, Haute Couture, Ready-to-wear, Mass Market." Accessed Jan. 13, 2012. http://www.textilesindepth.com/index.php?page=types-of-fashion.

Thompson, Derek. 2011. "Who's Had the Worst Recession: Boomers, Millennials, or Gen-Xers?" *The Atlantic,* Sep.13. Accessed Oct. 11, 2012. http://www.theatlantic.com/business/archive/2011/09/whos-had-the-worst-recession-boomers-millennials-or-gen-xers/245056/.

Ward, Susan. "6 Ways to Find Out What Your Competition Is Up To: How to Gather Competitive Intelligence on Your Competitors." *About.com Small Business: Canada.* Accessed May 1, 2012. http://sbinfocanada.about.com/od/marketresearch/a/comintelligence.htm.

3

Brand Personification

To cut through the clutter of product saturation, entrepreneurs utilize branding as an effective way to differentiate their products and to establish credibility with the consumer. One must carefully orchestrate interplay between inspired creativity and analytical rigor. Creating a brand perception requires intrusion—a remapping of a consumer's brand preference. The brand must be authentic and powerful enough to force consumers out of their routines and into newness. Consumers must remember the brand experience and note it for long-standing preferences. Iconic fashion brands begin with a collective synergy to create a first, lasting impression at a glance.

KEY CONCEPTS

+ Identify assessment tools for brand analysis.

+ Understand the components of a brand statement.

+ Explore the fundamentals of brand development.

+ Examine emotional drivers to make a brand connection.

+ Establish tactics to building brand equity.

Brand Power

A strong brand has incredible power—not just in how it is perceived in the world, but also in how it redefines the competitive landscape, connects with prospects and influencers, creates memorable experiences, builds lasting relationships, and helps entrepreneurs and corporate organizations better manage people, resources, and profits. The following images evoke the power and presence of internationally recognized brands (Figures 3.1, 3.2, 3.3, 3.4, and 3.5).

From a holistic perspective, a **brand** is a distinct entity with a name, sign, or set of perceptions intended to create an identity and differentiation among likeness. It represents a product, idea, or service. **Branding** is a vital strategy laced within brand development. It is the process of attaching a name, image, or reputation to a product, idea, or service.

Branding is a major force in the fashion industry. Effective entrepreneurs utilize branding as the solidifying precursor to a product. It is the fundamental voice that embodies the product. A relentless product differentiation strategy is needed to build recognition. Emotional engagement has become a dominant tactic to build consumer loyalty. From the idiosyncrasy to the obvious, a product's positioning is often conveyed through layers of reinforcement to establish and secure its identity in the marketplace.

Figure 3.1 Zac Posen ready-to-wear collection. Model: Liya Kebede. *Source: Fairchild Fashion Media.*

Figure 3.2 Gucci ready-to-wear collection. Model: Eugenia Volodina. *Source: AFP/Getty Images.*

Figure 3.3 Alexander Wang ready-to-wear collection. Model: Shu Pei Qin. *Source: Fairchild Fashion Media.*

Figure 3.4 Burberry Prorsum collection. *Source: Fairchild Fashion Media.*

Brand Analysis

When an entrepreneur enters into a branding arena that is laden with product saturation and heavy competition, it can be intimidating or over–whelming. Conducting brand analysis and setting strategy will eradicate uncertainty and ensure a firm start. **Brand analysis** involves sizing up the industry, evaluating the competition, and creating a strategic plan.

The entrepreneur should assess the market:

1. Market size—the scope of competition
2. Growth rate of their particular industry sector
3. Current growth cycle of the industry sector
4. Number of competitors and their relative size
5. Market saturation—price classifications
6. Number of customers and their relative size
7. Type of distribution channels used to access existing/potential customers

If these crucial market assessments are not executed, an entrepre–neur may find that the brand may not fit well with the intended sector of the industry or may not be capable of establishing and maintaining a competitive advantage for the new product. Once the assessments are determined as a prosperous opportunity, the long-term direction, objectives, and strategies can be developed. Designer, Rebecca Minkoff explains her well-devised brand formula to enter into a competitive market in Box 3.1.

As a step in assessing the market and conducting brand analysis, entrepreneurs must determine the appropriate price classification for their niche products.

Price Classifications

In the fashion industry, products are segmented by price classifications. Based on the retail price range of a product, a brand will position into a specific price category. Entrepreneurs must evaluate their products to ascertain the extrinsic value that correlates to quality. In ready-to-wear, fabric, construction, and fit are significant factors that dictate quality and steer the price classification. Ready-to-wear apparel is mass produced and manufactured to standard size specifications generated by the brand entity. Consumers often utilize fit as a fundamental factor to garner a price-to-quality relationship. Traditionally, the brand entity allows tolerances per size specification that directly impact fit. Tolerance is a measurement that varies from the desired size specification. The higher the price classification, the lower the allowable tolerance permitted for each size specification, whereas the lower the price classification, the higher the allowable tolerance for each size specification. Size categories are based upon fit, also referred to as the body type, of the targeted consumer. An example in women's apparel is junior, misses, petite, or plus. Junior is an adolescent or youthful body type indicated by sizes with an odd numerical sequence 00–11. Misses is a fully developed woman's body type indicated by an even numerical sequence 0–12. Specialty sizes are plus, petite, and tall. The fit of the garment caters to average body specifications for the stated category.

There are six major price classifications in the fashion and beauty sector: designer, bridge, contemporary, better, moderate, and budget.

Figure 3.5 Christian Louboutin footwear. *Source: Corbis.*

1. *Designer.* This is the highest price point in luxury ready-to-wear, accessories, footwear, and beauty. Prestigious designer brands such as Prada, Yves St. Laurent, Balenciaga, Ralph Lauren, and Christian Louboutin are in this price sector. Designer boutiques, luxury multibrand boutiques, and specialty stores, such as Bergdorf Goodman, Neiman Marcus, and Saks Fifth Avenue, retail these products. This category has the most astute quality in mass-produced goods. The price points range into the thousands from brand to brand.

2. *Bridge.* This price point positions slightly lower than designer. It consists of designer diffusion collections—strong aesthetics but in lower quality, thus lower prices. Notable collections are C by Chloe, D&G by Dolce & Gabbana, Elie Tahari, CH by Carolina Herrera, and Michael Kors. The prices vary by designer or manufacturer.

3. *Contemporary.* Products in this classification market to youthful-spirited consumers. Notable brands are Rag & Bone, Marc by Marc Jacobs, Alice + Olivia, and Elizabeth and James. Retailers such as Barneys, Nordstrom, and multibrand boutiques carry this price point, which varies for each brand and typically ranges from $300 to $1,000.

4. *Better.* This price point caters to the mass market—the largest consumer segment. Manufacturers such as Liz Claiborne and

BOX 3.1 Rebecca Minkoff

How to Break into a Crowded Industry

Rebecca Minkoff's fast-track growth is particularly notable because she found success in an already crowded and fiercely competitive fashion industry. While the number of fashion-design houses has decreased 2.3 percent annually since 2005, industry revenues have been growing 0.6 percent per year, giving the remaining players an increasingly bigger piece of the market, according to IBISWorld, a market-research firm based in Los Angeles. Here, Minkoff shares her top three tips for launching a business in a competitive industry:

1. **Be unique.** Piggybacking on an existing product or service usually won't get your business noticed in competitive markets, Minkoff says. Yours should fill a need and stand out from the competition. "I created a line for what I wanted to wear—and what I saw there was a lack of in the market—in terms of design and function at an affordable price," she says.

2. **Know your price point.** Regardless of the industry, customers want a quality product for a great price, Minkoff says. Setting an appropriate price for a product or service is crucial. Minkoff learned that lesson after she downgraded the leather for a particular handbag without lowering the retail price. "I didn't put a tag on it saying it was made with this other type of leather, but the bag didn't look the same, and my customers knew it," she says. "We recognized that immediately when sales for the item didn't perform."

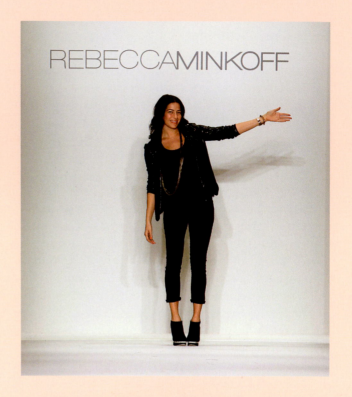

3. **Listen and respond.** Establishing communication with customers and making them feel a part of the decision-making process has been important to Minkoff's success.

Source: J. Fell. 2011. Partial interview from "How a Young Fashion Designer Stands Out in a Crowded Market." *Entrepreneur.com*, May 5. http://www.entrepreneur.com/article/219578

Jones New York provide quality products at affordable price points. Department stores such as Macy's and Dillard's carry these lines. Brand retailers such as Ann Taylor, Banana Republic, and J.Crew focus on this price sector. The retail price points are typically under $200.

5. *Moderate.* These are affordable fashion products for the mass-market consumer. Products have a lower quality to maintain their low-price stance. Brand retailers such as Gap and Zara and department stores such as Kohl's and JCPenney cater to this price segment. The price range is typically below $100.

6. *Budget.* This is the lowest price-point class. Fast-fashion goods positioned in this price sector are trend-driven products that are low-quality goods and sold in high volume at low price points. Retailers such as Forever 21 and H&M and big-box stores such as Kmart and Walmart cater to this price segment.

Brand Statement

To plan for brand development there needs to be an overarching focal point. Much like the mission and vision statements for the company, many entrepreneurs create brand statements. A **brand statement** is a touchstone to communicate the intrinsic value of the brand and provides direction for where the brand is going in the market. A brand statement defines the company's brand message and promise. It identifies where the company is and is used as a tool to guide the company in the future. A brand statement also can be used as a consistency test to ensure all brand efforts are promoting the brand, and not confusing consumers.

Questions to examine when developing a brand statement:

- What is the brand message?
- How does the consumer experience the brand?
- What brand concepts are compelling and differentiating?

Figure 3.6 Brand synergy. Brands have a unique intersection of strategy, communications, design, and technology.

Brand Building

In today's competitive industry, entrepreneurs must harness traditional communications, digital media, mobile devices, and social networks to make every touch point speak in unison. In every price classification, powerful brands have a unique intersection of strategy, communications, design and technology—the synergy of brand building (Figure 3.6).

CASE STUDY 3.1   **The Top Ten Designers**

In [2012]'s top ten list of most-recognized designer brands, Calvin Klein, Tommy Hilfiger and Ralph Lauren take the three top spots—and for good reason. Each of these brands stands for a particular genre of Americana that U.S. consumers react to emotionally, and likely identify with. There's no denying the fact that when it comes to brand awareness, American consumers like to keep things close to home.

Calvin Klein, for instance, is a homegrown megabrand with an offering that spans three retail tiers (designer, bridge, and better) and a variety of categories. Tommy Hilfiger's take on preppy-with-a-twist designs offers a novel vision of American East Coast dress codes, and Ralph Lauren, like no other U.S. designer, embodies quintessential luxury rendered through an American lens.

Brand proclivities aside, these three brands are also masters at conveying their messages to consumers. Gucci, in fourth position, knows a hot commodity when it sees one. The Italian fashion company secured Charlotte

Casiraghi, the beautiful yet press-shy daughter of Princess Caroline of Monaco. Coming in at number five, Vera Wang. Besides her high-profile bridal and ready-to-wear collections, Wang has a significant presence at Kohl's with Simply Vera Vera Wang and the Princess Vera Wang junior collection. She also offers more affordably priced bridal gowns through a deal with David's Bridal and the Vera Wang Love collection of wedding bands at Zales.

The Top 10:

1. Calvin Klein
2. Tommy Hilfiger
3. Ralph Lauren
4. Gucci
5. Vera Wang
6. DKNY
7. Louis Vuitton
8. Chanel
9. Dolce & Gabbana
10. Giorgio Armani

Source: Marc Karimzadeh. 2012. "The Top 10 Designers." *Women's Wear Daily,* December 13. http://www.wwd.com/fashion-news/fashion-features/the-top-10-designers-6521785

Brand building is comprised of innovative insights and strategies, brought to life by a product message that engages the consumer.

Core aspects of brand building:

- *Emotion:* Brands drive growth by connecting to emotion and reason in equal measure. For example, Bobbi Brown Cosmetics has redefined beauty to enhance one's unique beauty, not cover it up. The products are formulated to create a natural and healthy appearance. The duality of branding self-esteem and enhancement through product gives an emotional stance to the consumer.
- *Creativity:* Brands are crafted and expressed through inspiration and creativity to generate preference and loyalty. For example, Anna Sui collections are riddled with colorful patterns and prints and the mixing of each. This creative use of texture, color, layering, and mixing is the brand's signature. It has created brand recognition and consumer loyalty. Missoni has masterfully intrigued and maintained consumer loyalty with their iconic pattern, robust color palette, and modern knitwear collections. Both designers have created brand recognition and consumer loyalty with strategic tactics in textiles and design.
- *Longevity:* Brands must retain relevance and appeal over time, using intelligent brand management techniques and metrics. An example, Ralph Lauren collections expand across multiple categories of business and price point. The brands have an aura of timelessness that gives them life beyond the season of purchase. This longevity factor has made the brand a classic.
- *Financial:* Brands, if managed well, enable companies to embody their vision and inspire stakeholders—customers, employees, partners, and the investment community. Brands are economic assets to be invested in and managed for financial returns. For example, lululemon athletica is a publicly traded company that embodies a proven brand strategy with financial stability for the company and its investor.

As a brand owner or creator, entrepreneurs have a unique perspective that builds the brand identity.

Brand Identity

An entrepreneur must create a brand identity that evokes dynamism within its sector of the industry. It must have a point of origin, a storyline, and a concise vantage point to generate consumer interest. Consumers are highly discerning and have myriad choices to satisfy their needs and wants. Brand identity and product consistency ensures a concise vantage point the consumer can rely upon. The repetition and evolution secures and strengthens the identity of the brand in the marketplace.

Brand identity is the personality of a product. It is a set of distinct characteristics that provides identity cues to the consumer. It can be a visual or physical aesthetics or mental association, such as a symbol, of the brand.

- *Color:* Valentino red
- *Graphic:* Target bullseye
- *Logo:* Movado dot (Figure 3.7)
- *Packaging:* Tiffany blue box (Figure 3.8)
- *Typography:* H&M font

Figure 3.7 Brand identification with a symbol: A Movado timepiece with the iconic dot. *Source: Denis Beyeler/Alamy.*

Brand Name

What sets the trajectory of a brand's identity often begins with its name: as the adage claims, everything is in a name. The foundation that brings a product to life starts with creating the **brand name.** A brand name is a symbol, word, logo, or set of perceptions intended to identify or represent a product or service. A fundamental goal in developing a brand name is to create a unique identity. The same principle is applicable for an **eponymous brand.** Eponymous brands reflect the name of a person who inspired, designed, or created the idea, product, or service (e.g., Patrick Kelly, Christian Dior, Carolina Herrera, and Marc Jacobs).

Although the formation of a company name is important, it can differ from the product's brand name. The product name, often referred to as the brand name, will permeate the market and establish a relationship with the intended consumer. The brand name can be suggestive or arbitrary rather than descriptive. This approach will allow unlimited flexibility for future brand extension growth.

When a brand name is applied to a product, it should require imagination, thought, or perception to determine the nature of the goods. It should complement the company's positioning and resonate with the target market.

The juxtaposition and dichotomy of the brand name also can evoke emotions of interest and curiosity. For example, the brand name

Figure 3.9 *d*irt, a luxurious natural body scrub collection. *Source: Erthe Beaute, LLC.*

of a luxurious natural body scrub collection is *d*irt (Figure 3.9). The company's name is Erthe Beaute. The product's natural ingredients and earth-inspired essence support the brand name. The name resonates with the contemporary consumer and ecoconscious users because of its earthy, whimsical brand name. Its luxury packaging and suitable product names further define the brand. Furthermore, *d*irt's tagline, "groundbreaking beauty," reinforces the brand's product philosophy of being a niche, underground, natural beauty product. A **tagline** is the verbal or written portion of a message that summarizes the main idea in a few memorable words.

Company Name

Unlike a brand name, a company name provides legal identity to the business entity in a specific trade sector. The company name can be separate and distinct from the brand name of a product or service, or it can be the same. When a company's name is different from their brand name, a

Tip 3.1 **Create-a-minute!**

Remember: Quality is often revealed in the details. In accessories and personal care, packaging is an extension of a product. It often defines the brand image in the mind of the consumer.

term that often is used to describe the brand name is a "DBA," which is the acronym for "doing business as." An example would be the company Erthe Beaute LLC, whose product brand name is *dirt*. The company is legally recognized as the limited liability corporation; however, it conducts business as *dirt*. A core reason to separate the company name from the brand name is for growth or dissolving a brand without interfering with the legal business entity.

Creating a company/business name is a significant task for an entrepreneur. Here are basic guidelines:

- Create a company name that is meaningful and distinct from direct and indirect competition.
- Create a name that resonates with the trade sector and target market.
- Create a name that can be effortlessly pronounced.
- Be mindful of creative name spelling. It can be misinterpreted as erroneous.
- Be mindful that if you use an eponymous name, it will be associated with the success and failure of the company.

Another example of company delineation is subsidiary structuring of secondary business units under a parent company. Louis Vuitton Moët Hennessy (LVMH) has different business entities under its umbrella. Each business is independently operated, yet maintains a relationship with the others through the parent ownership. Examples include LVMH and Donna Karan (Figure 3.10).

As an entrepreneur, one must complete due diligence by researching the availability of the company and brand name. The most common way to ensure name availability is by searching a state's Secretary of State website. Registering a limited liability or corporation business entity/company name is mandatory. In most states, a company will register its name at the county level, but some states require the name to be registered at the state level. It is important to research the law of the state where the business will be formed to see the requirements. A second search option is in the United States Trademark and Patent Office (USTPO) website. Not all companies file claims of ownership of the company or brand mark. Lastly, conduct a name search on all online search engines to see if the name is available. It is critical to conduct thorough name research to avoid trademark infringement.

Brand Positioning

At the creation of a brand, the product's price classification must be established to position it into a sector of the fashion industry and gain

Figure 3.10 Donna Karan collection. *Source: Victor VIRGILE/Gamma-Rapho/Getty Images.*

Tip 3.2 **Create-a-minute!**

Remember: When creating your company name or brand name, research is critical! Be sure the name you choose is available but, equally important, not similar to an existing brand.

identity with the intended consumer. Price classifications are the core determinant of a brand's positioning strategy. The six price classifications for mass produced consumer products are designer, bridge, contemporary, better, moderate, and budget. The highest price classification is designer and descends to budget. The actual price point categories come from the items' industry sector—ready-to-wear is a different price classification than beauty.

Brand positioning is a company's intended posture and image of the brand in the mind of the consumer. It highlights its differentiation among the competition and its advantage in the price classification. Differentiation reflects what is unique or distinctly sets a brand apart from the competition.

In the designer market, Louis Vuitton is positioned as a luxury brand in the designer price sector of the fashion industry (Figure 3.11). The company has successfully personified its consumer as the consummate

Figure 3.11 Louis Vuitton has superior high-quality travel luggage. Product shown was featured at a new store opening celebrating Vuitton's 150th anniversary, February 10, 2004, in New York City. *Source: Peter Kramer/Getty Images Entertainment/Getty Images.*

Tip 3.3 **Create-a-minute!**

Remember: The psychographics of your customer can easily be identified in their daily routine—from sunrise to sunset.

luxury traveler. Its positioning was created upon introduction of the brand. The brand's point of origin was established in 1854 with its high quality travel luggage that in this modern day is still touted as the Art of Traveling. The company has capitalized on its heritage of superior quality through a succession of brand extensions.

Successful brands have the target customer in mind when creating the product collection. A muse is a personification of the target customer that inspires aesthetics of the brand's image. To capture the essence of the brand persona, entrepreneurs often create a visual board using consumer magazine tear sheets to identify who the muse will be for the brand. This aids in knowing the psychographic matrix for the targeted consumer. Here are questions to consider to aid in harnessing and personifying the brand's positioning:

- What is the targeted consumer demographic—age, education, income, etc.?
- What is the targeted consumer personality type?
- What is the consumer's style—apparel, home décor, etc.?
- What is the consumer's career/lifestyle?
- What are the targeted consumer's hobbies, habits, passions, and pursuits?

By researching the aforementioned questions, an entrepreneur will generate the ideology of the targeted consumer and define the parameters for designing, branding, and selling the product. It's a process of creating a narrative about the consumer in order to identify and ultimately satisfy that consumer's needs or wants: How well do you know your customer and does your brand reflect their interest and mirror their lifestyle? A creative tool that merges technology with fashion is the collaboration between Samsung and Polyvore. With the Samsung GALAXY Note II smartphone, consumers can explore their creativity and put together their own fashion style with the enhanced Easy Clip feature (see Box 3.2 consumer profile and Figure 3.12 GALAXY Note II Smartphone).

Brand extensions are product lines marketed under the same general brand as a previous item or items. Ralph Lauren is touted as the authority on lifestyle branding. His empire ranges from designer to moderate price classifications across apparel product categories. The company stretches its branding strategy into home furnishing collections and his RL restaurants. In apparel, Ralph Lauren has successfully expanded different lines under his varied brands. Another example of brand extension is Louis Vuitton. The distinct brand extension difference from Ralph Lauren is that Louis Vuitton has expanded in a single price classification of prestige to remain solely accessible to their targeted consumer. Louis Vuitton has successfully spread the integrity of its positioning from luxury

BOX 3.2 Consumer Profile

Developing a consumer profile brings the consumer to life in the mind of the entrepreneur. By researching or extracting information about the targeted consumer, you essentially build the "ideal" target customer. This tangible set of demographic, geographic, and behavioral information will help shape the product attributes and benefits. This method of pinpointing a single person from a homogeneous group yields the model consumer for a product or service. This development process is considered idea generation, keeping the entrepreneur sharply focused on its targeted consumer.

Exemplify your target customer using the basic information below.

Name:

Gender:

Age:

Family status:

Annual income:

Geographic location:

Career:

Fashion style:

Brand loyalty:

Buying habits:

Leisure activities:

Travel destinations:

Social media favorites:

Pursuits and passion:

Must-haves:

Figure 3.12 Samsung GALAXY Note II smartphone muse board app. *Source: Samsung.*

travel cases into other product categories such as ready-to-wear, time-pieces, accessories, and footwear (Figure 3.13).

Brand Story

Consumers are intelligent, well-researched, and demanding. Technology has provided a wealth of trade knowledge to the consumer. Increasingly, consumers have fundamental information at their fingertips. They readily seek the story behind the brand and build a relationship with the brand. For many fashion companies, the dominant branding mission has become lifestyle driven. Brands are being introduced within the context of lifestyle utility, while romancing their features and benefits as the ancillary matter.

The entrepreneur must stay ahead of the consumer and create a lure of interest and entertainment that intrigues the target market. Many brands have extended the brand's voice and use a brand story to add meaningful depth and emotional integrity to the product. The core element of a **brand story** is a narrative that communicates the ethos of the brand. It's used to generate brand power through an emotional connection with consumers, whereas the brand is perceived as an extension of consumers' personalities and lifestyle. The most successful fashion brands evoke emotion thorough a series of lifestyle images in their advertisements, websites, and social media platforms. They reflect and confirm the consumer's aspiration, identity, and stature. These visual monologues beckon the consumer to live the brand (Box 3.3).

When a consumer inquires about the derivative of a name, history, or heritage, this is an entrepreneurial opportunity to tell the product or brand story. The story becomes the overarching strategy to engage the consumer and ignite brand loyalty. **Brand loyalty** is when a consumer buys the same manufacturer-originated product or service repeatedly over time rather than buying from competition within the category. Placing consumers outside of a brand story reveals that there are voids in their closets and reinforces the need for relationship with a specific brand by purchasing a product.

A product is a product and a dress is a dress, it seems. One brand story that permeates the industry is the legacy of the little black dress (LBD)

Figure 3.13 Ralph Lauren collection. *Source: Victor VIRGILE/Gamma-Rapho/Getty Images.*

BOX 3.3 *dirt*: Brand Story

Despite its grimy reputation, dirt is literally a natural substance that cleanses, nourishes, and stimulates growth, and produces beauty among other things. Organic in nature, it's the mastermind behind every harvest. We were inspired by its nutrient-rich properties, hence begins the story of our groundbreaking beauty… DIRT.

Created to nurture the body and broaden the landscape of beauty, the DIRT team hit the ground and stayed there. They dug in the garden, rummaged through the pantry and refrigerator to concoct exfoliation recipes from fruits, vegetables, and natural ingredients that could remove dead skin cells while infusing moisture for a healthy, radiant glow. In the laboratory, they refined culinary creations into formulas packed with antioxidants, vitamins, botanical and essential oils and cultivated luxurious body treatments that inspire personal beauty rituals.

Source: Courtesy of Erthe Beaute, LLC. www.dirtbeaute.com

Figure 3.14 Little black dress. Elie Saab ready-to-wear. Model: Drielle Valeretto. *Source: Fairchild Fashion Media.*

that began with Coco Chanel—a story wrapped into a single silhouette. Understanding the story behind the LBD brings interest. The ideology comes to life and creates a relationship with the wearer. It becomes an artistic expression that extends from one fashion generation to the next. It has become a staple in the wardrobe of women across the world. What was once merely a symbol of mourning has become a universal statement for understated elegance and a must-have item for designers and fashionable women across every price classification (Figure 3.14).

Brand Design

Once the company name is established, a brand name is created, the brand positioning is determined, and a story is developed, the brand aesthetics warrant development. The brand design aesthetics are the carriage of the product. They support the packaging of the brand and are the conduit to facilitate visual identity in tandem with the product.

Brand design, the micro level of brand identity, is where the details that settle into the mind of the consumer reside—the logo, the label, the color of the label, the shape of the label, the font, the hangtag, and so on. For a cohesive branding approach, use the same color scheme, fonts, and design for brand labels, marketing materials, business cards, letterhead, and websites and blogs.

At point of sale, there must be a continuum to the brand's dynamism and perception that extends beyond the product to maintain brand positioning and brand loyalty. A brand's logo is just as important as the name. The logo is the first visceral connection the consumer makes with the brand. It triggers the brand perception.

Practical considerations in logo design:

- It must be authentic and easily recognizable.
- Its intention and message should be perfectly clear.
- It must reflect the sensibilities of the targeted consumer.
- It must reproduce well in various sizes and media.

Brand Appeal

To truly captivate an audience, a brand must know itself. Entrepreneurs should be acutely aware of the product's point-of-difference. This will become the brand's competitive advantage.

A **competitive advantage** exists when the factors critical for success within the industry permit the brand to outperform its competitors. Advantages can be gained by having differentiation in terms of providing superior performance or unique attributes that are important to customers. A key to building the brand's image is to be unique within the positioned category.

Each price category has an observed set of aesthetics that reflect the target market. For example, the luxury market has an image of refined exclusivity that conveys simplicity or extravagance. The premium market has a youthful, innovative edge that conveys innovative rebellion with confidence. The better market has a practicality that reads as classic and enduring. The mass and fast-fashion markets have an explicit sense of bold urgency that reads now or never.

Brand Equity

Companies build brand equity through strategic branding execution that happens over time. Brand equity is achieved through brand recognition, brand image, product usage, and customer loyalty. **Brand equity** is the value of a brand. The three common ways brand equity is built:

- *Introduction:* Introduce quality products with the strategic intent to use the brand platform to launch product extensions. Example: Yoga Smoga is high performance, modern yoga clothing company that retains a connection to yoga's ancient Indian roots.
- *Elaboration:* Establish a memorable brand experience that is positive and encourages repeat purchases. Example: Yoga Smoga reiterates their wellness approach through their product and mantra of one breath at a time. Their iconic logo is based on traditional symbology that conveys a balanced and powerful energy center.
- *Fortification:* The brand should carry a consistent message that reinforces its positioning in the mind of the consumer. Example: YogaSmoga supports health, education, and financial support to small cottage industries through its Namaskar Foundation.

To effectively build brand equity, the distribution channels must be parallel in positioning to reach the consumer and solidify the brand message. An entrepreneur must consider the appropriate conduits to market and sell his or her product or service. The channels must mirror the brand personification or image. This is vital to the survival of the brand's identity in the marketplace. A brand must convey a singular brand message from conception to distribution to generated consumer loyalty and build equity.

Summary

Brand personification is a pivotal process that establishes a relationship with the consumer by providing consistent messages about a product or service using multiple platforms. Successful branding involves establishing a clear brand message. The development of a cohesive mixture of elements and strategies creates brand identity. Understanding what makes a product unique provides insight for differentiation and brand image. For branding success, an emotional connection must be made with the consumer. To create brand loyalty, consumers must view the brand as an extension of their personalities and lifestyle.

Online Resources

Entrepreneur.com
A publication that carries news stories about entrepreneurialism, small business management, and business opportunities.
www.entrepreneur.com

Marketing Scoop
A useful website for branding and social media. An Internet marketing expert reveals powerful marketing secrets.
www.marketingscoop.com

Activity 3.1 Brand Identity

1. What is your brand's distinct characteristic or point of difference?

2. Select an established fashion brand with which you've had a positive brand experience. Identify and list the factors about the brand that created the positive experience.

3. List factors that you perceive are pivotal to developing a positive brand experience for your new brand or brand extension.

TRADE TERMS

brand

branding

brand analysis

brand statement

brand identity

brand name

eponymous brand

tagline

brand positioning

brand extensions

brand story

brand loyalty

competitive advantage

brand equity

Activity 3.2 Brand Identity

1. What are three adjectives that describe your product?

2. Define your brand positioning.

3. Write a brand statement for your new product and/or brand extension.

Bibliography

American Marketing Association. "Dictionary." Accessed April 2013. http://www.marketingpower.com/_layouts/Dictionary.aspx.

Bobbibrowncosmetics.com. "Bobbi Buzz: Bobbi's Story." http://www.bobbibrowncosmetics.com/cms/bobbi_buzz/bobbi_story_index.tmpl?cm_sp=Gnav-_-BobbiBuzz-_-BobbisStory

BusinessDictionary.com. s.v. "Branding." http://www.business dictionary.com/definition/marketing.html

Hameide, Kaled. 2011. *Fashion Branding Unraveled.* New York: Fairchild Books.

Marketing Scoop. "Emotional Marketing." Accessed April 2013. http://www.marketingscoop.com/emotional-marketing.htm

Reiss, Craig. 2011. "How to Build a Winning Brand." *Entrepreneur .com.* Accessed April 2013. http://www.entrepreneur.com/article /219314

PART II
THE PRODUCT

New products creatively ignite the fashion world and stimulate the global economy. With enthusiasm and anticipation during fashion week, retail executives, editors, bloggers, celebrities, and consumers flank the perimeter of ready-to-wear runways to view collections that reflect the zeitgeist of each season. These products are the creative culmination of an entrepreneur's passion to create products that are relevant and timely for the brand.

New products and product extensions are the market lifeline for fashion entrepreneurs. Newness is often the acute response to market opportunities. Fashion entrepreneurs must create new products that not only envelop their company's mission and vision but also secure the brand's position in the market. Consumers and industry professionals rely upon the consistency and continuity of a brand's point-of-view through seasonal collections. It creates brand identity, recognition, and loyalty.

Fashion entrepreneurs can have a viable product, but unless it is priced to yield a profit the outcome can be detrimental to the company. They must set financial strategies for the cost, wholesale, and retail pricing and a foundation for strategically sourcing production with domestic or offshore contractors. We expound upon the elements of developing sound operational and organizational strategies to create a product with a solid pricing strategy to start and stay in business—THE PRODUCT.

4

Inspiration + Ingenuity

Successful entrepreneurs develop new products and product extensions that embody the company's mission, vision, and brand positioning. New products are integrated into a company's brand strategy to contribute to its perpetual growth and renewal (Box 4.1). Newness is often the acute response to market opportunities. The target consumer must remain at the crux of an entrepreneur's passion to create products that are relevant and timely for the brand (Figure 4.1). If new products are on the cusp of the market trend or are market sensitive, consumers will flee their existing brand preference for new options. A pivotal example is the H&M and Levi Strauss & Co. ban on sandblasting. Consumers have become increasingly eco-conscious and sensitive to the conditions of production facilities in the apparel industry. In response to the commitment to the health and safety of workers across the apparel industry, Levi Strauss & Co., and Hennes & Mauritz AB (H&M) plan to implement a global ban on sandblasting in all of their future product lines.

To establish context, the product development perspective explored in this chapter is intended for the entrepreneur or small manufacturer. In small companies, the owner or a small executive team commonly executes product development. To become proficient in manufacturing, the entrepreneur must engage in all facets of the product development process.

Product Development

A preemptive step for a fashion entrepreneur is to examine the framework of fashion and deconstruct the unpredictable nature of it. Although it vacillates on the axis of change and innovation, fashion can be comprehended and forecasted if intensely tracked and intimately followed from season to season. Fashion is immediate and competitive. Designers consistently manipulate fabrics, silhouettes, colors, textures, and other details to manifest their creative voice. Albeit individualized by brand, each component of fashion can be collectively observed and scrutinized to the

+ Understand how to conduct fashion trend research and forecasting.

+ Discover an origin of ingenuity to inspire design concepts.

+ Examine and engage the product development process.

+ Explore concepts of merchandise classification systems.

+ Identify and employ the development calendar.

+ Analyze the product life cycle for product introduction.

BOX 4.1 One-on-One with Vera Wang

LYSACEK: When you want to make something that's modern and exciting, how do you also make sure that it is comprehendible to a larger audience?

WANG: It's been challenging for me with my ready-to-wear line. Certainly a big challenge for me with evening wear is to make it look modern and artistic and avant-garde. In terms of bridal, I've tried everything. I've tried short, long, deconstructed, constructed, bustiers, working in fabrics, working in color. I've been working in color in bridal for probably fifteen years. Who else would do an entire collection dipped in tea? My design team dipped every single dress in tea in a bathtub. I did that just because I wanted to work out of the vocabulary of white. Those have been quite challenging parts. It's kind of hard when your moniker is "bridal" and "evening" for people to understand that I don't run around in a bridal gown all day, nor do I run around in an evening gown. I run around in clothes that resonate for me. I wanted to do those clothes in my ready-to-wear collection—because I don't know how you can be a woman designing for other women and not relate it back to yourself. I think the greatest women, the ones I most respect in design—Miuccia Prada, Jil Sander, and Rei Kawakubo of Comme des Garçons—are all women extremely confident about their vision. I think fashion is intensely personal. It should give a woman a creative outlet, it should give her a little bit of an escape, and it should give her a little bit of individuality that she can add to her life. It's important to view fashion as personal and creative—even for brides. To me it's about respect and self-understanding and honesty.

Image Source: David Livingston/Getty Images Entertainment/Getty Images

Source: Evan Lysacek. 2013. "Vera Wang." *Interview Magazine,* December. http://www.interviewmagazine.com/fashion/vera-wang#_

point of predictability. Entrepreneurs must be resourceful and relentless in pursuit of ingenuity. By conducting trend research, developing a creative voice, and understanding consumer readiness, an entrepreneur becomes primed for product development in the fashion industry.

Product development is the synergistic efforts of trend research, planning, designing, merchandising, and production processes to create a product for the intended consumer (Figure 4.2). Product development involves but is not limited to:

- Trend research
- Idea generation
- Product planning
- Product concepts
- Design development
- Production

COVENTRY UNIVERSITY LONDON CAMPUS

Figure 4.2 Product development steps.

Figure 4.1 Fashion entrepreneurs must harness their creative voice amongst the range and complexities of inspiration and ingenuity. Alexander McQueen. *Source: Fairchild Fashion Media.*

A **trend** is movement or the general direction that an item is moving in based on observation. Entrepreneurs must immerse themselves in the industry's current major and minor trends. The adage "timing is everything" is a truism. Identifying fashion trends while they are in progress can steer a brand's creative direction toward or away from innovative ideas. One must learn how to estimate the duration and the scope of a trend. Market pressures for condensed development cycles are forcing brands to implement lean and efficient processes in the front-end design and development processes. Timing is the baseline to ascertain the rise or fall of what is prevalent in the marketplace—it can unravel a product concept or stitch together an unforgettable collection.

Trend Research and Forecasting

Being engrossed in research is the starting point for product development. Fashion historians contend that fashion reflects the time in which it is created and worn. The entrepreneur must extrapolate the spirit of the times, the **zeitgeist**, as a critical variable to the direction of fashion. The purpose of **trend research** and **trend forecasting** is to provide actionable trade intelligence to improve a brand's overall strategic direction.

Trend research is conducted in all areas of the fashion industry: design, production, manufacturing, merchandising, marketing, product development, and management. Executives use forecasting as input for planning. Product developers use the short-term trend forecast of color, textile, and style direction to shape collections. Marketing managers use it to position products. An entrepreneur will need an all-encompassing posture to merge forecasts with the burgeoning brand's identity, product philosophy, and positioning. Trends can be magnified or diluted to reach the intended consumer (Figures 4.3 and 4.4).

Primary Sources

Surveying the retail environment, tracking prominent style innovators, and watching fashion unfold on the street are all basic forms of primary research for idea generation. If an entrepreneur is developing a brand extension, last year's sales and overall historical sales data from retail partners is equally important for insightful direction. To optimize the information, an entrepreneur must shift away from opinionated bias and adopt the vantage point of a product developer to gain forecasting competencies in trend research.

Figure 4.3 Designer trend sensitivity. Carolina Herrera Fashion Week in New York City. *Source: Frazer Harrison/Getty Images Entertainment/ Getty Images.*

Figure 4.4 Contemporary trend sensitivity. *Source: Kelynn Smith.*

CASE STUDY 4.1   **Kenji Ikeda Launching Chargeable Handbags**

Understanding the current trends and customers' needs will facilitate the development of a new product, as shown by Kenji Ikeda who launched chargeable handbags in 2012. Talk about a zap on the run. Kenji Ikeda, a Japanese designer known for his luxurious quilted leather handbags, joined forces with Tokyo-based electronics company, Amadana, to produce a collection of bags that can charge smartphones, portable music players and other small gadgets.

The line, called Kenji Amadana, hit stores in Japan in September 2012, with international distribution possible in the future. "I think of the [bags] as mainly men's, but … I don't think it would be strange to call them unisex," said Ikeda, adding that he hopes to add more feminine styles at some point. "Our target customer is anyone who uses a smartphone." Amadana is a ten-year-old consumer electronics company that makes products from media and audio devices to kitchen appliances.

After months of meetings and at least seven rounds of samples, the resulting products melded the innovative

and the practical. A rechargeable battery is sewn into the lining at the bottom of each bag, connected by hidden wires to two USB ports behind a metal logo plate. The bags can be fully recharged in five to six hours, at which point the built-in battery has enough juice to charge an iPhone two-and-a-half times. The bags are compatible with any device charged via a USB cable, and two gadgets can be charged at once. An external indicator at the base of the bag shows how much charge is left in the battery.

Source: Kelly Wetherille. 2012. "Kenji Ikeda Launching Chargeable Handbags." *WWD*, August 27. http://www.wwd.com/accessories-news/handbags/kenji-ikeda-launching-chargeable-handbags-6196883

For research to be useful, an entrepreneur must consider core and peripheral factors that influence fashion direction. The following questions should be used as the precursor for research:

Core
- What are the dominant fashion trends: silhouette, color, texture, fabric, and detail?
- Which trends are in saturation and excess?
- Which trends are unexpected and novel?
- Which trends can extend and translate forward?

Peripheral
- What is the dominating mood of the times—rebellious, political upheaval, war culture, recession or stability, clarity, and confidence?
- What is the market attitude and readiness?
- How can the trends be modified or comingle into wearable utility?
- How can the trends be re-interpreted to make them brand appropriate?

Trade Sources

For an authoritative daily dose of fashion news, *Women's Wear Daily* is the industry's leading source that professionals rely upon to stay abreast of all fashion-related information. *WWD* was founded by Edmund Fairchild as an outgrowth of the menswear journal, *Daily News Record*. Although editors did not always anchor the first row of couture shows, the publication has risen to be the noted as the bible of fashion. WWD focuses on fashion, designers, socialites, and the celebrities that follow and wear the work of designers from around the world. The publication can be accessed online and via paid print subscription.

For global and in-depth trend analysis, entrepreneurs rely upon research that is executed by industry professionals who have committed themselves to market intelligence. Being proprietary knowledge, many trade resources are subscription based. They are expensive; however, the information is affecting and priceless. *The Tobe Report* pioneered fashion trend forecasting. Since 1927, it has provided comprehensive and compelling content in trend and color forecasting, merchandising, and product development. Its parent company, the Doneger Group, is a trusted and highly recognized leading source of global trend intelligence, focused merchandising direction, expert analysis of the retail business, and comprehensive market information (Figure 4.5). Online resources, such as WGSN and TrendStop, are leading companies for fashion forecasting, trend analysis, and research. They provide a global perspective on comprehensive design and style.

Consumer Sources

With a haphazard understanding of fashion, consumers have taken control of their own fashion ideology. In today's progressive technology, fashion blogs, and websites have become an independent voice, readily identifying fashion trends as they occur. Although it is user-friendly and engaging, entrepreneurs can become misled by consumer-generated information that is unfounded and opinion based. There is a plethora of fashion information available to engage and inform the consumer, but these should not be confused with the trade resources.

Tip 4.1 **Create-a-minute!**

Hmm…fashion blogs are a great resource for fashion-conscious consumers, but not necessarily for trade forecasting the next product launch. Steer clear of opinions that are often conveyed as facts. You are the expert!

Figure 4.5 Design concept board from the Doneger Group. Source: Doneger Group.

Trade Driven Resources
Women's Wear Daily
www.wwd.com
The Doneger Group
www.doneger.com
WGSN
www.wgsn.com
TrendStop
www.trendstop.com

Consumer Driven Resources
Style.com
www.style.com
Stylelist
www.stylist.com
The Sartorialist
www.thesartorialist.com
Rookie
www.rookiemag.com

Figure 4.6 Trend resources: trade versus consumer.

As a fashion professional, use fashion trade resources as the predominant research tool, in lieu of consumer resources (Figure 4.6). A focal point of trend research for the entrepreneur is to explore the opportunity for product development and estimate market potential for the brand. By using trade resources to conduct research, entrepreneurs can garner niche opportunities and emerging trends that lead to timely new product development.

Idea Generation

Fashion is a medium often used to reveal creativity. From minimalism to avant-garde, new product ideas can be inspired by a myriad of sources.

Intrinsic

To ignite creative direction, an entrepreneur can tap into his or her ingenuity through a **multisensory experience.** This is a holistic combination of sensory information that filters through the five senses: sight, smell, touch, taste, and hearing. The senses can be used as a primary conduit to inspire silhouette, color, texture, detail, fabrication, and other factors. The multisensory experience has the power to reinforce and subtly reinvent the brand's personality through a new product or brand extension. Ingenuity also can derive from emotions. A reaction to tangible things can trigger feelings that can be conceptualized into a product with the intent to evoke parallel emotions from the wearer. From the celebrity to the reality show phenomenon, inspiration also can be derived from entertainment triumph and tragedy as seen in the Jean Paul Gaultier Spring 2012 Couture collection (Figure 4.7). He memorialized the life of Amy Winehouse in a dynamic apparel collection inspired by her eclectic and glamorous style. Inspiration can evolve from the life and lifestyle of the famed or everyday person.

Extrinsic

Understanding the world around us is a complex task; however, utilizing the wealth of visual inspiration can induce creativity that can translate into a design aesthetic. Ingenuity can be unveiled by exploration of:

- *History:* Visit local art museums to become inspired by different periods and the attire adorn during that time.

Figure 4.7 Jean Paul Gaultier's haute couture show at the 325 rue Saint-Martin, inspired by Amy Winehouse. Model: Joan Smalls on the runway. *Source: Fairchild Fashion Media.*

Figure 4.8 Art parallel of two images by movement and philosophy. *Left:* Ann Demeulemeester. *Source: Victor VIRGILE/ Gamma-Rapho/Getty Images. Right: Abstraction White Rose, Georgia O'Keeffe, 1927. Source: Georgia O'Keeffe Museum/Artist Rights Society.*

- *Culture:* Research an ethnic group that is unfamiliar. Allow an indigenous group to inform and inspire authenticity. Be mindful to respect what is considered sacred by the group to avoid a slanderous or offensive representation.
- *Art:* Study the works of an artist—painter, musician, and vocalist. Transcend the philosophy or movement into creative inspiration (Figure 4.8).
- *Travel:* Visit a familiar or unfamiliar place and gather the unique traditions and norms. From a local bed and breakfast or summer cottage to an international destination, geographic history can inspire creativity.
- *Architecture:* Seek insights from buildings, unique structures, churches, and the usage of lines and angles to inspire silhouettes and patterns.
- *Nature:* Mother Nature has given a rainbow of options—use them to flaunt ingenuity. A sunrise or fall foliage can reveal inspirational color schemes (Figure 4.9).

Figure 4.9 Natural parallel of two images by color and silhouette. *Left:* Couture collection by Emanuel Ungaro. *Source: Corbis. Right:* A blue butterfly isolated on a white background. *Source: Sofiaworld /Shutterstock.*

Idea Generation   **63**

P.S. ... allow sensory elements to guide creativity. Look for intricate shapes in architecture. Look for unusual colors in nature. Be open to what is ever present. The world around you can often be a catalyst to inspire and evoke ideas for your collection. Use your senses as primary research.

Product Concept

After an entrepreneur becomes a creative purveyor, the next step is to harness the inspiration onto a concept board. A **concept board** is a product developer's visual montage of images, color palettes, swatches, textures, and miscellaneous items that inspire creative excitement toward a cohesive product collection. It becomes a harmonious focal point that captures the essence of the intended product concept for the targeted consumer (Figure 4.10).

Figure 4.10 Example of a concept board, which becomes a harmonious focal point that captures the essence of the intended product concept for the targeted consumer. *Source: 911 Pictures.*

The concept board becomes the visual statement that translates into an entrepreneur's creative statement for the product. The **creative statement** communicates the point of origin, the point of view, the color story, fabric selection, texture, silhouette, and the overarching creative aesthetic for the product. Once the creative statement is established, the product concept is awakened. The style direction is determined for execution and development. Depending on an organization's structure and management hierarchy, the product concept is thoroughly discussed to ensure that it reflects the brand positioning and natural progression to reinforce the brand's identity.

Product Planning

For product concepts to become tangible prototypes, it starts with planning. Creating a merchandise plan will help steer product concepts into a solid assortment of goods. **Merchandising** is the masterful combination of having the right product at the right time in the right quantities and in the right distribution channel, with the right marketing to reach the target consumer (Figure 4.11).

In this day, time, and age of product saturation and cost consciousness, creating an apparel **line** or **collection** that has a compelling point of view with a limited number of silhouettes is often the goal. The strongest collections are sharply focused with a clear creative message that is salable and competitive in the marketplace. An entrepreneur must adapt the vantage point of the merchandiser to plan a cohesive and balanced assortment. A **balanced assortment** is a well-planned variety of products that appeals to a specific market. Building a **product assortment** involves creating a range of choices to offer the consumer at a particular time. It is planned according to the desired number of stock-keeping units (SKUs), styles, colors, and sizes included in the line. The combination of unique SKUs will create a related group, often referred to as a "story" or "collection."

Collection Aesthetics

To create a cohesive line or collection, there is a centralized theme that establishes and binds the group to make a single statement. Beyond the

Figure 4.11 Merchandising formula.

Figure 4.12 Cohesive factors.

silhouette, color, texture, detail, and fabrication, the aesthetic focus of an assortment often includes a myriad of considerations (Figure 4.12):

- *Style:* Appropriate trend adoptions for the target consumer
- *Key Item:* A core item that is a staple or platform of the collection
- *Fringe Item:* An add-on, often a test piece in the collection
- *Range:* Styles that appeal to varied retail channels in the price zone
- *Fluidity:* Pieces can work together to generate different looks
- *Consistency:* Product reflects the brand integrity and positioning
- *Packaging:* Reinforces the product image and convey the brand's positioning

Classifying Merchandise

An effective merchandise classification system facilitates planning and developing a comprehensive product collection for consumer selection.

A **merchandise classification system** (Table 4.1) consists of alpha and numeric codes that provide identity to products. It is the platform used to develop a unique style number for each item in a collection. Furthermore, it organizes product into specific group categories. It provides structure to eliminate unplanned duplication or style redundancy in a collection.

Merchandise classification systems are developed by organizations to uniquely suit the identification needs of their product. It is detailed information that fits within the context of an assortment to distinguish one item from the other. For example, a product classification may be a sweater; a subclassification of sweater is a cardigan. As an example, J.Crew has an extensive knit collection with several cardigans in the collection. Often, the cardigans are distinguished by fiber and style treatment—sleeve, detail, hemline, and color, for example.

Tip 4.3 **Create-a-minute!**

Note: When developing a collection it must be cohesive. Have a central theme with a point of view that tells a consistent story.

TABLE 4.1 **CLASSIFICATION PLAN**

MERCHANDISE CLASSIFICATION SYSTEM	
YEAR	
1	2014
2	2015
3	2016
SEASON	
A	Spring
B	Summer
C	Fall
D	Winter
CLASS	
1	Duvet
2	Sheets
3	Pillowcases
4	Shams
SUBCLASS	
1	Duvet
	1 Goose Down Fill
2	Sheets
	1 Fitted
	2 Flat
3	Shams
	1 Standard
	2 King
4	Pillowcases
	1 Standard
	2 King
FABRICATION	
1	Cotton
2	Sateen
3	Velvet
COLOR	
1	Ivory
2	Sandstone
3	Burgundy
SIZE	
1	Double
2	Queen
3	King
4	California King

Design Development

During design development all approved styles are produced to create a **sample** or **prototype** of the design. All specifications are developed for patterning and sewing. Styles are produced in the median size for the prototype. For example, in ready-to-wear a size run may be XS, S, M, L, XL, so the medium is selected as the sample size. The samples are to reflect the exact design specifications as the production product. Preliminary costing starts to render decisions that affect cost: for example, the change of a button can augment cost higher or lower; adding a dart or princess seam for shaping will augment labor cost.

Once the sample line has been created, all garments are fitted on a live person who fits the specification size. This person is called a fit model. Fit models can be contracted from local modeling agencies. This allows the entrepreneur to see the product for corrective purposes and make changes as it relates to fit or styling preferences. Once corrections are made, a second sample is produced and refitted—it becomes a production sample. The timeline between a first and second sample depends on the modifications required. Upon fit approval, the style is ready for production. Final costing is executed. Additional production samples are often made for seasonal markets and shown to retailers for order placement, determining successes and failures.

Production

Mass production is the actual development of product in bulk quantity. Industry professionals abbreviate the term to "production" as a quick reference point to the specifications of a finished good (Figure 4.13). After

Figure **4.13** Production. *Source: Alaettin YILDIRIM/Shutterstock.*

an entrepreneur and the sales team have secured orders from showing the sample collection at market, orders are tallied to reflect the units sold by style. A buyer's acceptance or rejection of a style is reflected in order placement. If a style is rejected or doesn't yield orders, it is usually cancelled off the line and no longer available to sell to retail stores. Sales indicate strong styles in the collection, also called **best sellers.** In polarity, if a particular item does not generate orders or the quantity is insufficient to yield profit, the item is typically cancelled from the collection.

Based on cumulative wholesale orders, an entrepreneur will contract to purchase fabric and components. Most often a cut-and-sew contractor is used to facilitate mass production. Negotiating skills are needed to maximize cost efficiency and to acquire the best prices for components and labor. To aid an entrepreneur and streamline distribution, many contractors have the ability to provide the full, comprehensive service of grading or sizing, cutting, sewing, and applying hangtags and price tags. For an additional cost, a contractor can provide hangers, shipping boxes, and carton labels to expedite distribution efforts. Once all of the sourced fabrics, materials and trims are secured, production is scheduled.

Development Calendar

The time to shift product from a concept to fashion markets has become increasingly shorter. The product development process has become complex, with the challenges of balancing cost efficient workflow with product style variation and product quality requirements. A robust tool for aligning and coordinating design, technical development, and specification processes is the development calendar. A comprehensive time and action calendar is needed to enable the entrepreneur and preproduction team to proactively track major milestones, incorporating production and delivery lead times for both sample and bulk production. Major milestones include market research, design development, sourcing, first samples, fittings, production samples, wholesale orders, production, and delivery.

The **product development calendar** provides a cross-functional view of the entire product development cycle from concept to production on a single system of record. The format and tracking software varies by company. For the entrepreneur, a simple spreadsheet is typically the genesis for the calendar. Entrepreneurs develop and maintain the calendar. Entrepreneurs, in tandem with product design and development or contract teams, can easily work together and collaborate on designs by working in parallel in functional areas such as sourcing materials, artwork, product variants, care instructions, and sample management. As part of product development, a company's approval processes can be executed and tracked against the calendar established for that season, and the interface allows the entrepreneur to quickly identify outstanding tasks. This coordination helps the entrepreneur to manage and track a collection's development to ensure product accuracy, availability, and profitability. Calendar visibility beyond product development activities, preproduction, and production will increase an entrepreneur's control and reduce the risk of unexpected delays that can result from micromanagement.

Bookmark this: A development calendar is a critical tool in product development. Maintaining a record of each activity in tandem with an action plan and deadline will eliminate missteps and production delays.

Product Life Cycle

Once a new product or brand extension is distributed to the direct or indirect distribution channel for retail, the **product life cycle** begins. (Direct and indirect sales channels are defined in-depth in Chapters 8 and 9.) It is used to effectively ascertain and understand the possible

TABLE 4.2 **DEVELOPMENT CALENDAR**

DEVELOPMENT CALENDAR						
PHASE I	**SEPT**	**OCT**	**NOV**	**DEC**	**JAN**	**FEB**
Step 1	Market					
	Research					
Step 2		Inspiration				
		Concept Dev.				
Step 3			Design			
			Source Materials			
Step 4				Sample		
				Development		
Step 5					Production	
					Samples	
Step 6						Market
						Sales
PHASE II	**MAR**	**APR**	**MAY**	**JUNE**	**JULY**	**AUG**
Step 7	Market					
	Sales					
Step 8		Market				
		Sales				
Step 9			Production			
Step 10				Production		
Step 11					Shipping	
Step 12						Shipping

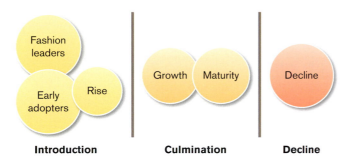

Introduction	Culmination	Decline

Figure 4.14 Product life cycle.

evolution of and response to new products. The **product life cycle** is designed to identify the maturation stage of a product by customer acceptance. Every product has a life cycle; however, the movement along the cycle varies based upon consumer acceptance (Figure 4.14). There are four distinct stages that a product goes through at varied velocity rates.

1. **Introduction to the market**
   During the introduction phase of the product life cycle, the product sets a firm positioning statement. Product knowledge, advertising, press, and public relations usually support this phase of business. Fashion leaders and early adopters purchase product. Sales slowly begin to rise as brand awareness begins.
2. **Growth in the market**
   During the growth phase of the product life cycle, brand awareness increases. A significant portion of the target market gravitates to the product as it becomes more established and available in the marketplace. Sales increase, and so does competition.
3. **Maturity in the market**
   During the maturity phase of the product life cycle, sales peak and begin to slow down. The mass consumers readily identify the brand. Laggard consumers become informed and engage as active buyers during this phase.
4. **Decline in the market**
   During the decline phase of the product life cycle, sales of the product begin to taper off and new products are being introduced. Strategic decisions are made to continue or discontinue a product. Production will eventually cease and existing product will be marked down and out of stock.

The product life cycle is an important tool that an entrepreneur can use to measure timing factors for product introductions, brand extensions, as well to make strategic decisions to discontinue products. Identifying the stage of adoption and the readiness of the target market is critical for future growth and development.

Summary

By comingling trend research and ingenuity, an entrepreneur sets the foundation for creating a product for the brand's target market. Product development is not a solitary journey. The entrepreneur may spearhead the creative direction; however, it takes the combined wherewithal of industry experts to contribute to the development of a product assortment. Building a new product or brand extension requires an entrepreneur to consider the budgetary constraints and creative ingenuity to compete in a saturated market. Having the ability to develop a merchandise assortment that is balanced to generate interest of the consumer is vital. Knowing the development process and product life cycle is critical for a successful entrepreneur.

TRADE TERMS

product development

trend

zeitgeist

trend research

trend forecasting

multisensory experience

concept board

creative statement

merchandising

line

collection

balanced assortment

product assortment

merchandise classification system

sample

prototype

best seller

product development calendar

product life cycle

Online Resources

TrendStop
Trend forecast up to 18 months ahead of the season
www.trendstop.com

WGSN
Business-to-business site for fashion industry trends
www.wgsn.com

Fashion Snoops
Trend forecasting
http://fashionsnoops.tumblr.com/

Activity 4.1 Idea Generation

Conduct trend research in the appropriate market segment that is being considered for a new product introduction or product extension. Generate ideas using intrinsic and extrinsic factors to trigger creative thoughts for the product.

1. Create a concept board at Polyvore.com. http://www.polyvore.com/cgi/app

2. Write a creative statement for the new product or brand extension.

Activity 4.2 Product Development

Create a collection of ten to twelve products for the fall or spring season in the next calendar year. Consider the current season's trends and the trend cycle. Allow for an eight- to twelve-month development period. There must be a unifying creative philosophy that ties the collection together, yet differences that make each piece unique and desirable to the target consumer. Keep in mind the integrity of the brand and the readiness of your targeted customer. Create flats or sketches.

Consider the following components of fashion to create an overall mood:

- Silhouette
- Color—consider multiple colors for certain items
- Fabric/Texture—swatches will be needed for cost sheet
- Texture
- Details

All designs must be original ideas. Be mindful of silhouettes that may be appealing in more than one color. Think about the retail environment and how certain items are desirable in multiple colors—knits, shirting, etc. For fabric selections and material cost, remember price is important to keep within the boundaries of the targeted price classification segment. Be sure to scan the renderings so they can be reproduced and scale in future activities.

Activity 4.3 Merchandise Classification

Create a merchandise classification system. Each product within your collection will need to have an identification style number. Each digit has significant meaning to the company/brand. It is a code that reveals detail information for internal usage and provides differentiation and identity of the product to the retailer and consumer. Style numbers can range in length and can include alpha or numeric symbols. An example of developing a classification system follows.

PART I: Developing a Classification System
The first digit can reflect the year:

1. 2014
2. 2015
3. 2016
4. 2017

The second digit can reflect the season code of the collection:

1. Spring
2. Summer
3. Transition
4. Fall
5. Winter/Holiday
6. Resort

The third digit can reflect the classification of product suitable to your collection, for example:

Clothing: 1. Shirts 2. Pants 3. Skirts 4. Blazers

Accessories: 1. Bracelets 2. Necklaces 3. Rings 4. Earrings

Home Collection: 1. Pillowcase 2. Sheets 3. Comforter 4. Shams

Cosmetics: 1. Blush 2. Lipstick 3. Eye shadow 4. Lip-gloss

Personal Care: 1. Soap 2. Shower Gel 3. Moisturizer 4. Scrub

The fourth digit can reflect the subclassification. This digit further refines the product classification into attributes and into descriptive segments for your product to differentiate it by distinct characteristics. Based upon the aforementioned product classes, here are subclasses:

Skirts—the subclasses, depending on your collection: A. Mini B. Maxi C. Pleated

D. High-waist (these can be numbered, or alpha)

Earrings: A. Drop B. Hoop C. Stud

Sheets: A. Fitted B. Flat

Blush: A. Matte Powder B. Cream

Handbag: A. Clutch B. Hobo C. Shoulder strap

The fifth digit can vary by significance in the collection. It can be fabrication, color, scent, etc.

Color: 01-Black, 02-White, 60-Red 99-Multi

PART II: Create Style Numbers
Based on your style numbering system, create style numbers for each item within your collection. Be mindful, if you have multiple colors of a product, each color will have a style number. List each style number, and state the product description.

EX. #12465-01 Tailored Trouser Pant—Black

BIBLIOGRAPHY

Brannon, Evelyn. 2005. *Fashion Forecasting*. 2nd ed. New York: Fairchild Publications, Inc.

BusinessDictionary.com. s.v. "product life cycle." *Business dictionary.com,* Dec. 23. http://www.businessdictionary.com/definition/product-life-cycle.html

Doneger Group. http://www.doneger.com/web/

Fiore, Ann Marie, and Patricia Ann Kimle. 1997. *Understanding Aesthetics for the Merchandising and Design Professional.* New York: Fairchild Publications, Inc.

Jennings, Tracy. 2011. *Creativity in Fashion Design: An Inspiration Workbook.* New York: Fairchild Books.

Kunz, Grace I. 2010. *Merchandising, Theory, Principles and Practice.* 3rd ed. New York: Fairchild Books.

Rath, Patricia, Jacqueline Peterson, Phyllis Greensley, and Penny Gill. 1994. *Introduction to Fashion Merchandising.* New York: Delmar Publishers Inc.

Rookie. http://rookiemag.com/

Rosenau, Jeremy, and David Wilson. 2006. *Apparel Merchandising: The Line Starts Here.* New York: Fairchild Books.

Stall-Meadows, Celia. 2011. *Fashion Now: A Global Perspective.* New Jersey: Pearson Education Inc.

Stone, Elaine. 2008. *The Dynamics of Fashion.* 3rd ed. New York: Fairchild Books.

Tobe Report. http://www.tobereport.com/pages/

WGSN. http://wgsn.com

5

Strategic Sourcing

Strategic sourcing identifies steps involved in the production process. During the start-up phase of business, most entrepreneurs will need to find domestic contractors to facilitate production. Depending on the product, they might also consider offshore production. Entrepreneurs need to take an authoritative stance as the purchaser of contract services to negotiate the best price. Typically, budget constraints will force entrepreneurs to quickly assess how to maximize their production as they manage sourcing and handle minimum quantities and contractor relationships. An emphasis will be placed on the strategic and operational elements of establishing and maintaining domestic supply chains. Production standards are extremely important and failure to meet standards can hurt the reputation of a brand.

Strategic Sourcing Decision

Not all fashion brand entrepreneurs can sew, but every fashion brand entrepreneur has an idea and vision of what niche product to create. If, in fact, an entrepreneur does have the ability to produce her own products, there is still a need for outsourcing all or some of the work. **Strategic sourcing** refers to finding the most cost-effective way to manufacture one's product, either locally or in a foreign country. International sourcing is used to provide mass volume to retailer needs comapred to local sourcing, which provides a shorter lead-time. For the purposes of this text, the authors focus solely on domestic sourcing, since international information is usually not the first route for a start-up business.

Entrepreneurs must seek a contractor or manufacturer to produce their goods upon development of the product idea. A **manufacturer** is an entity that makes goods through a process involving raw materials, components, or assemblies, usually on a large scale, with different operations divided among different workers.[1] Within manufacturers are three types: **a cut-make-trim (CMT)**, who will only cut and assemble products from specifications that are given to them; a **full package program**

KEY CONCEPTS

+ Examine strategic sourcing and contract relationships.

+ Explore domestic sourcing and negotiation tactics.

+ Analyze production labor.

+ Examine quality control with the standardization of production.

+ Understand the basics of international outsourcing. Evaluate key agreements and laws in the global market.

Figure 5.1 A manufacturing facility: the lingerie company Les Atelieres in Villeurbanne, France, on January 14, 2013. *Source: Jeff Pachoud/ AFP/Getty Images.*

(FPP), who will source all materials, develop patterns according to the entrepreneurs guidelines, and create the product; and a **contractor**, an independent entity that agrees to furnish a certain number or quantity of goods, material, equipment, personnel, and/or services that meet or exceed stated requirements or specifications at a mutually agreed–upon price and within a specified timeframe[2] (Figure 5.1).

The primary objectives of domestic outsourcing are:

1. **Quality:** Domestic suppliers make it easier for buyers to maintain communication and control. Working with someone domestically will alleviate a possible language barrier, cultural issues, and time zone constraints. A supplier that is located locally makes it easier to visit the manufacturer and look over the product and its quality.

2. **Shorter lead times:** A supplier that is located domestically reduces the lead-time versus a global supplier that can take up to 180 days. If a product is a best seller, then it will be possible to reorder and get the product sooner.

3. **Smaller quantities:** Small quantities can allow flexibility for the brand and thus the buyer. The entrepreneur will be able to purchase smaller quantities to see what the demand is for the product. Yet, a buyer should be sure that they strategically place product with the retailers so no one is stuck with unsellable

inventory. Unfortunately, smaller quantities almost always equate to a higher cost to the entrepreneur, so that it may become difficult to make a profit.

4. **Design protection:** The United States has a high level of intellectual rights protection. In 2012, an estimated 576,763 people applied for an intellectual property (IP). In 2012, 2.35 million patents were registered worldwide. If a product is manufactured in low-cost countries, then patents, copyrights, and trademarks could be compromised. In 2013, the United States has called for China to advance on their IP rights and protection. Entrepreneurs should take steps to protect their innovations.

5. **Positive brand image:** A large part of the American retail industry is manufactured overseas. Many people like seeing American-made products, and it gives them a sense that the brand is loyal and believes in the economy of the country.

6. **Reducing tariff and duty burdens:** Tariffs and duties do not need to be paid when using a domestic supplier. Tariffs or duties (the words are used interchangeably) are taxes levied by governments on the value including freight and insurance of imported products.[3]

Table 5.1 shows international trade terms used in the importing and exporting industry. Congress establishes all duty rates for goods entering the United States, and the U.S. Customs and Borders Protection collects these duties. The Harmonized Tariff Schedule (HTS) lists all imported goods and the duty rates that are applied to each good. HTS classifies all goods and posts these rates online.

When deciding to source, it is important to know what criteria are needed in selecting a manufacturer. Criteria that one should look for are experience and past performance with similar products, types of systems

TABLE 5.1 **TRADE TERMINOLOGY**

Import quota	A quantity control on imported merchandise for a certain period of time.
Tariff-rate quota	Import quota allows a limited quantity of goods into a country at a reduced duty rate during a specified period.
Absolute quota	No more than the amount allotted can be allowed entry during a quota period.
Dumping	Exporting goods at prices lower than the home market prices.
Duty-free	Goods on which import duty is not charged, usually only on items sold to departing passengers in an airport.
Tariff or **duty**	Is a tax levied by governments on the value of goods based on freight and insurance of imported products.
Exports	Products of local producer sold to other countries.
Imports	Products of a foreign producer brought into a country.
Transshipping	Transferring for further transportation from one shipment to another.

Sources: International Trade Association, Office of Textiles and Apparel. http://web.ita.doc.gov/tacgi/eamain.nsf/6e1600e39721316c852570ab0056f719/e881952e8c64f497852576850049c6dc?OpenDocument
Business Directory. http://www.businessdictionary.com/definition

TABLE 5.2 **LIST OF WEBSITES FOR SOURCING**

Apparel News	www.apparelnews.net	Reports and analyzes the apparel industry, trends resources, finance, textiles, and sourcing. Based in California.
Apparel Search	www.apparelsearch.com	Apparel industry directory that provides members of the fashion industry with information regarding virtually every aspect of the apparel and textile industry.
Cotton Incorporated	www.cottoninc.com	Website exclusively about cotton.
Emerging Textiles	www.emergingtextiles.com	A textile information service covering the global textile and clothing trade.
Fashion Coop	www.fashioncoop.com	Provides up-and-coming designers with a network of resources in the industry, and knowledge about business strategy, public relations, and creativity.
Garment District Alliance	www.garmentdistrictnyc	Information about everything in the Garment District in New York City.
Infomat	www.infomat.com	Gathers reviews and ratings from leading editors and ranks with a variety of top lists, how-to guides, and articles to show how items compare.
Premiere Vision	www.premierevision.com/en	Worldwide information about textile news.
Thomas Register	www.thomasnet.com	Supplier directory for almost all materials and services.

and machinery in place, financial stability, technical support, and capacity requirements. A manufacturer can be found through contacts, sources on the Internet, trade publications, local merchandise marts, governmental agencies, trade shows, and trade associations (Table 5.2 contains a list of resources for sourcing). When selecting a manufacturer, it is important to get referrals from people in the industry who have used them before, checking the manufacturers history and financials; be sure to interview them. Financials can be found in *Dun & Bradstreet* or other publicly available financial reports. An agent can also be hired to assist in finding a manufacturer that is a right fit. An apparel manufacturer will assist in product development—the product transition from design concept to a finished product. The manufacturing company needs to be a good fit on both ends. The manufacturer's location as well the company's sourcing philosophy is a good start. The United Nations Global Compact (UNGC) is a program that promotes human rights, labor standards, and environmental awareness, as well as being anti-corruption (Box 5.1). A manufacturer that is chosen should embrace, support, and enact these core values. A manufacturer should be able to offer

- Prototypes to your specifications
- Samples to your specifications
- Specification sheet showing yields, sizes, pricing
- Estimates on manufacturing costs
- Fabric/material quality and availability
- Product evaluation and testing
- A formal quote with the cost and specifications

Contractor Relationships

Once a contractor is selected, it is important to build a beneficial relationship. The following are steps to building a strong relationship with a supplier/vendor.

1. **Share Priorities.** Communication is key when dealing with the manufacturer. It is important to lay out all priorities, goals,

BOX 5.1 The Ten Principles

Human Rights

- *Principle 1:* Businesses should support and respect the protection of internationally proclaimed human rights; and
- *Principle 2:* make sure that they are not complicit in human rights abuses.

Labor

- *Principle 3:* Businesses should uphold the freedom of association and the effective recognition of the right to collective bargaining;
- *Principle 4:* the elimination of all forms of forced and compulsory labor;
- *Principle 5:* the effective abolition of child labor; and
- *Principle 6:* the elimination of discrimination in respect of employment and occupation.

Environment

- *Principle 7:* Businesses should support a precautionary approach to environmental challenges;
- *Principle 8:* undertake initiatives to promote greater environmental responsibility; and
- *Principle 9:* encourage the development and diffusion of environmentally friendly technologies.

Anti-Corruption

- *Principle 10:* Businesses should work against corruption in all its forms, including extortion and bribery.

Source: United Nations. "The Ten Principles." *United Nations Global Compact.* Accessed Jan. 15, 2012. http://www.unglobalcompact.org/aboutthegc/thetenprinciples/index.html.

Tip 5.1 **Create-a-minute!**

A manufacturer's sourcing philosophy, such as owning their footprint and shaping sustainability, can speak volumes about the company. It is important to know a manufacturer's philosophy and that it aligns with the company's.

objectives, and expected outcomes. The earlier this is done, the better. It is easier to make any changes deemed necessary earlier in the process rather than later.

2. **Negotiate.** All terms should be negotiated up front. It is wise to include any penalties for late deliveries, insurance, and ensure that all workers are legal.

3. **Listen.** Manufacturers should be looked at as partners, so it is important to listen to their insights. A manufacturer's job is to produce products, so she has an understanding of the process and may be able to offer ideas that can make the product more economical and save money.

4. **Written Contract.** Create a written detailed contract with the manufacturer before production is started. The contract will help to clearly define the business relationship and can avoid any surprises that were not agreed on. Have a lawyer look over the contract to make sure there are no misunderstandings or surprises.

5. **Touch Base Often.** Meetings should be scheduled periodically to discuss the progress. Inquire for the preferred method to communicate with the contractor, whether it is through email, text, or phone calls. Also, if the contractor is not available, then find out who the next person in command is. Regular meetings will commit the contractor to stay on schedule. Ongoing communication is essential to preserve a strong working relationship. The meetings do not need to take place face-to-face every time and should be kept short and with an agenda in mind.

Sourcing Raw Materials

Part of the sourcing process is to be responsible for purchasing production fabric. For entrepreneurs, it is easier and more cost efficient to source fabric within the United States, to avoid the cost of duties and tariffs. But buying domestically is not always possible, and sometimes materials must be purchased outside the United States. Bamboo is an example of a good that must be purchased overseas. Tables 5.3 and 5.4 show lists of domestic and international textile markets.

There are several different sources that can be used to find and purchase fabric according to Fashiondex[4]:

- *Textile mill:* A weaving or knitting company that manufactures fabrics and textile products.
- *Textile converter:* A person or company that purchases woven or knitted greige goods directly from a fabric mill, then proceeds to dye, finish, print and/or wash the goods into a full line of finished fabrics.

TABLE 5.3 **KEY DOMESTIC TEXTILE MARKETS**

NAME	WEBSITE	EXPLANATION
Magic Online	www.magiconline.com/ sourcing-at-magic	Information about SOURCING at MAGIC, North America's largest, most comprehensive sourcing event.
Shows Northwest LLC Textile Trade Show	nwfabricshow.com	A regional textile show out of Seattle and Washington, DC.
Texworld USA	texworldusa-us. messefrankfurt.com	Sourcing apparel trade show from countries around the world and USA.

TABLE 5.4 **KEY INTERNATIONAL TEXTILE MARKETS**

NAME	WEBSITE	EXPLANATION
Premier-Vision	www.premierevision.com/en	Worldwide information about textile news and trade show information.
Messe Frankfurt	texpertise.messefrankfurt.com	Information about textiles and trade shows.
Textile Source	www.textilesource.com/	International wholesale textile sourcing directory.

Buying from jobbers can be beneficial if you are looking for small minimums. Great deals can be found, but goods cannot be returned and many times they cannot be reordered.

- *Fabric representative:* An agent who shows fabrics from one or more mills and works directly with manufacturers and other textile customers in a predetermined territory.
- *Fabric wholesaler:* A general term for all other secondary fabric sources, this includes any other person or company that purchases excess finished fabrics from mills, converters, jobbers and large apparel, accessory, and home furnishings manufacturers and sells direct to small manufacturers and small retail fabric stores.
- *Fabric jobber:* A person or company that purchases large quantities of excess finished fabrics from mills and converters and then sells them wholesale, and in smaller quantities, to small design companies, manufacturers, and retail fabric stores.

Contact a textile mill's sales representative and request **textile headers,** which are free textile sample cuts being manufactured by the mill. When selecting fabrics it is wise to select product that has a lower minimum and color purchase requirement. When choosing fabric, try to avoid prints, since it may be hard to reorder, and be cautious of colors that might not appeal to the core customer. This is also the case when it comes to selecting ingredients within the beauty industry. Remember the budget set in place throughout this process. A manufacturer may request 1,000 yards per color or 1,000 units per container depending on the product being manufactured.

When selecting trim, it is important to visit several manufacturers to compare their styles and pricing structures. Most trim manufacturers will offer free samples during their meetings. When dealing with other products such as personal care, choosing packaging that is considered an in-stock item will ease the reorder lead time. Trims and notions can also increase the price to a product.

Prior to product development, brand label, care labels, size tags, clothing hangers, price tickets, and packing materials need to be sourced and ordered. The contractor or manufacturer will need these items during production.

Negotiation Tactics

Part of selecting a manufacturer is the art of negotiation. When negotiating, it is important to know the goal and intended outcome. Common topics that can be negotiated are

- Price
- Quality

- Quantity
- Delivery time
- Payment terms
- Service levels
- Support

The goal for negotiation should always be to reach a mutual agreement that meets the intended goal. The objective is to execute negotiations using the SMART concept, which is the acronym for *s*pecific, *m*easurable, *a*ttainable, *r*elevant, and *t*ime-bound. Here is an example:

S: The objective is to have a price reduction.
M: The price reduction should be $.25 per piece.
A: The current market trend will allow this reduction to be more competitively priced.
R: This reduction is for the current order.
T: The current order that will be placed during a specific time period.

When negotiating overseas it is important to consider[5]:

1. The negotiating environment
2. Cultural and subcultural differences
3. Ideological differences
4. Foreign bureaucracy
5. Foreign laws and governments
6. Financial insecurity due to international monetary factors
7. Political instability and economic changes

It is wise to compare different manufacturers and secure bids from each one. When selecting a manufacturer, entrepreneurs must weigh all options. Although price is critical, it is not the sole factor for choosing a partner. Quality assurance and ethical conditions are equally important to price.

Production Labor

On an industrial basis there are certain areas or sequences through which products are manufactured. The entrepreneur or the manufacturer provides the initial sketch. For apparel, flat drawing helps the patternmakers understand the construction and assists in developing the first pattern for the design. The first pattern is sent to the contractor to create a sample. Depending on the item, the sample is often in muslin fabric to reduce cost. If changes are needed, they are made on the first sample. It is important to thoroughly examine the sample during this time period. The initial sample will be the guide to the production sample.

Samples vs. Production

It is important to first have a prototype created and then a production sample. A **prototype** is an initial sample that is created to test a concept.

Figure 5.2 A production sample garment.

It is the first opportunity to make adjustments to the product. Figure 5.2 shows a sample garment. Most often, a supplier will require a fee before creating prototypes. After the prototype is made, all corrections are made and a second sample is developed. Upon approval it will be considered a production sample. A **production sample** is a product that is given to the buyer to view before committing to a purchase. The production sample is graded into different sizes based on the entrepreneur's product specifications. It is imperative that the samples are produced on the same machinery and equipment as the final product so that there are no surprises with the end product. In addition, preproductions must be requested to make certain that the product is to specification before production begins.

Communication is key, so it is important to be in constant contact with the manufacturer and to speak or write clearly. It is best if a drawing, photo, or actual sample can be given, so the manufacturer has a visual idea of what to create. Be aware that many times a physical piece will be duplicated, so if changes are to be made, give very specific instructions.

Manufacturers require production **minimums**—the lowest quantities that one can order from a supplier. If the minimums are 1,000 units, entrepreneurs can negotiate a plan to meet the minimum by item/SKU. Orders are typically planned by cut-to-order or cut-to-stock. The best route is cut-to-order plus an additional 15 percent to the initial order. This allows an entrepreneur to plan cut tickets by items/sizes sold to guide early production. A major production can take eight to ten weeks. Table 5.5 shows a fashion merchandising production-planning calendar.

Quality Assurance

Quality assurance is all activities that seek to guarantee the quality of work. It is important to conduct quality assurance before, during, and after production. Most manufacturers perform quality control, but it is imperative that the buyer does their own inspection. The ISO 2859 standard (derived from MIL-STD 105 E) defines an **inspection** as

TABLE 5.5 SAMPLE OF A DOMESTIC SOURCING PROCESS

MONTH	STEP
July	1) Research market packaging and scents
August	2) Begin to design sketches
September	3) Swatch and begin to make samples
October	4) Early production, retail orders placed
November	5) Major production begins
December	6) Major production continued
January	7) Major production…
February	8) In-store promotions
March	9) Shipping period, in-store promotions
April	10) Shipping continued…Record period
May	11) Store set-up
June	12) Track retail, plan for next year

Source: *Columbia College Merchandise Management Book.* River Forest, IL: Dominican University, 2012.

an "activity such as measuring, examining, testing or gauging one or more characteristics of a product or service, and comparing the results with specified requirements in order to establish whether conformity is achieved for each characteristic."[6]

The 1:10:100 Ratio

Research has shown that that there is a cost and time ratio for the development, production, and delivery of an item that has been manufactured. The 1:10:100 ratio shows that for each error it will cost *10 times more* in dollars and in time to fix in production than it would to fix in development, and *100 times more* if the mistake in fact reaches the customer. Table 5.6 shows 6 ways to deal with defects. If the problem is not corrected in a timely manner, then it will cost time, money, and customers.

TABLE 5.6 QUALITY ASSURANCE

STAGE	PREVENT ERRORS	CHECK AND CORRECT ERRORS	1:10:100 RATIO	TIME CONSEQUENCES	COST CONSEQUENCES
Development of style (samples)	Adapted design, capable factory		x1	Best option	Best option
		Early review of technical files	x1	Might cause slight delay	Very low cost
Mass production (workshop)	Good production and quality assurance		x10	Good option	More expensive
		Quality control after production	x10	Delays if repair is necessary	Expenses can balloon
Delivery to customer (shop/mail)	Exchange bad products		x100	–	Very high cost
		Customer keeps bad products	x100	–	Loss of future business

Source: Renaud Anjoran. 2011. "What Is a QC Inspection?" *Quality Inspection Services in China: Advice for Importers,* Dec. 6. Accessed Jan. 15, 2012. http://www.qualityinspection.org/qc-inspection/

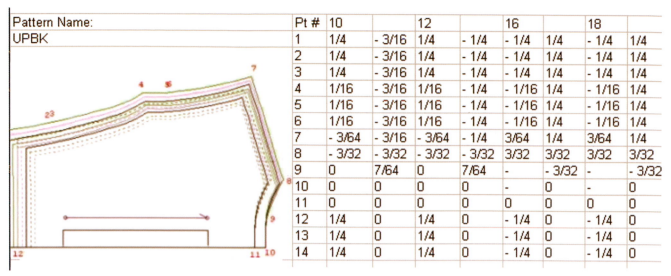

Pattern Name: UPBK	Pt #	10		12		16		18	
	1	1/4	- 3/16	1/4	- 1/4	- 1/4	1/4	- 1/4	1/4
	2	1/4	- 3/16	1/4	- 1/4	- 1/4	1/4	- 1/4	1/4
	3	1/4	- 3/16	1/4	- 1/4	- 1/4	1/4	- 1/4	1/4
	4	1/16	- 3/16	1/16	- 1/4	- 1/16	1/4	- 1/16	1/4
	5	1/16	- 3/16	1/16	- 1/4	- 1/16	1/4	- 1/16	1/4
	6	1/16	- 3/16	1/16	- 1/4	- 1/16	1/4	- 1/16	1/4
	7	- 3/64	- 3/16	- 3/64	- 1/4	3/64	1/4	3/64	1/4
	8	- 3/32	- 3/32	- 3/32	- 3/32	3/32	3/32	3/32	3/32
	9	0	7/64	0	7/64	-	- 3/32	-	- 3/32
	10	0	0	0	0	-	0	-	0
	11	0	0	0	0	0	0	0	0
	12	1/4	0	1/4	0	- 1/4	0	- 1/4	0
	13	1/4	0	1/4	0	- 1/4	0	- 1/4	0
	14	1/4	0	1/4	0	- 1/4	0	- 1/4	0

Figure 5.3 Pattern grading.

Entrepreneurs can be at the manufacturing site for inspection during all three phases of production. It is best to catch errors during preproduction. It is imperative to verify all production changes with the factory. An entrepreneur or their development team is responsible for conveying any prerequisites to the manufacturing team. The first items off of the production line allow the entrepreneur to evaluate the product and gauge the completion schedule. The final check should be done after production, prior to shipment. Most manufacturers only inspect 10 percent of a random sampling of the finished product. The product is checked against a list of criteria to be sure that they have been met. The criteria list will depend on what agreement the entrepreneur and the manufacturer have. A grading rule should be provided so that the vendor has a range and standard for each product size. **Grading** of a pattern or grading of size spec measurements means adding or decreasing inches (or other measurement units such as millimeters), to a specific part of the sample-sized pattern in order to size up or size down.[7] Figure 5.3 shows a grading sample.

Once production is complete, distribution can begin. The product can be boxed, hung, or packaged and shipped to the customer or a place where the product will be housed until sold, such as a warehouse. It is important to state in the contract who will be handling the final packaging (as discussed further in Chapter 6).

Global Sourcing

The primary objectives of global outsourcing are to reduce cost (see Box 5.2 for a comparison of average wages for labor) and a more specialized workforce. Currently, China and India are the world's largest apparel exporters. Table 5.7 shows the top ten countries that export to the United States as of November 2013. Global sourcing is a good option for a company that is able to purchase large quantities, so they can price their goods competitively in the market.

The global sourcing of product has advantages and disadvantages. Low cost is usually the greatest advantage. Many countries have skills or resources not found domestically. Some key disadvantages of global sourcing are increased risk of loss of intellectual property. Monitoring the process and quality can be difficult, and being in a different time zone can

Hourly Wages in Apparel Manufacturing in Selected Countries*

United States	$17.31
Brazil	$3.08
Canada	$16.95
Mexico	$2.06
China, Mainland	$.40–$.53
China, Coastal	$.60–$.70
France	$22.97
Dominican Republic	$1.62
Guatemala	$.90–$1.12
Honduras	$.82–$1.31
India	$.51
Vietnam	$.26

*These hourly compensation costs data were updated on November 20, 2009, to reflect the latest available information.

Source: U.S Department of Labor, Bureau of Labor Statistics. "International Hourly Compensation Costs for Production Workers, by Sub-Manufacturing Industry." *U.S. Bureau of Labor Statistics.* Accessed Jan. 24, 2012. http://www.bls.gov/fls/flshcpwindnaics.htm.

add to that frustration. Culture and language barriers are also a hindrance. The lead times have been increasing over the years. When sourcing internationally, it is important that the entrepreneur have an understanding of the political and economic climate, natural resources and specialties of the country, labor cost and practices, proximity to markets, and legal structures of the country in question. Examples of some of these factors affecting global sourcing are:

- Shortages of raw materials, such as cotton, are causing fabric prices to increase.
- Labor cost is increasing in many countries.
- Oil prices have increased, which have caused transportation costs to increase.

TABLE 5.7 **U.S. IMPORTS OF TEXTILES AND APPAREL (IN MILLIONS OF DOLLARS)**

RANKING	COUNTRY	CALENDAR YEAR 2011	CALENDAR YEAR 2012	% CHANGE
1	China	$25,165.761	$25,637.383	5.44
2	India	3,306.168	3,435.247	7.72
3	Vietnam	3,130.100	3,167.365	14.59
4	Pakistan	2,484.283	2,445.290	0.98
5	Mexico	2,545.376	2,414.447	−0.96
6	Bangladesh	1,749.767	1,764.632	10.76
7	Indonesia	1,771.733	1,734.477	0.90
8	Korea Republic	1,292.649	1,350.422	−2.27
9	Cambodia	1,097.761	1,115.364	2.26
10	Honduras	1,210.844	1,155.006	−4.84

Source: *Major Shippers Report: Total Textile and Apparel Imports (MFA)*. Office of Textiles and Apparel (OTEXA). Department of Commerce. United States of America, Nov. 2013. http://otexa.ita.doc.gov/msr/cat0.htm.

- Political volatility is affecting delivery reliability, chiefly from suppliers in North Africa and the Middle East.
- Stable currency is important. The region's currency should be stable so that agreed-upon pricing does not fluctuate.

The United States has agreements and laws in place with other countries to facilitate the importing and exporting of products. Table 5.8 is a representative list of laws and agreements that the United States has in place. The North American Free Trade Agreement (NAFTA) was established in 1994, connecting Canada, the United States, and Mexico. The three countries were able to reduce or eliminate tariffs. The success of NAFTA has led the way for other similar agreements with other countries such as Korea. The United States entered a free trade agreement with the Republic of Korea, also known as **KORUS FTA.** The agreement went into effect in March 2012, which will allow for U.S. exporters to sell additional made-in-America goods, services, and agricultural products to the Korean market, which in turn will support products made in the United States.

Case Study 5.1 gives some insights into the realities of sourcing in the current market.

TABLE 5.8 **AGREEMENTS AND ACTS IN TRADE**

North American Free Trade Agreement (NAFTA) www.ustr.gov/trade-agreements/free-trade-agreements/north-american-free-trade-agreement-nafta	An agreement reached by the United States, Canada, and Mexico that eliminated a variety of fees to encourage free trade between the countries.
Caribbean Basin Initiative (CBI) and the Caribbean Basin Economic Recovery Act (CBERA) www.ustr.gov/trade-topics/trade-development/preference-programs/caribbean-basin-initiative-cbi	Intended to facilitate the development of the Caribbean Basin economies. The act provides the countries with duty-free access to the U.S. market for most goods.
Andean Trade Preference Act (ATPA)/Andean Trade Promotion and Drug Eradication Act (ATPDEA) www.ustr.gov/trade-topics/trade-development/preference-programs/andean-trade-preference-act-atpa	Created to help the Andean countries (Bolivia, Colombia, Ecuador, and Peru) in their fight against drug production and trafficking by expanding their economic alternatives and providing duty-free treatment for certain products.
U.S.–Israel Free Trade Area Agreement www.ustr.gov/trade-agreements/free-trade-agreements/israel-fta	Expanded trade and investment between the United States and Israel by reducing barriers and promoting trade transparency.
Jordan Free Trade Area Agreement www.ustr.gov/trade-agreements/free-trade-agreements/jordan-fta	The act expanded the trade relationship between Jordan and the United States by reducing barriers for services, providing protection for intellectual property, and requiring effective labor and environmental enforcement.
African Growth and Opportunity Act (AGOA) www.ustr.gov/trade-topics/trade-development/preference-programs/african-growth-and-opportunity-act-agoa	Created to expand U.S. trade and investment with sub-Saharan Africa to stimulate economic growth, encourage economic integration, and facilitate sub-Saharan Africa's integration into the global economy.
Caribbean Basin Trade Partnership Act (CBPTA) www.ustr.gov/trade-topics/trade-development/preference-programs/caribbean-basin-initiative-cbi	Expanded the CBI to include a free trade agreement between the United States and Barbados, Belize, Guyana, Haiti, Jamaica, Panama, St. Lucia, Trinidad and Tobago.
U.S.–Chile Free Trade Agreement (US-CFTA) www.ustr.gov/trade-agreements/free-trade-agreements/chile-fta	Eliminated tariffs and opened markets, reduced barriers for trade in services, and required effective labor and environmental enforcement.
U.S.–Singapore Free Trade Agreement (Singapore FTA) www.ustr.gov/trade-agreements/free-trade-agreements/singapore-fta	Expanded U.S. market access in goods, services, government procurement, intellectual property, and provided cooperation promoting labor rights and the environment.

Source: Office of the United States Trade Representative. "Trade Agreements." USTR. www.ustr.gov/trade-agreements.

An interview with neckwear designer/entrepreneur, Steve Mayer, owner and founder of Bird Dog Bay.

When and how did you start your neckwear business?

I started Feb. 2006, launched Bird Dog Bay's first collection Fall 2006. I simply design neckwear that I think is witty, fun, and would proudly wear myself. The ties are all 100 percent 18 momme silk twill, handprinted and handmade. They're just a hair longer than most regular ties, cut to 58" long and 3-1/4" wide at their widest spot on the front apron. All of our ties have a long center-stitched self loop and have our Bird Dog Bay custom tipping.

Did you start your business initially manufacturing domestically?

No. There isn't a handprinted silk mill in the United States that can handle my kind of work, so I worked with one of the most respected print mills in the world, which is in Asia. Most of our cut, make, and trim work are done there, though I still have some of my more specialized work done in the States.

When I started, I didn't know if I was going to get backlash for working mostly overseas, though I don't have a business partner, and I knew enough that managing the production in itself is a full-time gig here in the States, so I choose to take a bit of branding hit solely to not bring in a partner. Plus, the CMT work in the States for the type of handmade prints that I make are not very good; there is more talent overseas.

How did you find a manufacturer? What steps were taken to find the right one?

Printed silk was a dying art in the '90s, and there were very few places left in the world that still did it, so I was lucky that I had used this specific mill before prints came back into fashion around 2003 to 2005. So, even though I was a small, upstart company, they still took my business because I'd worked with them in the past.

What were some challenges that arose with manufacturing overseas?

The language, obviously. Though out of dumb luck, the woman who set up my accounting program the day I started became a good friend of mine and now is my

full-time accountant. She is from Shanghai and moved to America within months of me launching BDB; if I have any real communication problems with the mill, she can jump in and speak Mandarin to get the problems resolved.

How do you evaluate a manufacturer?

I simply look at what like-brands they are producing. Is the quality at a level that we strive to be? Plus, how are they working with brands of my size? Right now I'm working with a large cotton mill in Peru and am getting swallowed up with poor communication, though the quality is spot on. I'm a very small fish in a big pond, and sometimes that's worth the hassle, sometimes it's not. It helps to get a point person at the mill that you communicate well with.

On average what can the lead times be?

From the day I put in an order it takes about three to four months to manufacture the goods.

Is it crucial for you to travel overseas and visit the manufacturing plant that you are using?

It depends. Some mills have great representation here in the States if it's a larger company, and you can get all your work without having to leave the United States. Sometimes the reputation of the mill is so great that we just reach out to them directly, and our business has enough value at this point they're willing to entertain

(continues)

our requests. That is followed by many, many FedEx packages of back-and-forth sampling. And, finally, sometimes it's just best to show up. Yeah, it's the most expensive way to get your brand going, but you'll learn more and possibly save more money in the long run by cutting brokers out of the mix.

Are there any incentives to bring back your manufacturing to the US?

All of the handprinting of the silks has to be done overseas. It's simply not done in America, and if someone were to ever build out a U.S. handprinted silk mill, I'd be selling a product that would be so costly my brand would crumble. And don't think that Made-in-the-USA means the actual goods are manufactured here; more times than not, the term is referring to the "assembling" of the made-overseas pieces that grant the finished product that Made-in-the-USA [label].

Though we flirt with the idea of "assembling" the bulk of our products in the United States all the time, my head in-house seamstress would have to build a much larger new team, and at this point it's not cost effective for the amount of work we produce a season. We could outsource this to another CMT shop, though making a printed silk tie is much more difficult to hand-make than a woven silk tie. The talent would have to be there, and I've never come across a [U.S.] shop that is consistent … with my medium.

What advice would you give to an entrepreneur who is trying to manufacture a product overseas?

They have wholesale sourcing shows in Las Vegas and China where you can meet with the reps for the manufacturing plants.

Acts

The Federal Trade Commission (FTC) Act regulates any misleading trade practices by a business that are considered to harm or defraud consumers. There are several laws under the United States FTC, some of which are listed in Table 5.9. When it comes to manufacturing product, it is important to have an understanding of these laws. Under the FTC labeling

TABLE 5.9 **LAWS, RULES, AND GUIDES**

Labeling Act	States information that must be included on product labels, depending on the consumer good.
Wool Product Labeling Act	Wool products must be marked in the form of a stamp, tag, or label showing the fiber content, country of origin, and identification number.
Fur Products Labeling Act	Every fur product should be labeled and invoiced according to the requirements of the act and rules and regulations. This includes the name of the animal (not breed name), country of origin, and dyeing information.
Flammable Fabrics Act	Bans the use of highly flammable textiles for use in clothing.
Textile Fiber Products Labeling Act	Requires each textile product to have a label listing the generic names of the textiles used.
Fair Packaging and Labeling Act	Requires that all consumer goods be labeled to disclose net contents, identity of good, and name and place of business of the product's manufacturer, packer, or distributor.
Federal Trade Commission Act	Gives the commission the power to use law enforcement against false claims that a product is of U.S. origin.
Made in USA	Means that a product must be completely made in the USA.

Source: Bureau of Consumer Protection. business.ftc.gov/legal-resources/17/33

TABLE 5.10 LABELING REQUIREMENTS IN VARIOUS COUNTRIES

COUNTRY	LANGUAGE	FIBER CONTENT	ORIGIN	CARE	MANUFACTURER/ IMPORTER	SIZE
China	Chinese	Mandatory	Mandatory	Mandatory	Manufacturer	Mandatory
India	English and Hindi	Mandatory	Mandatory	Optional	Both	Mandatory
Vietnam	Vietnamese	Mandatory	Mandatory	Mandatory	Manufacturer	Optional
Mexico	Spanish	Mandatory	Mandatory	Mandatory	Either	Mandatory
Pakistan	English or Urdu	Optional	Mandatory	Optional	Manufacturer	Optional
Bangladesh	Neligh or Bangla	NA	Mandatory	NA	NA	NA
Indonesia	Indonesian	Optional	Optional	Optional	Optional	Optional
Canada	English or French	Mandatory	Mandatory	Optional	Either	Optional
Honduras	Spanish	NA	Mandatory	NA	Manufacturer	NA
United States	English	Mandatory	Mandatory	Mandatory	Manufacturer	Optional

Office of Textiles and Apparel. "Labeling Requirements." *International Trade Administration.* Accessed Jan. 24, 2012. http://web.ita.doc.gov/tacgi/overseasnew.nsf/d1c13cd06af5e3a9852576b20052d5d5/fad8900a6a29da2b8525789d0049ea04?OpenDocument

act, all manufacturers and importers are required to attach labels to all clothing that is being sold in the United States. These laws were put in place so that customers know what they are paying for. Labels must contain the following information:

- Fiber content
- Country of origin
- Identification of the manufacturer
- Importer
- Care instructions

Table 5.10 shows the labeling requirements for various countries. It is imperative that these steps are followed to ensure proper labeling according the FTC labeling law.

The FTC act gives the commission the authority to take action against any business that is falsely misleading consumers with claims that a product is "made in the USA." The commission requires that all or virtually all of the parts, processing, and final assembling of the product is made in the USA in order to carry that label. If a product is not entirely made in the United States, then "Made in the USA of imported products" can be stated.

The economy can affect the perception of "Made in the USA." According to research conducted by Perception Research Services International (PRS), the "Made in the USA" label matters very much. PRS research shows that 4 out of 5 shoppers notice the "Made in the USA" claim when shopping, and many (76 percent) say the claim influences their purchase decisions. When there is a recession, it is wise to market the brand as "Made in the USA" if that is the case. Table 5.11 is a list of companies that manufacture their goods in the

TABLE 5.11 **U.S. VENDORS/MANUFACTURERS**

This table is a sampling of 10 vendors that manufacture in the United States of America.

COMPANY	LOCATION	PRODUCT	WEBSITE
Ofabz Swimwear	Fort Wayne, Indiana	Swimwear	http://www.ofabz.com/
Optimo Hats	Chicago, Illinois	Hats	http://www.optimohats.com/
Joshu + Vela	San Francisco, California	Bags	http://joshuvela.com/
American Apparel	Los Angeles, California	Knits, wovens, clothing	http://www.americanapparel.net/
Hart Schaffner Marx	Chicago, Illinois	Tailored clothing	http://www.hartschaffnermarx.com/
Raleigh Denim + Workshop	Raleigh, North Carolina	Denim	http://raleighworkshop.com/
J Brand	Los Angeles, California	Denim	http://www.jbrandjeans.com/
Wigwam	Sheboygan, Wisconsin	Socks	http://www.wigwam.com/
Rising Sun	Pasadena, California	Denim	http://www.risingsunjeans.com/
Black Sheep and Prodigal Sons	New York, New York	Accessories	http://blacksheepandprodigalsons.com

United States. Figure 5.4 is a brand named Joshu + Vela, which is made in the USA.

Labeling Requirements

Products must have labels on them. The FTC requires that all clothes sold in the United States be properly labeled. A label must be securely attached to the product until it reaches the consumer, but does not need to be permanently affixed. An example of not having a label permanently affixed would be when an article of clothing is reversible and there are no pockets. The label must be clearly visible at the point of sale. Cosmetics products must follow the both the Federal Food, Drug, and Cosmetics Act (FD&C) and the Fair Packaging and Labeling Act (FPLA) for

Figure 5.4 Joshu + Vela, an example of a brand made in the United States. *Source: Joshu + Vela.*

As Made in the USA products continue to gain ground with consumers, domestic manufacturers are stepping up their commitment.

The nonprofit Save the Garment Center now lists an assortment of resources for apparel labels that want to manufacture in New York, and the new website keepinitlocal.org was created to help emerging designers do just that.

Gary Wassner, co-chief executive officer of factoring firm Hilldun Corp., said, "More than ever, people are asking us for local resources. They are finding it more expensive and more difficult to source overseas, and the quality of production in China is going down. They also need to be in their factories more frequently to get their products quicker. Every day somebody is asking us how they can bring production or some part of their production back."

The United States is expected to see a manufacturing renaissance within the next five years, according to a report released this spring by the Boston Consulting Group. With wages in China climbing at an annual rate of about 17 percent and the value of the yuan also on the rise, the gap between American and Chinese wages is narrowing. In addition, government incentives

in Mississippi, South Carolina, and Alabama are making these and several states more competitive alternatives for companies with U.S. clients.

In the wake of the dust-up over Ralph Lauren's Made in China opening-ceremony uniforms for American athletes at the London Olympic Games in 2012 and the brand's—as well as the U.S. Olympic Committee's—commitment to make the 2014 team's uniforms domestically, U.S. Senator Sherrod Brown (D-Ohio) has introduced a "Buy America" plan to ensure that the federal government purchases apparel that is 100 percent American made.

Source: Rosemary Feitelberg. 2012. "New York City's Garment Center Revs Up." *WWD*, Sept. 5. http://www.wwd.com/markets-news/textiles/new-york-citys-garment-center-revs-up-6220400

labeling requirements. These laws were put in place to protect the consumer. Labelmakers can be used to create these labels and can be found in trade papers or trade directories.

The FTC requires that the following information be listed on a label:

- *Fabric content:* If the product is covered by the Textile or Wool Act rules, then it must list the fabric content. Trim, linings (unless used for warmth), small amounts of ornamentation, and the threads that hold the garment together do not need to have their fiber content listed.
- *Care instructions:* The care and labeling rule states that washing and care instructions must be shown on the label. The care symbols from the American Society for Testing and Materials (ASTM) may be used instead of words.
- *Country of origin:* The country where the product was manufactured as well as the origin of the materials must be listed.
- *Company's registration number (RN):* A registration number is needed to identify textile, wool, or fur products.

Having a product that is "Made in the USA" can create jobs and stimulate the economy.

Beyond the FTC requirements listed, the Federal FD&C Act and the Fair Packaging and Labeling Act (FPLA) require the following:

- *An identity statement:* The product label should state its intended use.
- *The net quantity of content:* What is the weight of the content?
- *The name and place* of the business, the manufacturer, packer, or distributor.
- *Distributor statement:* Who the product is being manufactured or distributed for.
- *Material facts:* Any imperative information about the product. If the product must be used in a certain way for safety issues, that information must be listed.
- *Warning and caution statements:* Anything that might be hazardous to the consumer.
- *Ingredients:* All ingredients must be listed in descending order of predominance.

Anyone not adhering to the Federal Trade Commission Act, the Federal FD&C Act, and the FPLA can be fined up to $10,000 for the offense.

TRADE TERMS

strategic sourcing

manufacturer

cut-make-trim (CMT)

full package program (FPP)

contractor

textile header

import quotas (Table 5.1)

tariff-rate quotas (Table 5.1)

absolute quota (Table 5.1)

dumping (Table 5.1)

duty-free (Table 5.1)

tariff or duty (Table 5.1)

exports (Table 5.1)

imports (Table 5.1)

transshipping (Table 5.1)

textile headers

prototype

production sample

Summary

Strategic sourcing is crucial when it comes to finding a manufacturer who can create the intended product. Companies are choosing to source locally due to longer lead times and a more complex supply chain. Sourcing locally has many benefits to the entrepreneur who is just beginning a venture. Once a manufacturer is found, it is important to have a set of objectives to facilitate the process of manufacturing the product. Relationships need to be built along with an understanding of the process to have a successful partnership.

Once the product is manufactured, it is important to ensure that the same quality is maintained during production and throughout the supply chain. If issues are not caught right away, then valuable time is wasted. Manufacturing locally can make it easier to visit the manufacturing company to monitor how the production process is going. It is more difficult to be able to monitor when manufacturing overseas, but the benefit remains being price competitive. When working with manufacturers, locally or abroad, it is important to have an understanding of all trade terminologies and laws, whether regarding labeling or quotas. It is also necessary to understand agreements, such as NAFTA, when doing business with other countries. It is also imperative to follow labeling requirements to make sure that the company is in compliance with any label laws.

Online Resources

Textiles in Depth

Textiles in Depth is a nonprofit company that offers general information related to specific categories, such as the apparel industry.
www.textilesindepth.com/index.php?page=buyinghouses-unitedstates

Emerging Textiles

Emerging Textiles.com is a textile source that offers information regarding the global textile and clothing trade.
www.emergingtextiles.com/?q=com&s=daily-yarn-fiber-prices

United States Fashion Industry Association

The USFIA represents the fashion industry: textile and apparel brands, retailers, importers, and wholesalers based in the United States and doing business globally.
www.usfashionindustry.com

Activity 5.1 Sourcing

Research and find three manufacturers in the United States that may be partners in the manufacturing process. What does each manufacturer have to offer? What are they lacking in service? Create a list of questions that you would ask a manufacturer you were contemplating doing business with.

Notes

1. BusinessDictionary.com. "Manufacturer Definition." *BusinessDictionary.com.* Accessed Jan. 22, 2012. http://www.businessdictionary.com/definition/manufacturer.html.

2. BusinessDictionary.com. "Contractor Definition." *BusinessDictionary.com.* Accessed Jan. 22, 2012. http://www.businessdictionary.com/definition/contractor.html.

3. "Eight Tips on Selecting Domestic Sourcing." 2011. *Purchasing and Procurement Center,* Dec. 21. http://www.purchasing-procurement-center.com/domestic-sourcing.html.

4. Fashiondex.com. "How to Shop the Fabric Market." *Fashiondex.com.* Accessed Oct. 16, 2012. http://www.fashiondex.com/howtos/htstfm1.php.

5. Salacuse, J.W. 1991. *Making Global Deals: Negotiating in the International Marketplace.* Boston: Houghton Mifflin.

6. Anjoran, Renaud. 2011. "What Is a Quality Control Inspection?" *Quality Inspection Tips,* Dec. 06. Accessed Jan. 20, 2014. http://www.qualityinspection.org/qc-inspection

7. ApparelSearch.com. "Grading Fashion: Grading Clothing—Terms of Interest to the Fashion Industry." *Apparel Search.* Accessed Jan. 20, 2012. http://www.apparelsearch.com/terms/G/Grading_fashion.htm.

Bibliography

Ahman, Gul Naz. "The Step-by-Step Process of Garment Manufacturing." *HubPages,* last updated April 3, 2011. Accessed Jan. 22, 2012. http://gulnazahmad.hubpages.com/hub/A-Step-by-Step-of-Garment-Manufacturing.

Bureau of Consumer Protection Business Center. "Legal Resources." Accessed Jan. 24, 2012. http://business.ftc.gov/legal-resources/17/33.

BusinessDictionary.com: Online Business Dictionary. Accessed Jan. 24, 2012. http://www.businessdictionary.com/definition.

Export.gov. "Tariffs and Import Fees." Last updated July 13, 2013. http://export.gov/logistics/eg_main_018130.asp.

Globalsources.com. 2011. "Challenges with Preproduction Samples." Oct. 17. Accessed Jan. 15, 2012. http://www.globalsources.com/NEWS/SIC-Challenges-with-pre-production-samples.html

Hyde, Vicky. 2005. "Changing Global Economies Create New Global Sourcing Opportunities for the Fashion Industry." *Manufacturing & Logistics IT Magazine,* Nov. 3. Accessed

Jan. 22, 2012. http://www.logisticsit.com/absolutenm/templates/article-supplychain.aspx?articleid=1671.

just-style. 2013. *Tomorrow's Apparel Industry: Products, Markets, Sourcing, and Processes Forecasts to 2019,* June. http://www.just-style.com/market-research/tomorrows-apparel-industry-products-markets-sourcing-and-influences-forecasts-to-2019_id171243.aspx

Keiser, Sandra J., and Myrna B. Garner. 2008. *Beyond Design: The Synergy of Apparel Product Development.* 2nd ed. New York: Fairchild Publications.

'Made in the USA' Matters to Shoppers - Perception Research Services International." *PRS - Perception Research Services International.* Web. 24 Jan. 2012. http://www.prsresearch.com/about-prs/announcements/article/made-in-the-usa-matters-to-shoppers-including-millennials/

Morrell, Liz. 2010. "The Benefits of Local Sourcing." *Retail Week,* Feb. 26. Accessed Jan. 15, 2012. www.retail-week.com/in-business/supply-chain/the-benefits-of-local-sourcing/5010688.article.

TRADE TERMS *(continued)*

minimums

quality assurance

inspection

grading

North American Free Trade Agreement (NAFTA) (Table 5.8)

Caribbean Basin Initiative (CBI) and the Caribbean Basin Economic Recovery Act (CBERA) (Table 5.8)

Andean Trade Preference Act (ATPA)/Andean Trade Promotion and Drug Eradication Act (ATPDEA) (Table 5.8)

U.S.–Israel Free Trade Area Agreement (Table 5.8)

Jordan Free Trade Area Agreement (Table 5.8)

African Growth and Opportunity Act (AGOA) (Table 5.8)

Caribbean Basin Trade Partnership Act (CBPTA) (Table 5.8)

U.S.–Chile Free Trade Agreement (US-CFTA) (Table 5.8)

U.S.–Singapore Free Trade Agreement (Table 5.8)

U.S.–Korea Free Trade Agreement (KORUS FTA)

Office of the United States Trade Representatives. "U.S. Korea Free Trade Agreement." Accessed Oct. 13, 2012. http://www.ustr.gov/trade-agreements/free-trade-agreements/korus-fta.

Sollish, Fred, and John Semanik. 2011. *Strategic Global Sourcing Best Practices.* 1st ed. Hoboken, NJ: John Wiley and Sons, Inc.

United States Patent and Trademark Office. *U.S. Patent Statistics Report.* Web. Accessed Jan. 19, 2014. http://www.uspto.gov/web/offices/ac/ido/oeip/taf/us_stat.pdf.

U.S. Department of Commerce, Office of Textiles and Apparel. "Importing into the U.S." *International Trade Services Administration.* Accessed Jan. 24, 2012. http://web.ita.doc.gov/tacgi/eamain.nsf/6e1600e39721316c852570ab0056f719/e881952e8c64f497852576850049c6dc?OpenDocument.

U.S. Department of Labor, Bureau of Labor Statistics, Office of Productivity and Technology. 2009. "Hourly Compensation Costs for Production Workers in Manufacturing." November 20. Accessed Jan. 24, 2012. ftp://ftp.bls.gov/pub/special.requests/ForeignLabor/pwcountrytables.txt.

U.S. Food and Drug Administration (FDA). "Cosmetic Labeling & Label Claims." Last updated Jan. 23, 2012. Accessed Aug. 15, 2012. http://www.fda.gov/Cosmetics/CosmeticLabelingLabelClaims/default.htm.

Valladares, Mercedes. "How to Start a Clothing Manufacturing Business." *EHow.com.* Accessed Jan. 22, 2012. http://www.ehow.com/how_5951094_start-clothing-manufacturing-business.html.

van der Heide, Marjolein. "US wants China to improve intellectual property rights protection." *Future of Copyright.* N.p., 27 Dec 2013. Web. 22 Jan 2014. Accessed Jan. 19, 2014. http://www.futureofcopyright.com/home/blog-post/2013/12/27/us-wants-china-to-improve-intellectual-property-rights-protection.html.

Yuka-Alpha. "Pattern Making." *Yuka & Alpha.* Accessed Jan. 23, 2012. http://yuka-alpha-eng.seesaa.net/article/5721543.html.

6

Pricing the Product

Entrepreneurs can have a viable product, but unless it is priced to yield a profit, the outcome can be detrimental to the company. Developing a solid pricing strategy is critical for an entrepreneur to start and stay in business. Having a comprehensive understanding of the pricing components will enable an entrepreneur to set margins that yield profitability. Establishing the cost, the wholesale price, and manufacturer suggested retail price are fundamental for market penetration.

Price Components

Understanding how to price a product will drive the success of the company. Successful entrepreneurs have a comprehensive understanding of three price components: cost, wholesale, and manufacturer's suggested retail price (MSRP).

- **Cost** is the total dollar amount of materials, trims, packaging, and labor used to develop a single unit of product. The optimal cost strategy is sourcing fabrics, materials, packaging, and labor that reflect the quality standards for price classification and negotiating the lowest price for the highest quality of goods and labor. If applicable, shipping or transportation of goods is also factored into the cost component.
- **Wholesale** is the price at which the entrepreneur sells the product to the retailer. It is a dollar amount set by the entrepreneur that is at least double the amount of the cost of a single unit of product. By minimally doubling the cost, the entrepreneur will cover the actual cost of a single product unit and variable operational expenses such as sales collateral, website hosting, telephone, rent, or storage facility.
- The **manufacturer suggested retail price (MSRP)** is the price the entrepreneur recommends the retailer sell the product to the consumer. It is a set dollar amount that is at least double the amount of the wholesale. By providing an MSRP, the retailer has a price guideline

to benchmark and competitively position the brand within their store environment. Furthermore, it ensures consistency in the marketplace. Be mindful as an entrepreneur, it is illegal to dictate or control the actual retail price. It can only be suggested.

- Quick costing, also known as **keystoning,** is a quick way of figuring out wholesale or retail by doubling the cost of goods or wholesale. Quick costing is not used as often anymore due to market pricing, but is a quick way to gauge what the wholesale or suggested retail may be.

Example: Quick Costing

Cost of goods:	$ 70.00 (actual amount to create product)
Wholesale:	$140.00 (2x marked up from cost)
Suggested Retail:	$280.00 (2x marked up from wholesale)

The cost is the single most important variable that sets the overall price positioning for the product. It is the primary component entrepreneurs can single-handedly control at the beginning of their venture. The cost component of a product can vary depending on the materials, trimmings, packaging, labor, and shipping.

Pricing Strategies

Sourcing

It is the trade intelligence of the entrepreneur to make the appropriate material selections and sourcing partnerships to position in a specific or desired price classification. Material cost and manufacturing cost of a product will dictate the pricing structure. If the cost of goods is higher than anticipated, the entrepreneur must find alternate sources to accommodate the budget or pricing constraints of creating a single product unit. It is important to source manufacturers and contractors for production. Seek quotes to examine cost differences. Negotiating cost is typically tied to meeting minimum quantity requirements. Typically, the more units being produced, the better the price. A manufacturer or contractor's production cost is not final; it can be negotiated, so it is important to source the market.

Competition

The competition will provide insight to price. Each competitor's product should be examined according to quality, material, and packaging. An entrepreneur can assess price by reviewing the retail price ranges of the competition. Reverse the quick cost by taking the suggested retail, divide it in half for the wholesale. Next, divide the wholesale in half and that will provide an idea of cost of the product. Entrepreneurs in the industry are continuously editing and reworking product to get it to the best possible cost. Consumers can examine multiple black dresses and understand the differences in construction, details, material, quality, and/or name brand.

Example: A women's black silk sheath dress

Manufacturer Suggested Retail Price	$100.00
Estimated Wholesale Price	$100.00/2 = $50.00
Estimated Cost	$50.00/2 = $25.00

This should only be used as a guideline to estimate the price components.

Today's customer is Internet savvy and can search online to comparison shop. Make sure you are not pricing yourself out of the market.

Position in the Market

When examining the competition it is important to realize positioning at the lowest price might not be an effective strategy. It may be difficult to compete with large organizations that have the resources and funding to negotiate low cost. The Camuto Group, which provides design, sourcing, marketing, and production services, can offer a sharper price than a small startup brand with limited resources. Figure 6.1 is a dress by Vince Camuto. A brand needs to look at the competition to create a strategy for how to price the product:

1. *Competitive Analysis:* Price is not the only factor to consider when looking at the competition. The product as a whole needs to be examined, such as the style, quality, material, details, trim, and packaging. Who is the customer? What image are the competing brands trying to portray? Do competitors use any type of marketing tools?

2. *Maximum Pricing:* What is the most a customer is willing to spend on a given product? The target market must be looked at to get an understanding of maximum pricing. If the intended target market will not shop at a high-end department store such as Neiman Marcus, then do not use their price points to determine the maximum price.

3. *Price Flexibility:* If the competition is scarce, then a higher price point can be achieved. The consumer will not pay a premium price when many comparable items are readily available. The product needs to speak for itself when it comes to price.

An entrepreneur may want to enter into the market with a competitive price to be able to get a foothold in the marketplace, but the cost should never compromise the brand's profit margin. A competitive price is one that does not stunt financial growth. In other words, an entrepreneur should not forfeit or erode the price margin by selling at a steep discounted wholesale price. This will cause a decrease in the ability to cover company expenses, produce the next collection, and possibly stunt overall growth. However, circumstances that could warrant a slight wholesale discount would be an overstock position or end-of-season reduction of inventory. An effective approach would be to price the product competitively or slightly higher, rather than to enter the marketplace at a lower retail price point. A higher price point will position the product as better quality and make certain there is a likelihood of a profit. If the product has been priced too high, then it will be easier to lower the cost. A thorough understanding of the industry will assure that the item is being priced where it should be.

Figure 6.1 A draped dress by Vince Camuto, which is owned by the Camuto Group. *Source: Fairchild Fashion Media.*

As WWDMAGIC reshapes itself as a preeminent fashion expo appealing to Baby Boomers, Kellwood Co.'s Democracy aims to carry that mandate.

Two years after building a business at Dillard's, Nordstrom, Von Maur, Amazon.com, and specialty stores in the United States, South America, Mexico, Germany and Canada, the denim and sportswear label is making its debut in WWDMAGIC's White section with spring looks loaded with bright colors, lively prints, and stylish silhouettes that can be worn in various facets of a multitasking woman's life.

There's a textured jacket in soft, unstructured tweed that's suitable for the office, for instance. Plus, a dip-dyed chambray shirt that can be knotted in the front as a weekend get-up. Budget-conscious fashion lovers who can't decide between a solid color or print can settle on

$78 reversible jeans that pop in a coral tint on one side and are printed with tonal lace on the other.

Democracy tries to enhance every shape between sizes 4 and 16 with wider waistbands, forward seams, and angled pockets. Its strategy is that its combination of trends and accessible retail prices between $39 and $128 will attract independent specialty stores, many of which are owned by women.

After all, the company's motto states that it's for the "woman who grew up with fashion and got busy with life," according to Caren Lettiere, president of Democracy in Los Angeles. "Her priorities in life are such that she isn't going online and searching for key fashion to wear," she said. "We're trying to streamline that fashion message."

Source: Rachel Brown. 2012. "WWD MAGIC: Ones to Watch." *WWD,* August 21. http://www.wwd.com/markets-news/ready-to-wear-sportswear/wwd-magic-ones-to-watch-6183256

Figure 6.2 Entrepreneurs need to be excellent negotiators and should avoid price wars that cause revenue loss. *Source: moodboard/ Cultura/Getty Images.*

Pricing the Product

When pricing the product, it is important to stand out from the competition. The product may get lost in a store's merchandise mix, so steps should be taken to differentiate the product in ways that are not based on pricing alone. Figure 6.2 shows that the last thing a brand wants to do is to have a price war with another brand to which it is too similar in style and quality.

- *Quality:* Complicated designs or better fabric in a garment could give perceived value. A better-fitting garment often justifies a higher retail price.
- *Benefit:* Does the product offer a benefit that the customer is looking for? The brand *d*irt highlights the natural benefits of body care by emphasizing that it's formulated to nurture the skin with earth-derived ingredients instead of synthetic chemicals. Figure 6.3 illustrates natural ingredients that are used by *d*irt to nourish the skin.
- *Branding:* Develop the brand name to generate a positive viral buzz about the product. Often, the price is related to the brand. Dior mascara can retail at $25 versus Maybelline mascara that retails at $5.
- *Packaging:* In the beauty industry, product packaging forms a customer's first impression. The consumer will often purchase a product based on the packaging alone. Yet, the quality must be inherent or a customer will not become a repeat buyer. The apparel industry does not need to focus on the packaging, but it must consider the product presentation with display components such as hangers.

Figure 6.3 *d*irt utilizes earth-derived, natural ingredients as a core strategy. *Source: Erthe Beaute, LLC.*

Costing Principles

The **initial cost estimate** is an approximation of what the item might initially cost. During this process a prototype is created to estimate the initial cost. The initial cost estimate is referred to as "pre-costing" or "quick costing" in the industry.

Cost components

- Product development
- Apparel patternmaking and grading
- Marker making and plotting
- Cutting and sewing
- Quality assurance
- Finishing

The estimated cost should be in alignment with the product's positioning and price classification. Working with a contractor that can provide various samples is invaluable when it comes to breaking down and pricing new garments. Creating a single sample will cost more per piece than manufacturing a production run. Sample cost and small production runs are generally higher. These costs can be twice of the actual production run. Figure 6.4 shows an illustration of a full-service apparel manufacturer based in the northeastern United States.

Samples

Entrepreneurs must consider the cost to create market samples and consumer samples. Showroom samples must also be accounted for when producing samples. If multiple sales representatives are hired to sell

Figure 6.4 Exacta is a full-service, garment-cutting contractor based in Bloomfield, New Jersey. *Source: Exacta Garment, Exacta Industries Incorporated.*

the line, then sets of samples must be made for each sales representative to show potential buyers during seasonal markets. Depending on the industry segment, samples are often marked out of stock and given to retail buyers to entice partnership. The buyer will try the product to determine whether to purchase it. For example, a beauty product production cost may be $15.00 a unit. If 100 units are required for prospective buyers, it will cost the company $1,500.

In the beauty industry, entrepreneurs often develop amenity–sized products. These items are considered samples and given to retailers and consumers free of charge. Companies such as are Birchbox and Total Beauty welcome samples as a part of their sales strategy. According to Total Beauty founder and chief executive officer Emrah Kovacoglu, "It is not cheap providing these samples. It is hard for [beauty brands] to measure direct ROI [return on investment]. They aren't looking just to get their products into the hands of people. They are really looking to get their products into the hands of people that are in the market and are influencers. Those are all things that we understand." Figure 6.5 shows one company's sample room.

Tip 6.2 **Create-a-minute!**

When creating a sample for a body product, consider creating sample sizes to cut down on cost.

Figure 6.5 The Tibi sample room in the basement of the Wooster Street store. *Source: Fairchild Fashion Media.*

Direct Costing

There are variable costs that determine the actual cost of the product. To determine the cost of goods sold, one must cost out the different components of the actual production process. The **cost of goods sold** is what the designer/entrepreneur will pay to manufacture each product. During the manufacturing process, the entrepreneur reviews the direct cost to begin the costing process. **Direct cost** is the actual cost to produce the product.

Materials

Materials are the most significant component of any costing. They may include fabric for apparel or the formulation for a beauty product. The materials must be measured by yardage or ounces, depending on the product. Fabric yardage is determined by the design and size specification of each garment. It's common to use the median size for sample development.

> Example: Wool pencil skirt. Sized 2 to 12. The sample size could be a size 6 or 8. Depending on the width of the fabric, the skirt may require 1.5 yards of fabric. If 24 pieces were sampled for that style, and the size run is 2 to 12, with a size scale of 2–4–6–6–4–2, respectively,
> A quick yardage estimate: 24 pieces × 1.5 yards = 36 yards

Trimmings

The number of trims used for the product (if any) would be priced out.

> Example: The skirt needs one zipper.
> 1 zipper × the cost $0.25 = $0.25

Labor

Labor costs could include marking, construction, grading, and cutting if the product is a garment. Marking is laying out all the pieces of the garment; grading involves developing a size range; cutting is the actual cutting of the pieces; and construction is bundling, sewing, pressing, trimming, and inspection of the garment. In the beauty industry, labor involves product development, formulation, and testing.

> Example: Marking cost of $.60 + grading cost of $.55 + cutting cost of $.90 + construction of $5.00 = Total labor cost of $7.05 per piece.

Packaging

The packaging of a product can involve tissue, polybag, and the inner and outer box when it comes to garments. Beauty industry packaging may consist of plastic or glass jars, bottles, and tubes, along with secondary packaging that often costs more than the actual product itself. Packaging can represent a significant portion of a product's selling price. The cosmetic industry estimates that the cost of packaging is up to 40 percent of the product's selling price. The packaging decisions should be highly considered, so that the cost is not exuberant. Figure 6.6 shows a limited-edition Swarovski crystal bejeweled Vaseline Lip Therapy valued at $62.00. The standard jar is retailed at $1.99. If a customer does not see the value in the product, then most likely they will not purchase the product.

> Example: A 12-oz. acrylic jar $4.50 + the secondary package $1.25 = Packaging cost of $5.75.

Transportation

Transportation cost depends on where the product is being shipped. If the product is manufactured overseas, then an export agent should be appointed to assist with the goods that are to be exported to the United States. Goods should almost always be shipped ocean freight versus airfreight. Ocean freight is much more cost effective, but the drawback is

Figure 6.6 Vaseline created a limited-edition Swarovski crystal bejeweled Vaseline Lip Therapy valued at $62.00. The standard jar MSRP is $1.99. *Source: Vaseline.*

the lead-time it takes to deliver the goods. Airfreight might be necessary if the goods being shipped could be damaged due to moisture, humidity, or cold that could occur during ocean travel. When starting up a brand, it might be wise to manufacture locally where minimums might be lower and the transportation cost is less. Make sure shipping from the manufacturer does not eat up too much in the cost of goods.

Indirect Costing

When creating a product, the business as a whole needs to be taken into consideration. **Indirect costs** are all the other costs that are not part of the direct costs. Indirect cost could be fixed or a variable cost. Figure 6.7 illustrates some various indirect expenses, such as advertising, marketing materials, and photography costs, but there are various other expenses including rent, insurance, phone and other utility bills, bank charges, travel expenses, website maintenance, and office supplies. These indirect costs are necessary for the day-to-day operation of the business regardless of whether sales are being made. The entrepreneur needs to figure out what the yearly cost will entail to cover these expenses so that the company will at least break even. A company's **break-even point** is the point when sales cover all direct and indirect expenses.

> Example: The direct and indirect costs for a product come out to $30,000 a year. An estimated 3,000 units of a beauty product will be sold. That means that $30,000 divided by 3,000 units equals $10.00 per unit. The lowest amount that can be charged for the product is $20.00 just to break even.

Re-Costing

The cost sheet should be updated for every production cycle. The materials or labor can increase or decrease. For example, the price of cotton fluctuates continuously.

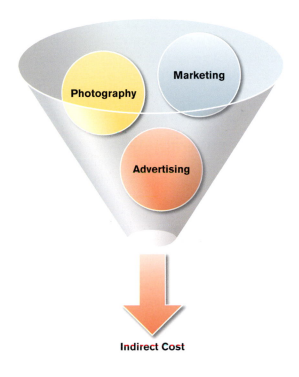

Indirect Cost

Figure 6.7 Brands must consider various costs to determine what the indirect cost will be and how they will affect how many units need to be sold to break even.

Chargebacks

Retail buyers often seek financial assistance when issues arise with a product. **Chargebacks** represent payments back to the retailer due to reasons such as late deliveries, issues with quality, or below or above receipt of product. According to Vano Haroutunian, a lawyer with Ballon Stoll Bader & Nadler, chargebacks now represent about 20 percent of yearly sales for many of his vendor clients, as opposed to 5 percent a decade ago. While some vendors are learning how to deal with the issue, smaller fashion companies are still suffering.[1] An entrepreneur needs to take chargebacks into consideration when calculating the cost of goods sold.

Final Costing

Pricing is a vital strategic matter because it is integral to the position of the product. If a product is costed incorrectly, the product can result in a loss. It is important to understand and analyze all stages of the costing process to avoid any mispricing. A dress that was manufactured at $30.00 but was sold at wholesale for $34.00 would in turn affect the profit margin.

Production Costing

The cost of producing the product will command what the pricing structure will be. The cost of the material, trim, labor, packaging, minimum style per order, and transportation (depending on where the garment is being manufactured) will ultimately dictate the production cost. When dealing with a manufacturer, orders are priced by the piece.

> Example: Costs of material + trims + labor + business overhead + profit = Cost of finished product.

Wholesale Cost

The cost sheet will determine the total cost of goods and what the suggested wholesale price should be. The **wholesale cost** is what the retailer will pay to purchase the product. Retail buyers will attempt to negotiate the wholesale cost, but it is the entrepreneur's job to make sure that the planned profit margin is being achieved. A large order does not guarantee a large profit. The goal for the company is to sell product, but not if it means selling at a loss. There are three main approaches to how a brand may set their prices:

1. **Cost-based pricing:** Determining price by adding a profit percentage on top of the cost of manufacturing the product. A simple method for setting the wholesale price for a product is to keystone. **Keystoning** is a pricing method that doubles a product's cost to determine the wholesale cost.

   Example: A shirt costs $25.00 to manufacture, so it will be sold at wholesale for $50.00. This will equal a 50 percent gross profit margin.

2. **Customer-based pricing:** Pricing is established by having an understanding of what the customer will be willing to pay.

Example: Based on the target market research, it is concluded the target customer will pay anywhere from $50 to $75 for yoga wear.

3. **Competitor-based pricing:** The price structure will vary depending on where the competition is priced.

Example: Brand A is priced at $95.00, brand B is priced at $89.00, and brand C is priced at $109.00 for a similar solid cotton jacket. The product would then need to be priced between $89.00 and $109.00 to be able to compete with the market.

Regardless of what cost method is used, entrepreneurs should make it easy on themselves and the buyers by rounding up the wholesale and retail prices of the product.

Example: For a dress that costs $34.27, the wholesale should be rounded to $70.00; the MSRP would be $140.00.

Profit Margins

The goal of any business is to make a profit. The reason some entrepreneurs fail in the launch of a brand is due to not pricing their product correctly. The entrepreneur needs to price the product to cover all costs, not just the cost of manufacturing the product. It is vital to predetermine the profit margin in order to be fully equipped to eliminate relationships that erode the margins and stay on track to make a profit.

Example:

Wholesale cost	$28.00
Actual cost of product	−$12.32
Net profit	= $15.68
Net profit margin	$12.32 (actual cost)/$28.00 (wholesale cost) × 100% = 44%

Sell price

Once the wholesale price is calculated, then the suggested retail price will need to be set. **Sell price** is what the retailer will sell the merchandise for. Each category in the fashion industry has its own markup range, but the industry average is 2.5 times. This allows for unexpected cost variables and errors. The market must be studied to ensure retailers are guided to sell the product at a competitive price and avoid having to mark down the merchandise. For example,

Suggested retail price: $40.00 (wholesale price) × 2.5 = $100.00.

A retailer will take the suggested retail price into consideration but can increase it to account for markdowns, discounts, and losses.

Cost Sheets

A cost sheet is an important document for tracking the cost of a product. A **cost sheet** is used to calculate the total cost of manufacturing a product. Figure 6.8 is an example of a completed cost sheet. The cost sheet usually includes the total material cost, total trimming cost, and labor cost. The most important factor when filling out a cost sheet is

Date:	6/15/13			Style # :	AG1274
Product Description: Sleeveless Dress				Season:	Spring 2014
Sizes:	Missy Fit 2-12			COG:	$ 31.75
Colors:	Red			Wholesale:	$ 65.00
				Sug. Retail:	$ 130.00

MATERIAL	YARDS	PRICE	AMOUNT
Silk #543	2	$ 10.50	$ 21.00
Interlining #231	1	$ 1.50	$ 1.50
TOTAL MATERIAL COST			$ 22.50

TRIMMINGS	QTY	PRICE	AMOUNT
Zipper 8 nylon coil YKK	1	$ 0.80	$ 0.80
Brand Label	1	$ 0.10	$ 0.10
Care/Content Label	1	$ 0.10	$ 0.10
Size Label	1	$ 0.05	$ 0.05
TOTAL TRIMMING COST			$ 1.05

LABOR			AMOUNT
CMT - Cut Make and Trim			$ 4.00
Grading			$ 1.00
Packaging			$ 0.20
Transportation			$ 2.00
General Overhead			$ 1.00
TOTAL LABOR COST			$ 8.20

| TOTAL COST OF PRODUCT: | | | $ 31.75 |

PRODUCT SKETCH

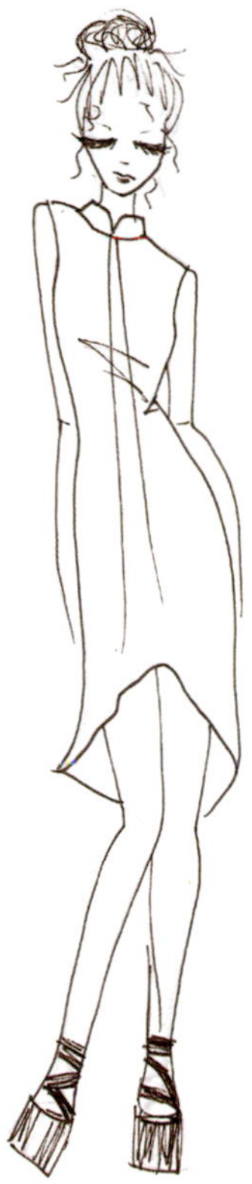

Swatch

Figure 6.8 An example of a completed sample cost sheet.

keeping in mind the gross profit margin. When filling out the cost sheet, make sure to include:

- *Date:* The date when the cost was agreed upon.
- *Style number:* An identifier for the product.
- *Description:* A written depiction of the item.
- *Sizes:* The size range of a garment or container sizes.
- *Color:* The color or color ranges of the product.
- *Season:* What time of the year the product is being produced for.
- *Materials:* The amount and cost of the material being used.

Date:				Style # :
Product Description:				
Sizes:				Season:
Colors:				Wholesale:
				Sug. Retail:

MATERIAL	YARDS	PRICE	AMOUNT	PRODUCT SKETCH

TOTAL MATERIAL COST _____

TRIMMINGS	QTY	PRICE	AMOUNT

TOTAL TRIMMING COST _____

LABOR			AMOUNT

Swatch

TOTAL LABOR COST _____

TOTAL COST OF PRODUCT: _____

Figure 6.9 A blank sample cost sheet.

- *Trimming:* The amount and cost of any trim being used.
- *Packaging:* Any material used to package the product, such as tissue, polybag, inner box, or outer box.
- *Labor:* The cost for grading, cutting, marking, or construction of the piece.
- *Shipping expenses:* What it will cost to ship the individual item.
- *Product sketch:* A rendering of the front and back of the product.
- *Swatch:* Actual material that is being used to create the product.
- *Total cost of product:* The total cost of producing a single item.
- *Wholesale:* The price that the buyer will pay.
- *Suggested retail:* What the recommended retail price should be.

The cost sheet should include all the pertinent information involved in constructing the product. Larger companies use industry-driven software, but an Excel spreadsheet is the most commonly used format when creating a cost sheet for a startup business.

TRADE TERMS

initial cost estimate

cost of goods sold

direct cost

indirect cost

break-even point

chargebacks

wholesale cost

cost-based pricing

keystoning

customer-based pricing

competitor-based pricing

sell price

cost sheet

Summary

An understanding of the target customer will aid in finding the key price points that will work for the brand. Negotiation skills along with knowledge of the industry will help in getting a fair price for the cost of goods sold. Being equipped with this knowledge and making sure the numbers are accurate will save a lot of time and alleviate headaches. An understanding of the costing process can help with the target price and make a profit for the company. More often than not, one may end up with a higher cost than was intended in the first place, so it is important to revisit the cost sheet and make changes to meet the targeted margin goals.

Online Resources

Fashion Incubator
This is an informative website that offers information on apparel manufacturing. http://www.fashion-incubator.com/

Online Clothing Study
Online Clothing Study is a blog with a database of e-publications, fact sheets, articles, and case studies connected to the apparel industry. http://www.onlineclothingstudy.com/2012/03/case-studies.html

Activity 6.1 Competitive Costing

Shop at retail stores for competitive purposes. Find two comparable items for your product that is being created. Based on the retail price, estimate what the wholesale and cost of goods are by using the quick-cost method shown in the example at the beginning of the chapter. In addition, examine and list each product's quality, material, and packaging.

Activity 6.2 Cost Sheets

Complete a cost sheet for each product. Determine the wholesale price and suggested retail price for each unit that is appropriate for your targeted market segment. Use figure 6.9 form to complete the cost sheet.

Note

1. Adrianne Pasquarelli. 2010. "Retailer Fee Frenzy Hits Designers." *Crain's New York Business.com,* May 16. Accessed April 13, 2012. http://www.crainsnewyork.com/article/20100516/SMALLBIZ/305169962.

Bibliography

Brown, Rachel. 2012. "Total Beauty Leaps Into Sampling War." *Women's Wear Daily.* May 07. Accessed May 10, 2012. http://www.wwd.com/beauty-industry-news/products/total-beauty-leaps-into-sampling-war-5897396.

Camuto Group. "About Us." *Camuto Group.* Accessed May 2, 2012. www.camutogroup.com/about

Lipe, Jay B. "How to Set (and Get) the Right Prices Part II: Explore Pricing Methods." *About.com.* Accessed May 11, 2012. http://marketing.about.com/cs/advertising/a/pricingstrtgy_2.htm

Riley, Jim. "Marketing - Pricing approaches and strategies." *Tutor2u.* Updated Sept. 23, 2012. Accessed May 15, 2012. http://tutor2u.net/business/gcse/marketing_pricing_strategies.htm

Valladares, Mercedes. "Pricing Strategies for the Apparel Industry." *eHow.* Updated June 22, 2013. Accessed May 18, 2012. www.ehow.com/way_5765621_pricing-strategies-apparel-industry.html

Zahorsky, Darrell. "Super Charge Your Business With Profit Pricing Strategy." *About.com.* Accessed May 6, 2012. http://sbinformation.about.com/cs/marketresearch/a/pricing.htm

7

Commerce Checklist

One of the most riveting moments in an entrepreneur's career is launching a product. The elation and anticipation of product readiness, reaction, and results quickly can turn into anxiety if one lacks foresight and preparedness. Entrepreneurs must have astute business acumen in the industry sector of their product. As with most endeavors, the success or failure of a new product launch is often directly tied to the planning process. To establish context, the market preparation explored in this chapter is intended for the entrepreneur who plans to sell products to retailers. The entrepreneur or a small executive team commonly executes and oversees the preparatory material needed to market and sell their products.

KEY CONCEPTS

+ Understand how to develop sales projections.

+ Examine the tools needed for sales preparation.

+ Analyze basic vendor compliance requirements.

Commerce Checklist

Creating a stellar prototype or actual product is the starting line for the launch phase. Proactive entrepreneurs will set the trajectory for success with a well-developed sales forecast and collateral material to support the selling and exposure of the product (Case Study 7.1).

Sales Projections

Sales projections are also known as sales forecasts. They provide an estimate of a company's prospective sales for a given timeframe. A seasonal sales plan is often six months and divided into two seasons: Spring: February–July and Fall: August–January. Creating sales projections for the product assortment will enable an entrepreneur to monitor selling by unit for each product. Building a sales projection spreadsheet that reflects

Kaitlyn Kirby believes that style never sleeps. It's a motto that would serve her well within the fashion industry, but when the twentysomething Kirby decided to start her own online publication, she made the choice to fill a *Cookie*-sized hole instead.

A lifestyle publication for the modern mother, *Cookie* was founded in 2005 by Conde Nast and closed in 2009, alongside other magazine staples like *Gourmet* and *Bride* magazine. The close of the magazine left a void behind for readers, and Kirby took that as her opportunity to launch *Babystyle Magazine* in December 2011. In its first month for the holiday preview issue, *Babystyle* received 50,000 unique visitors to the website and [featured] actress Jessica Alba and her two daughters on the cover of the spring [2012] issue. I got the opportunity to interview Kaitlyn about what makes *Babystyle* successful, the balance of her editorial life.

KAITLYN KIRBY: *Babystyle Magazine* is an online lifestyle publication for the modern parent. We cover style, design, trends, celebrity parents, and more. After the close of *Cookie Magazine,* there just wasn't another magazine for parents that focused on a mix of fashion, design, and entertainment. I started *Babystyle Magazine* to give modern parents what the market was lacking. *Babystyle Magazine* launched in December 2011 with a holiday preview issue and has since been covering topics in children's and maternity fashion, new products and trends, nursery and home design, travel and entertainment, as well as features on celebrity parents and tastemakers.

We focus on children from birth to 10 years of age and the style that encompasses every aspect of their lives and those of their parents. The magazine places significant emphasis on fashion, design, travel, and entertainment, all of which comes in the form of digital content accessible worldwide via computer, phone, and iPad.

Source: Deborah Sweeney. 2012. "Entrepreneur Spotlight... Kaitlyn Kirby of Babystyle Magazine." *Forbes.com,* May 5. http://www.forbes.com/sites/deborahsweeney/2012/05/01/entrepreneur-spotlight-kaitlyn-kirby-of-babystyle-magazine/

anticipated unit sales will assist in inventory management (Figure 7.1). This often will dictate the best sellers and slowest sellers in the collection.

Sales projections can often be planned by distribution channel categories. They can also be further mapped by sell-in opportunities: launch, immediate, and discontinued.

- *Launch:* Introduction of a new product to the market. The optimal opportunity to maximize sales based on newness and market readiness.
- *Immediate:* A term commonly used to replenish current/best-selling products into the current season's assortment.
- *Off Price:* Excess product that has shifted out of the production cycle and has been discontinued from the current season's assortment.

DIRT
SALES PROJECTION

Introduction/Launch

PRODUCT	BEG. ON HAND	PROJECTED SALES	ENDING ON HAND
73120 *d*irt Pumice Scrub	600	237	363
73110 *d*irt Salt Scrub	600	300	300
73120 *d*irt Luxe Salt Scrub	600	285	315
73135 *d*irt Orange Peel Scrub	600	230	370
73115 *d*irt Sugar Scrub	600	400	200
Total	3000	1452	1548

Immediate/Replenishment

PRODUCT	BEG. ON HAND	PROJECTED SALES	ENDING ON HAND
73120 *d*irt Pumice Scrub	363	200	163
73110 *d*irt Salt Scrub	300	250	50
73130 *d*irt Luxe Salt Scrub	315	285	30
73135 *d*irt Orange Peel Scrub	370	200	170
73115 *d*irt Sugar Scrub	200	180	20
Total	1548	1115	433

Off Price/Discount

PRODUCT	BEG. ON HAND	PROJECTED SALES	ENDING ON HAND
73120 *d*irt Pumice Scrub	163	163	0
73110 *d*irt Salt Scrub	50	50	0
73130 *d*irt Luxe Salt Scrub	30	30	0
73135 *d*irt Orange Peel Scrub	170	170	0
73120 *d*irt Sugar Scrub	20	20	0
Total	433	433	0

Figure 7.1 An example of a sales projection sheet. *Source: Erthe Beaute, LLC.*

With the phenomenon of e-commerce flash sales, such as HauteLook and MyHabit, entrepreneurs are wholesaling products off price. They are including current and discontinued products in their projections to liquidate inventory and reach a broader customer base (Figure 7.2). The length of time for each phase will vary by product sector and brand—apparel tends to have a shorter selling life than accessories and beauty.

Market Preparation

In tandem with the sales forecasts, entrepreneurs need an arsenal of documents to support the administrative and selling processes. Critical documents include line sheets, swatch cards, and order forms/purchase orders, account forms/credit applications, purchase invoices, and a cancellation and return policy.

Figure 7.2 MyHabit, a division of Amazon.
Source: Zuma Press, Inc./Alamy

Tip 7.1 **Create-a-minute!**

Sales projections are critical estimations that will enable me to manage my seasonal inventory stock levels and identify my best-selling styles. Done!

Line Sheets

A **line sheet** is a set of documents that communicate key product information to prospective buyers (Figures 7.3 and 7.4). They are used to assist buyers in writing product orders. They should be detailed so that a buyer does not need to see or experience the actual product. Many companies will provide a hard copy or provide an electronic file on a USB drive.

Line sheets include:

- Product season
- Product name and description
- Product flat or image
- Style numbers
- Size range
- Wholesale price
- Suggested retail price
- Color and fabric information
- Delivery dates and order cut-off dates
- Order minimums by item and/or total dollar amount
- Company and/or sales rep contact information

Order minimum: Many companies have two requirements: minimum quantity per style or per color and minimum dollar per order.

Figure 7.3 An example of a line sheet, which communicates key product information to prospective buyers.

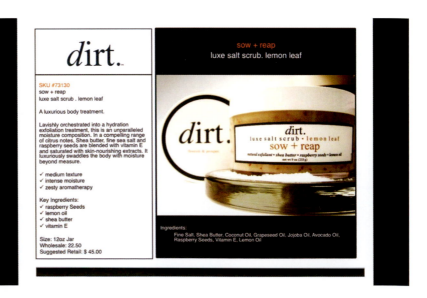

Swatch Card

A **swatch card** is a single card with multiple fabric pieces mounted on it or a set of individual fabric cards that correlate to the product assortment. Swatch cards provide a tactile and visual reference for buyers to plan their buy and order products without having tangible products in front of them. In the beauty industry, amenity-size samples are provided for a tactile and sensory experience.

Order Form

An **order form** is an imperative document to close a sale. It is an actual form used to record the order. Forms can be blank or preprinted with

Tip 7.2 **Create-a-minute!**

Although technology is the way of the world, providing a hard-copy order form is still an industry standard, especially for independent retailers. At trade-show events, receiving "paper" orders is a top priority!

product information. The form is usually a two-ply with carbon. The brand retains a copy and the account partner receives a copy.

Account Form and Credit Application

For administrative measures, an account form is needed to record core information about the account. From the corporate name and tax identification to contact information, information is needed for billing and shipping purposes. A credit application can be used if credit terms are requested. Basic bank information and account references are standard requirements to grant credit terms.

Purchase Order

Many large companies and retailers will use the line sheet to generate an internal document called a purchase order (PO) to buy products from vendors (Figure 7.5). **Purchase orders** are buyer-generated documents that authorize a purchase transaction. When accepted by the seller, it is considered a binding contract for both parties. Entrepreneurs must remember that an order is not confirmed until the retailer provides a purchase order or authorization with signature. They set forth the guidelines of the purchase such as product quantities, prices, discounts, payment terms, date of shipment and cancellation, and other terms and conditions. Vendors must confirm and verify that all information contained in the purchase order is correct. Best practices are:

- Confirm the purchase order with the buyer.
- Communicate any discrepancies on the purchase order with the buyer immediately.
- Follow the vendor guidelines completely and accurately.
- Ship orders in a timely manner.
- The purchase order will contain a ship date and an in-house cancellation date (known as "cancel date").
- Orders should be shipped in strict accordance with the schedule set forth in the purchase order.

Most often delivery of purchase orders earlier than the designated ship date will be refused, parallel to shipments after the cancel date. Entrepreneurs must be proactive by communicating and negotiating with the retail buyer

Ven#	Vendor Name		Beg. Ship	Complete	Terms	Label	Dept	Season	Buyer	Date	PO#	Retailer

New Order _____ Confirmation _____ Shipped: _____ Ordinary_____ Special_____

Style #	Description	Color	XS 2	S 4	M 6	L 8	XL 10	12	TTL Units	Wholsale	Retail	TWS	TR
1234	Sleeve Dress	01 -Black	2	2	4	4	2	2	16	$ 24.00	$ 48.00	$ 384.00	$ 768.00
												$ -	$ -
												$ -	$ -
												$ -	$ -
												$ -	$ -
												$ -	$ -
												$ -	$ -
												$ -	$ -
												$ -	$ -
												$ -	$ -
												$ -	$ -
												$ -	$ -
												$ -	$ -
												$ -	$ -
												$ -	$ -
												$ -	$ -
												$ -	$ -
												$ -	$ -
												$ -	$ -
												$ -	$ -
												$ -	$ -
												$ -	$ -
												$ -	$ -
												$ -	$ -
												$ -	$ -
												$ -	$ -
									16			$ 384.00	$ 768.00

Figure 7.5 Purchase order.

for early or extension dates. Buyers will often request wholesale concessions, such as discounts for late deliveries or extension dates.

Here are key terms often used on a purchase order:

- **Order date:** The date the PO was written.
- **Buyer:** The authorized personnel who issued the purchase order.
- **Ship date:** The earliest date that the retailer or distribution center will receive the merchandise.
- **Cancel date:** The latest date that the retail or distribution will receive the merchandise.
- **FOB (freight on board)** or **ROG (receipt of goods):** The point at which the retailer takes responsibility for the merchandise.
- **Ship via:** Direction on how to ship the merchandise.
- **Pre-ticket:** Determines whether we expect the vendor to pre-ticket/label the merchandise prior to shipping it.
- **Season:** The season the merchandise is intended for.
- **Channel:** What the merchandise is intended for (retail-stores, direct-website or catalog, wholesale).
- **Payment terms:** The terms at which the retailer agrees to pay the vendor for the merchandise. A common payment term is Net 30—payment will be issued within 30 days of ROG. Discount terms also are negotiated.
- **Currency:** The currency that your payment will be made in.

- **Order type:** The type of order (e.g., replenishment, late add, etc.).
- **Pack type:** The way the buyer is asking you to pack the order (loose or prepack).
- **Vendor style:** The style number assigned by the vendor.
- **Vendor description:** Describes the product.
- **Color:** The color of the merchandise (if applicable).
- **Size:** The size of the merchandise (if applicable).
- **Quantity:** The total quantity for that SKU.
- **Price:** Wholesale and MSRP.
- **Totals:** Units and dollars.

Purchase Invoice

Unlike the purchase order that's the sales contract, the **purchase invoice** is a document used for billing items purchased in a transaction. It is generated by the vendor and directed to the retailer once the product has been shipped. It indicates the amount due for the products purchased. Retail partners will render payment based upon the agreed payment terms. The retailer will have a maximum amount of time to pay and can be offered a discount if paid before the due date. An invoice contains parallel information from the purchase order, however it is directed to the billing department.

Cancellation and Return Policy

It is in the best interest of the entrepreneur to create a cancellation and return policy for retail partners. This document will serve as a guideline for the retailer in cases where it may be necessary to cancel an order or return product. The cancellation policy will provide a date range that allows the retailer to cancel due to unforeseen circumstance without penalty fees. For returns, a common practice is to require the retailer to contact your office for a return authorization (RA). This is a number/code that permits the retailer to return goods based upon set forth guidelines and authorization.

Vendor/Retailer Relationship

Parallel to any successful relationship, developing distribution relationships are unique to each account partnership. In a sales transaction, the entrepreneur will function as a vendor. A **vendor** is an entity that sells a product or service. Entrepreneurs can choose to sell products directly to consumers or through an intermediary. Entrepreneurs are responsible for establishing relationships with distribution channels to sell the products. A **distribution channel** is a path through which goods and services flow to the consumer. The channel can be direct from the vendor to the consumer, such as selling on the vendor's website, or include an intermediary such as retailer. Various distribution channels will be explored in the next two chapters.

Vendor Compliance

Established retailers have important policies and procedures that are required of all vendors. To ease the learning curve, many companies have specific websites for vendor registration. The vendor website is a reference tool to help guide vendors to partnership success. The registration process will generate vendor login information. Websites are updated regularly and contain information such as contacts, vendor guidelines, and billing information. If required, the retailer will also provide third-party sourcing information to assist vendors in pre-ticketing or bar-coding labels. Requirements may differ for domestic versus international vendors.

Vendor Code of Conduct

Established retailers will often inform vendors of their **code of conduct** statement and policy. Many corporate entities take human rights very seriously and insist that business be conducted according to the highest ethical standards. In tandem, they will insist on high standards from all vendors. Urban Outfitters requires vendors to commit to meeting important human rights standards and conditions of employment, including, without limitation, the following:

- *Compliance with law:* Vendors must be in full compliance with all laws, rules, and regulations applicable to the manufacturing of products, facilities where they are made, and accommodations made available to workers.
- *Child labor:* All workers must be at least the local minimum legal working age.
- *Forced or compulsory labor manufacturing:* Workers must be voluntarily employed and cannot be prisoners or any other kind of forced labor.
- *Nondiscrimination:* All hiring decisions must be based on the prospective worker's ability to do the job and may not be based on race, religion, gender, age, sexual orientation, disability, nationality, political opinion, or union membership.
- *Minimum wages, hours, and benefits:* All national laws regarding minimum wage, overtime, and hours and benefits must be complied with. In addition, hours per day and days per week shall not exceed the legal limitation of the countries in which any product is produced.
- *Health and safety:* Workers must be furnished with safe and healthy working conditions in compliance with local laws.
- *Corporal punishment:* Behavior, including gestures, language, and physical contact, that is sexually coercive, threatening, abusive, or exploitative is not be permitted.
- *Environmental protection:* Vendors shall comply with all applicable laws, rules, and regulations in respect of protecting the environment and maintain procedures for notifying local authorities in the event of an environmental accident resulting from vendors' operations.

Many established retail companies have compliance programs to monitor the ethics and compliance of each vendor. They will conduct inspections to ensure requirements are not violated. If vendors are in violation, the retailer may choose to cease the relationship.

Vendor Quality Assurance Guidelines

Established retailers have a quality assurance department. Once product is received by the retailer, it must pass a random quality audit. **Quality assurance** is ensuring quality product free of defects, poor workmanship, or color shading problems. An audit sample is random. The acceptance of the order will be based on the quality check. Products may be returned if they do not comply with the retailer's standards.

Product Safety and Liability

Retailers will have reiterated through documentation that all products meet all federal and state product safety statutes and regulations, including those that fall under the Federal Trade Commission Act and the Consumer Protection Safety Act. For example, the Flammable Fabric Act requires testing the flammability of clothing and textiles intended to be used in apparel. This minimum standard identifies textiles that are unsuitable for use in clothing because of their rapid and intense burning. The standard applies to all textiles used in adult and children's apparel. Most children's sleepwear must also meet more stringent flammability requirements. Most millinery footwear and fabrics used between the linings and outer fabrics of garments are not required to meet this standard.

Sample Requirements

At the vendor's expense, final production samples often are required when a retail buyer selects it for inclusion in their assortment. Failure to deliver all samples and information in a timely fashion may result in the cancellation of the purchase orders. For products being sold for direct/e-commerce, photography samples are required and should be a true visual representation of the final review sample. Samples are then sent to the appropriate department for inclusion in the catalog or website.

Vendor Chargebacks

Vendors incur penalty charges for not following the retailer's guidelines for partnership. A **chargeback** is obtaining compensation from a vendor for violations of the retailer's regulations, as stated in the Vendor Guidelines. Merchandise must be prepared and shipped in accordance with the instructions in the vendor guidelines. Shipments not in conformance with these guidelines may be refused and returned at vendor cost, or will be assessed a chargeback. Compensation can be in the form of cash payments, merchandise credits, or future discounts.

Vendor violations can be incurred as a result of packaging and marking requirements. Chargebacks also will be issued for internal damage related to insufficient packaging and vendor-related quality problems. Most retailers will provide photographs or documentation whenever possible. If this should occur, a return-to-vendor (RTV) will be negotiated.

Chargebacks are usually deducted from the next invoice payment for vendors shipping under net terms, otherwise payment is due upon chargeback notice. The statute of limitations for contesting chargebacks and shortages is six months. Most often, chargebacks are issued within a few days of the order being delivered. Commonly, all shortage claims and chargebacks are presented to the vendor within 30 days of the time that the order has been received.

Product Ticketing

Tickets or labels must be placed on the product and must not conceal any country of origin markings. Labels must be attached to the actual product, not to the packaging of the product. In cases in which the product is packed in a decorative display box or packaging, the label is commonly placed on the back, lower right corner of the box or the bottom of the box.

Vendor Shipping Guidelines

Retailers often require that each shipment contain a master packing list that provides a summary and detailed breakdown, by carton, of the total contents of the order being shipped. There is usually one purchase order per packing list. All packing lists must be legible and affixed to the outside of the lead carton, in a "packing list enclosed" envelope.

Key terms to be familiar with are as follows:

Freight Terms:

- **Freight-on-board (FOB) destination:** The vendor owns the cargo until it gets to the destination.
- **Freight-on-board (FOB) shipping point:** The retailer owns the cargo once in the hands of the shipper (Figure 7.6).
- **Pre-paid:** The vendor pays for freight to the retailer's warehouse.
- **Collect:** The vendor bills the retailer or uses the retailer's shipping courier service.
- **Cost, insurance, and freight (CIF):** The vendor/entrepreneur must pay cost, insurance and freight for the product to reach its destination.
- **Bill of lading:** A document that establishes the terms of a contract between the shipper and the carrier. Used to transfer ownership of a shipment between parties. The original bill of lading is required to gain release of a shipment from the carrier.
- **Country of origin marking:** The U.S. Customs and Border Protection Agency requires country of origin markings for virtually all products imported into the United States, and the Canada Broker Services Agency maintains similar requirements, that each item purchased be clearly and durably marked with the country of origin according to the regulations of the U.S. Customs and Border Protection Agency.

Figure 7.6 An FOB shipping point diagram.

TRADE TERMS

sales projections

line sheet

swatch card

order form

purchase order

purchase invoice

vendor

distribution channel

code of conduct

quality assurance

chargeback

Summary

A successful launch takes more than a remarkable product. It requires administrative documents to project, record sales and invoices, and ship product. Furthermore, to embark upon a relationship with an established corporate retail partner is no small undertaking. An entrepreneur must adhere to the guidelines set forth by the retailer to maintain an ongoing relationship. It is paramount to know the particular requirements of each retail partner to build a successful relationship and avoid vendor violations.

Online Resources

Federal Trade Commission, "Made in America"
business.ftc.gov/documents/bus03-complying-made-usa-standard

Wall Street Journal, "How to Get UPD Barcodes for Your Products"
http://guides.wsj.com/small-business/starting-a-business/how-to-get-upc-codes-for-your-products-2/

U.S. Customs and Border Protection, "Countries Eligible for Reduced Duty Rates or Duty-Free Treatment"
https://help.cbp.gov/app/answers/detail/a_id/586/kw/trade

Activity 7.1 Sales Projection

Create sales projections for your product. Include three phases of business for inventory management.

a. Introduction/Launch Phase

b. Immediate Phase

c. Off-price Phase

Bibliography

ApparelSearch.com. "Flammable Fabrics Act." Accessed April 2013. http://www.apparelsearch.com/flammable_fabrics_act.htm

Businessdictionary.com, s.v. "distribution channel," http://www.businessdictionary.com/definition/distribution channel.html#ixzz1x1s9FQmT

Businessdictionary.com. s.v. "purchase order," Accessed April 2013. http://www.businessdictionary.com/definition/purchase-order.html#ixzz1x1u9S5ph

Flammable Fabrics Act, Pub. L. No. 83–88; 67 Stat. 111, (1953, 2008).

Urban Outfitters Vendor Compliance Manual. Urbanvendor.com

PART III
THE PARTNER

Product placement is equally as important as the product itself. The most advantageous distribution is the multichannel retail environment. Consumers are intelligent, savvy, and discerning shoppers. Although they may have preferences, they will navigate a pop-up shop or swap meet as frequently as an established luxury specialty store, department store, or designer boutique. In tandem, e-commerce has become a dominant channel for everyone from established global businesses to start-up brands.

Fashion entrepreneurs probe distribution partners across the spectrum to interface with their target market. Distribution encompasses all the physical activities necessary to make a product or service available to the target customers when and where they need it. Determining the right strategy is a curious mixture of fact and insight, knowledge, experience, and creativity. A notable rule for seeking out the most suitable distribution partner is to seek distribution channels that mirror the characteristics of the product or service.

To maximize and sustain high sales performance, fashion entrepreneurs need to understand the buyer's perspective. Beyond the product, the buyer requires a team approach in all facets of the business for a successful relationship. Entrepreneurs also must adhere to the multiplicity of demand for vendor compliancy with larger retailers. We explore online distribution, the analytics, online sales applications, and ways to persuasively market product to induce sales through search engine optimization. Furthermore, we delve into the persuasive partnership and power of social media and blogs as avenues to launch and promote consumer and wholesale partners—THE PARTNER.

Resource-Based Projections

A resource-based sales projection determines future sales based on what the company is able to produce or sell. Many businesses, especially small and medium-sized companies, have a set maximum capacity. A company's capacity is often set by the financial capability or budget to produce a product each season. For example, if a company has an inventory budget of $30,000 and each item cost $4.00 to produce, the item capacity is 7,500 units. Meaning, the company cannot sell more than 7,500 units without spending more on production. Once a company's capacity is reached, these companies cannot increase sales without spending money to increase unit capacity. To create a market-based forecast, first determine your capacity. Entrepreneurs must determine the inventory cost and consider the overall budget for the product. This will dictate the unit capacity for the season. For example, the 7,500 units may wholesale to the retailer for $8.50 each. The total sales projection based upon the units and wholesale price would be $63,750.00. Small businesses also may be affected by the amount of cash flow, being able to purchase only a limited amount of stock each month. Once you have determined capacity, set your sales forecast at that capacity or at a level below it.

Seasonal Projections

Some types of business make a large part of their sales in certain seasons. Entrepreneurs with a new business collect information about seasonality in industry sales and factor this into monthly projections. Industry, market, and trend research is required prior to launching a product. This information should be gathered at the foundational level of the business. In the United States, weekend sales are typically stronger than weekday sales. Furthermore, in the fashion industry, fourth quarter sales generate a large part of the yearly revenue. Parallel to many businesses that sell products, it relies on holiday sales to generate revenue; other businesses may rely on summer sales. When developing sales projections, take seasonal factors into account.

Advantages of Sales Projections

There are a number of advantages to having up-to-date and accurate sales projections. One is that it may be easier to get financing. Banks often base their loan decisions on the time frame in which a business turns a profits. Established businesses may need to show growth potential and explain how they derived the numbers. The Small Business Administration recommends sales forecasts or projections as part of the loan application process. In large corporate entities, sales projections also enable marketing and other functional departments to create their budgets and plan projects. Favorable sales projections may interest potential investors, driving up value for shareholders.

Distribution Plan Development

Prior to positioning product in the marketplace, entrepreneurs define an effective multichannel strategy for selling. By reviewing the market and determining the most appropriate retailers—from brick-and-mortar to online—the entrepreneur can create a multichannel strategy to reach the maximum number of customers in its price classification segment. By visiting stores and checking the distribution strategy of the competition will often aid in knowing which stores are viable for partnership. The inherent agility of a strategy map is important since distribution can no longer be viewed as a random, standalone, or fixed activity. In a climate of constant change, the strategy has to be nimble and constantly fine-tuned in response to market conditions. For example the beauty brand, *dirt*, slowly shifted their distribution focus from retailers and apothecaries to spas based upon market demand and sales. Entrepreneurs are constantly researching, identifying, and evaluating multiple channels of distribution to determine which will yield the maximum sales for the product or service.

A **distribution strategy** is a plan that provides specific direction to how a company will sell its product to reach the end user. It is a highly significant tool created and utilized by companies that depend on a product to generate profits. The distribution strategy sets direction for positioning goods into the marketplace. A **distribution channel,** also called a marketing channel, is a path through which good and services flow from the company to the consumer (Figure 8.1). It can be direct from business to consumer such as online and catalog orders or may include several business-to-business intermediaries, such as wholesalers or retailers.

Beyond the tedious task of creating a distribution plan and determining the most viable channels, an entrepreneur must also develop channel management. **Channel management** relates to the policies and procedures that will be adopted in order for all members involved in the distribution channel to perform the required functions. Conflict between members of the distribution channel is common, therefore good communications, trust, and understanding among all members, along with contracts are key to the effective functioning of the channel. For example, retailers will often voice concern if the brand is sold by competitive retailers in what's perceived as too close proximity. Furthermore, in accessories, specifically timepieces, channel partners must be authorized dealers, meaning, each location that sells the brand must be an authentic corporate partner and not a secondary relationship.

Market Analysis

Entrepreneurs explore their market segment in order to define the appropriate distribution alignment. The way a product is distributed, including the place where it is offered for sale and the reputation of the reseller along with the experience with the purchasing process, is important because it impacts customers' feelings about the product and how it

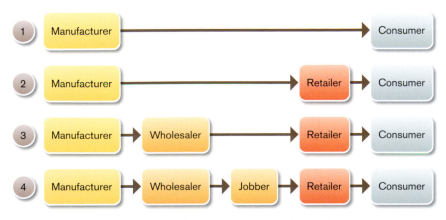

Examples of Customer Marketing Channels

Figure 8.1 Diagram of channel distribution.

Fashion Brain Academy is a business coaching and training company specializing in emerging fashion designers and creative types. Our primary focus is to jump-start new companies and boost existing ones by generating a solid sales and marketing plan while keeping you accountable and focused. Fashion Brain was founded by Jane Hamill, a successful ex-designer and retailer, who saw a growing need in this niche for information and specific step-by-step strategies to start and run a profitable fashion business.

Get your next three clients. Here's what you can do:

1. Locate

You have to know who you really want to sell to and what it is they are looking for. For instance, a designer came to me a few weeks ago and said she was having trouble finding her niche. So I asked her, "What have you done to research your audience? Have you offered to take a key influencer in your niche out to lunch or

coffee? Have you stopped by stores and talked to the salespeople?" The answer was no. You have to know who you're looking for and what their needs are before you can locate them.

2. Get out from behind your computer

That's right, most of the great stuff starts with real people. Let's say you are out and someone compliments your product, which you made and want to sell. Maybe you hand them a card (though 95 percent of people will do nothing with this card). It should be on US, the entrepreneurs, to take the lead.

3. Get back in touch

This is another strategy based on old-school marketing. I absolutely *love* Internet marketing, Facebook, Twitter—all of it—and they are important for most businesses. I also know that if you want three paying customers *now,* you might need to get on the phone.

Source: Jane Hamill. 2013. "Where to Find Your Next 3 Customers." *Fashion Brain Academy,* Aug. 12. http://fashionbrainacademy.com/blog/where-to-find-your-next-3-customers/

positions in their minds. A primary question to distribution planning is—where does the targeted consumer shop?

Entrepreneurs must define key channel partner groups and leading channel partners in their market segment that serve the targeted consumer. An effective way to do this is by collecting information such as the company profile, the geographic regions where they operate, the price classification they target, and the strength of their customer base. This will help shape a solid list of prospects for distribution partnership. Once the list is formed, the decision of which channels will yield the best conduit to the consumer is often revealed by what is termed as "shopping the market." Literally, visiting the prospect's retail environment or e-tail environment to examine the market position and competitive brand are the most viable way to assess suitable channel partnerships. Generating this type of distribution prospect list will result in a more unified and effective go-to-market approach, thus strategy.

Market Reassessment

Successful entrepreneurs have learned to survey the market demand since the development of the product or service. Innovation and technology have forced entrepreneurs to remain market researchers pre- and post-product development. To effectively plan channel distribution, an entrepreneur must conduct a brief market reassessment upon product readiness. By revisiting the market conditions, market demand will become apparent. **Market demand** is the demand generated from all potential customers for a specific product at a specific period of time. The market reassessment process enables executives to ascertain the best market entry at the pulse point of launching new products. By re-examining the market demand and target customer profile, the entrepreneur can adapt to and accommodate any market shifts since product development. Furthermore, an entrepreneur can capitalize on any newly developed or emerging social media opportunities to reach the target consumer. For example, blogs and online consumer interaction conduits have become authoritative tastemakers that continually sway consumer buying habits and product preferences (Case Study 8.1). Although social media is opinion based, consumers trust the word-of-mouth information as well as facts.

For the beauty brand *dirt*, product development of their natural body scrubs took twelve consecutive months. In Fall 2010, it launched with a distribution strategy to reach its target consumer through channel partners such as apothecaries, spas, and online retailers. During market reassessment, the team discovered Birchbox, a company that is changing the way consumers discover and shop for beauty, grooming, and lifestyle products (Figure 8.2). Birchbox also launched in the fall of 2010 and is one of the fastest growing companies of its kind. It combines a personalized subscription service that delivers high-end samples directly to members with an online magazine and store. Its platform provides brand partners with a more effective way to access customers, such as with blogs

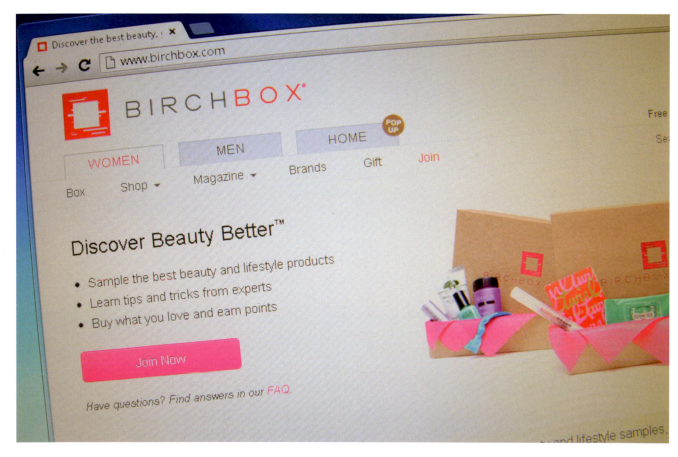

Figure 8.2 Birchbox launched in Fall 2010 as a subscription service that delivers luxury product samples. Courtesy of Birchbox. *Source: Web Pix/Alamy.*

BOX 8.1 Birchbox Blog on *d*irt

We Dig These Yummy Body Scrubs

"I spent this past winter in semi-hibernation mode, bundled up in sweaters and hiding my legs in thick jeans. But when the weather finally warmed up last week, I took one look at my newly exposed arms and legs and realized they were mega-dry after a season's worth of neglect. In search of a solution, I tested out *d*irt, an eco-friendly brand that is new to the Birchbox Shop. Each of their all-natural body scrubs is formulated around a single hero ingredient—like salt, sugar, and pumice—and they work to moisturize skin as they exfoliate."

Source: dirt.com. "We Dig These Yummy Body Scrubs." *d*irt. http://blog.birchbox.com/post/20366388050/we-dig-these-yummy-body-scrubs

Image source: Birchbox.com

(Box 8.1). Furthermore, Birchbox consumers sample top products from established and emerging high-end brands and create YouTube videos of themselves opening the boxes and evaluating products each month. Reassessment allowed *d*irt, Erthe Beaute LLC, executives to include this new channel in their strategic distribution map.

Market reassessment includes but is not limited to an examination of:

- *Buyer characteristics:* The target customer assessment provides insight to any demographic shifts in consumer behavior or purchasing habits. It helps answer the question: Do you *still* know your customer?
- *Market sensitivity:* New products can fill a void or harness a niche position in the market. A new survey of the competitive analysis will enable an entrepreneur to gauge the market demand of like products.
- *Market trends:* Conduct an overall analysis of emerging and regressing trends. Highlight any trends that may affect the target consumer's perception of the new product (Create Tip 8.1).
- *New distribution channels:* Ingenuity is the epicenter of the fashion industry. New technology driven channels are constantly emerging as outlets to reach the ultimate consumer.

Market Penetration

Every entrepreneur with a new product penetrates the market with an initial goal to establish sales. **Market penetration** is the amount of sales or adoption of a product compared to the total theoretical market for that product or service. The ultimate goal would be to garner increased sales and market share. **Market share** is the percentage of industry or a market's sales generated by a particular company. Distribution plan development inadvertently involves market share projections. Arriving at a projection of the market share is a subjective estimate. It is based on not only an analysis of the market but on highly targeted and competitive distribution strategies. The entrepreneur's basic principle, for market

Emerging trends are my friend! I must stay ahead of the curve by researching new opportunities in my business sector.

share projection or forecasting, is to define what business exists or remains within the market and how best to pursue that business with a strategic distribution plan. The approach is subjective and measured by the overall size of the market.

Establish entities, assess the company's current business, quantify the business that remains, and then adopt strategic planning initiatives that increase sales or garner market share from the competition. For instance, JCPenney's 2012 Strategy: With newly appointed executives from Apple and Target came new strategies and a bold overhaul. JCPenney has shifted from a coupon-driven sales-oriented destination in favor of everyday low pricing of "fair and square." The fun advertising campaign is reminiscent of Target, and the new logo has a fresh, clean, modern appeal. The redesigned stores reflect a well-needed update. Although the aesthetics have changed, the challenge is convincing the city-slick, suburban savvy consumer to flee from their tried and true brand-loyal Target commitment to JCPenney's new look. It is apparent that the strategy was developed to increase sales, radically penetrate a new market, and steal market share from the competitors. The strategy has since yielded a negative response (Box 8.2). Consumer readiness is a significant variable that proved the new strategy to be a failed attempt to modernize a fixed strategy employed by the company.

Distribution Factors

Beyond selecting the best distribution channels to reach the consumer, the entrepreneur must be sensitive to balance in the marketplace. To avoid the sporadic approach of random distribution, a distribution plan is also a balancing tool for product dissemination. It is equally important to consider the proximity of channel partners for balanced exposure in the marketplace. If distribution is concentrated, it may cause unnecessary competition between channels and may suppress sales for one or both channel partners.

Entrepreneurs need to know who their potential buyers are, where they buy, when they buy, how they buy, and what they buy. The level of distribution coverage needed to effectively address the customer's needs is measured in terms of the intensity with which the product is made available. The density or number of stores in a particular geographical area and the type of intermediaries used constitute the basics of distribution coverage.

Entrepreneurs are typically conscious of channel **distribution intensity.** This is the availability and the level of saturation of the product in the marketplace in a concentrated geographic area or channel. Market saturation occurs when the product is offered in so many channels that the product is no longer demanded or desired by the targeted consumer. If a brand is distributed in various retail outlets in a concentrated area

BOX 8.2 JCPenney's Strategy Shift

JCPenney: Was Ron Johnson's Strategy Wrong?

JCPenney Co. [JCP] has ousted its CEO, Ron Johnson, the chief executive who reinvented retail at Apple Inc. [AAPL] and who arrived at JCPenney just 17 months ago. Mr. Johnson had a bold vision for JCPenney. On joining the firm, he said, "In the U.S., the department store has a chance to regain its status as the leader in style, the leader in excitement. It will be a period of true innovation for this company."

Mr. Johnson abruptly scrapped JCPenney's dubious pricing policies of marking up prices and then offering discounts with heavy promotions and coupons. He proposed to offer more interesting products, from lines like Martha Stewart and Joe Fresh, at reasonable prices all the time.

The approach didn't fare well with Penney's customer base of bargain hunters. They rebelled, traffic declined, sales fell, and JCPenney slowly returned to the prior era of pricing, with lots of promotions, lots of price-focused ads, and marked-up prices that would be later marked down.

Nor did shoppers respond when Penney started to reintroduce markdowns last year. Sales fell 25 percent in the year that ended Feb. 2 [2013], depriving Penney of $4.3 billion in revenue and causing analysts to ask whether it might run out of cash needed to fund its overhaul.

Above all, Mr. Johnson destroyed his existing business model before the new business model was put in place. As David Cush, Virgin America CEO, said this morning on CNBC's *Squawkbox:* "Don't destroy your old revenue model before you have proved your new revenue model. It was a great idea. But you have this massive structure that you need to support. Revenue supports your structure. You've got to make sure that the new model works before you destroy the old one."

Source: Steve Denning. 2013. "J.C. Penny: Was Ron Johnson's Strategy Wrong?" *Forbes,* April 9. http://www.forbes.com/sites/stevedenning/2013/04/09/j-c-penney-was-ron-johnsons-strategy-wrong/

Figure 8.3 Chloé is a youthful, modern designer collection with very selective distribution channels in the United States market. *Source: Victor VIRGILE/Gamma-Rapho/Getty Images.*

with parallel consumers, the saturation of product will stagnate sales. To avoid market saturation or the cannibalism of sales, entrepreneurs will strategically select channel partners to sell products (Create Tip 8.2). This is referred to as **selective distribution.** Selective distribution is a preferred method of distribution for prestigious brands. For example, Chloé is a youthful, modern, and slightly bohemian designer collection with very selective distribution channels in the United States market (Figure 8.3). The retail partners are noncompeting geographic areas and adhere to image criteria set by the manufacture.

Relative to Chloé, in the contemporary price classification, Free People is a youthful bohemian brand that has **intensive distribution** (Figure 8.4). This distribution approach concentrates product into channels for the targeted consumer to encounter the product at maximum

Tip 8.2 **Create-a-minute!**

I must pick and choose my retail partners and select the preferred geographic locations for distribution to avoid market saturation.

Figure 8.4 Free People is a youthful, bohemian-styled brand that has intensive distribution. *Source: 911 Pictures.*

capacity without saturation. In tandem, in the fragrance sector, the long awaited Lady Gaga Fame perfume was introduced to the market with intense distribution (Figure 8.5). On the release date, it was featured in Sephora, Nordstrom, and Macy's stores and online among other outlets.

Another opportunity that can create sales demand is **exclusive distribution.** This is a strategy where as a company will distribute their products to a limited channel or single channel partner. For example, CH by Carolina Herrera employs an exclusive distribution strategy (Figure 8.6). Another example is a private label brand, such as Macy's INC International Concept Brand, or a license agreement, such as Vera Wang's Simply Vera Vera Wang for Kohl's collection. The timeline for exclusivity can vary from a short-term to a permanent commitment. Premium brands will often launch with an exclusive partner and eventually released to the other channel partners.

Distribution Channel Expansion

Distribution assessment is an ongoing process. Entrepreneurs are market opportunists. They seek innovative and insightful ways to boost revenues and maintain profitability. Conducting distribution assessment also enables channel expansion. Companies will often survey the market for new channel opportunities that were not initially considered or are now

Figure 8.5 The long-awaited Lady Gaga Fame perfume was introduced to the market with intense distribution. *Source: Fairchild Fashion Media.*

Figure 8.6 CH by Carolina Herrera employs an exclusive distribution strategy with its perfume campaign. *Source: Fairchild Fashion Media.*

"Fashion in some people's eyes is very untouchable and super-indulgent," he said. "For me, it's just clothes to be worn. And at the end of the day, the point is to sell the product."

That sounds pretty hard-nosed, coming as it does from fashion's latest It Child, a lanky, tousled design-school dropout who, in a scant five years, has leapfrogged from toting garment bags for *Vogue* to mapping out the vision behind a $25-million family business that is growing at a gallop. Mr. Wang's aggressively street-inflected collections are as avidly monitored by fashion insiders as they are by the shoppers who snap up his leather leggings, draped jersey dresses, and biker vests.

Mr. Wang's success is partly an outgrowth of his unstudied sexy aesthetic, a tough but sultry look that is as much his stock in trade as his signature filmy T-shirts. But lately this go-to designer for models and assorted urban sylphs has shown signs of growing up. His

sophisticated shapes and wallet-friendly prices are now speaking compellingly to a mature population of bankers, teachers and Botoxed social dragonflies who aspire to his brand of urban cool.

Mr. Wang runs his mini-empire without outside backers or benefit of a family fortune. He works alongside his mother; his sister-in law, Aimie Wang, an accountant; and his brother, Dennis Wang, who brings to the enterprise a background in international business development. "Alexander is the ultimate shopper," Dennis Wang said. "He's very aware of what's out there—the different looks, the different price points. He has a very innate sense, a clarity of vision, of where he sees the company going. Everybody we bring on, from accounting to production, he has an interest in meeting."

Source: R. La Ferla. 2009. "Alexander Wang, For Cool Kids, and Now You." *The New York Times,* Dec. 9. http://www.nytimes.com/2009/12/10/fashion/10WANG.html?pagewanted=all

emerging due to a market shift. The strategy has to be an inextricable part of a broader performance management regime that constantly tests and refines the distribution strategy as new information comes to light.

For example, Alexander Wang's women's collection demographic was centered on city–chic, young women who desired an edgy yet effortless look (Box 8.3, Figure 8.7). Distribution channels that cater to that consumer were boutique retailers, such as Jeffery in the meatpacking district of New York. As Wang's collections gained momentum and became more defined, the brand started to appeal to a slightly older, more refined customer who desired the same look. This new demographic triggered a need to broaden channel distribution to reach the new market segment. Products are now positioned into specialty store retailers such as Barneys New York, Bergdorf Goodman, and Fred Segal.

Summary

Entrepreneurs need to define an effective multichannel strategy for selling. Successful companies prioritize the markets they plan to target and outline routes to reach the targeted consumer. The ever-changing business environment allows for a greater need to pursue several sales channels at the same time. Entrepreneurs must develop channel routes that are balanced and used to inform, interact, transact, and deliver. By selecting distribution channels with a parallel brand image and price classification range, the brand integrity remains intact and a unified brand message echoes to the targeted consumer.

Online Resources

U.S. Small Business Administration
www.sba.gov/content/ideas-growing-your-business

Figure 8.7 Alexander Wang's women's collection demographic was centered on city chic, young women who desired an edgy yet effortless look. Alexander Wang, 2012. *Source: Fairchild Fashion Media.*

Activity 8.1 Sales Projections

Create a sales projection plan—by unit, by phase of business.

As an entrepreneur, you will build a sales plan to project how you will sell the product inventory across your seasonal selling period. Consider the number of units you will sell per week for each item. Selling should vary to establish best sellers from fringe or secondary selling.

Determine how many units of your inventory will sell across the three phases of business: introductory, maintenance, and clearance. Then determine the estimated duration of each phase of business. A best practice for unit projections is to determine what percentage of sales will occur in each phase.

Will 30 percent of your total inventory sell in the first 2 weeks and 50 percent during the next 3 weeks, then 20 percent the last 2 weeks? Toggle the numbers/units sold on the basis of how you believe your product will sell.

Activity 8.2 Distribution

What is the intended distribution strategy for your product extension? Explain why?

Bibliography

Burns, Leslie Davis, Kathy K. Mullet, and Nancy O. Bryant. 2011. *The Business of Fashion.* 4th Ed. New York: Fairchild Books.

Businessdictionary.com, s.v. "distribution channel." Accessed May 2013. http://www.businessdictionary.com/definition/distribution-channel.html#ixzz1x1s9FQmT

Businessdictionary.com, s.v. "distribution intensity." Accessed May 2013. http://www.businessdictionary.com/definition/distribution-intensity.html#ixzz23ePqRPD2

Businessdictionary.com, s.v. "exclusive distribution." Accessed May 2013. http://www.businessdictionary.com/definition/exclusive-distribution.html#ixzz23eNUT2R3

Businessdictionary.com, s.v. "market demand." Accessed May 2013. http://www.businessdictionary.com/definition/market-demand.html#ixzz24nZsaGxh:

Businessdictionary.com, s.v. "selective distribution." Accessed May 2013. http://www.businessdictionary.com/definition/selective-distribution.html#ixzz23eMx4xg7

Cron.com. "Small Business." Accessed August 31, 2012. http://smallbusiness.chron.com/

Investopedia.com, s.v. "market penetration." Accessed May 2013. http://www.investopedia.com/terms/m/market-penetration.asp#ixzz2548b52un

La Ferla, Ruthe. 2009. "Alexander Wang For Cool Kids and Now For You." *New York Times,* Dec. 10. http://www.nytimes.com/2009/12/10/fashion/10WANG.html?pagewanted=all

Mourdoukoutas, Panos. 2012. "JCPenney's Strategic Mistake." *Forbes,* Aug. 10. Accessed August 31, 2012. http://www.forbes.com/sites/panosmourdoukoutas/2012/08/10/j-c-pennys-strategic-mistake/

9

Direct and Indirect Sales

Entrepreneurs are the driving force behind determining the best distribution channels to introduce their product or service to the marketplace. For optimal market exposure, a mix of direct and indirect distribution channels often is used to establish and sustain high-sales performance. Entrepreneurs and their management teams must quickly identify suitable distribution channels and channel partners for market coverage to meet revenue goals.

Direct Market Distribution

A **direct market channel** is any conduit that connects the product producer to the end user. In all situations, there is no intermediary involved. It is the touch point of a business-to-consumer relationship. Direct market distribution allows the entrepreneur the opportunity to develop relationships with the product's target market This can provide insightful interaction and feedback to respond to the needs and wants of the customer. Furthermore, the entrepreneur will yield the full retail price, less cost of development, by selling direct to the consumer. Commonly used and highly effective direct market distribution strategies include direct sales force, e-commerce websites, email blasts, trunk shows, consumer trade shows, and other one-to-one techniques to communicate and sell to the customers and clients. In this day, time, and age, many entrepreneurs are using direct market distribution exclusively or in concert with other marketing channels. Collaborations can also boost distribution visibility and increase sales, for example designer Jason Wu and Lancôme launched a partnership in 2013 (Case Study 9.1).

Direct Sales Force

One of the oldest distribution methods is direct selling. This face-to-face distribution approach is the most traditional direct market channel.

The one makeup look from the Fall 2013 shows that we still find ourselves wistfully daydreaming about is Jason Wu's. Those indigo eyes were like a shimmering beacon crying out to our beauty-gripped hearts, and we were nothing but moths to a flame. You can imagine, then, the collective wheeze of excitement that occurred when Lancôme announced an upcoming collection with the visionary NYC-based designer.

The details behind the limited-edition line slated to launch in September have recently been released. The 15-piece offering, which will be sold exclusively at Nordstrom and Bergdorf Goodman, includes three hyacinth-streaked eye shadow palettes ($49 each), three neutral pressed powder shadows ($24.50), three red-hued lipsticks ($26), matching nail polishes ($15), a navy mascara ($27), a black liquid eyeliner pen ($30), and a dual-ended shadow and liner brush ($32.50). All the products are outfitted in dove gray packaging to reflect Jason Wu's signature color.

Christiana Molina. 2013. "Why Every Woman Wants Jason Wu's Beauty Line for Lancôme." *Elle*, August 15. http://www.elle.com/news/beauty-makeup/jason-wu-for-lancome-collection

We caught up with Wu at [the] launch party, where he told us his inspiration behind that unforgettable ultramarine runway hue, his multicultural approach to the collection, and how this line is finally his chance to unleash his secret inner drag queen.

Why was Lancôme a brand that really resonated with you for a beauty collaboration?
Well, in my opinion, Lancôme is the best in the world. They make some of the most high-quality, beautiful products, and they're luxurious. I'm flattered to collaborate with a cosmetic giant like Lancôme. This line is a true testament to my dedication to the beauty market, because I'm really devoted to this. I'm so proud of this product. Every girl in my studio wants it. The samples came in yesterday and everyone took them already. They stole everything! I was like, "Oh my God, at least save one set for me! Those were for my archives!" But I guess that means I'm doing something right I suppose, because the girls are already embracing it and wearing it.

Sales Consultants

Direct selling is the sale of a consumer product or service, person-to-person, that's away from a fixed-retail location, and marketed through independent sales representatives. Direct sellers are not employees of the company whose products or services they sell. Instead, they are independent contractors who market and sell the products or services of a company in return for a commission on those sales. Orders are usually placed in person, via telephone, or via the salesperson's website. In menswear, J.Hilburn is a growing tailored-clothing menswear company that utilizes direct selling to reach its target customer. With a network of more than 2,000 sales consultants who are trained and certified to measure, this antiquated model is still proving to be a successful for J.Hilburn. Entrepreneurs also execute direct selling by wardrobe and style management of private clientele. Another example of this type of person-to-person service is Michael Newell menswear furnishings (Figure 9.1). Direct selling can be an effective channel for an entrepreneur with strong management and training skills.

Private Parties/Charitable Events

Private shopping parties are the most widely recognized direct selling method, where friends, family, or acquaintances get together for a few hours to learn about or sample a range of products or services. This direct market channel has proven to be a socially evoked, destination-driven event. The product presentation tends to be intimate; sales are impulsive and immediate. The salesperson's product knowledge and persuasive demonstrations often render immediate brand loyalty.

Figure 9.1 A woven silk neckwear collection by Michael Newell, sold and distributed direct to consumer and indirect to luxury-driven retailers in the United States. *Source: Michael Newell.*

Tip 9.1 **Create-a-minute!**

Party time! What ever shall I do? Priority #1: everything must resonate and reinforce the brand image. From food to décor, the customer is the focus; selling is the mission!

Mary Kay Cosmetics is an exceptional organization, which utilizes home parties as a touch point to expand its customer base (Figure 9.2). Entrepreneurs can use this distribution channel to garner immediate feedback and market response during the introduction of the product launch. This can create immediate word-of-mouth market buzz with

Figure 9.2 Mary Kay Independent Beauty Consultants have embraced the company's mission statement. Mary Kay: Signature at the Chaz Dean Studios in Los Angeles, California. *Source: Rebecca Sapp/WireImage/Getty Images.*

targeted consumers. Local social media influencers and bloggers attend the events to generate editorial press.

Nonprofit organizations are excellent direct sale partners. They are always conducting fund-raising events. Often, there are seasonal opportunities for entrepreneurs and small businesses to participate in events as vendors. The typical sales agreement is a percentage of sales generated as a donation to the sponsoring organization or a flat fee for participation. Partnering with charitable organization is also a strategic alignment for social responsibility efforts and giving back to the community at large.

Corporate Sales Associates

In a retail environment, an in-house sales force personally sells to the potential or established consumer. This type of interaction is typical in the company's brick-and-mortar retail operation. For example, Moncler sales associates are trained to sell its products directly to the customer in its retail store environment (Figure 9.3). The brand experience is often magnified and personified by the sales associates.

Figure 9.3 Moncler visual display. Moncler cocktail party during Milan Menswear Fashion Week show on June 24, 2013, in Milan, Italy. *Source: Venturelli/Getty Images.*

Internet Market Distribution

The Internet has revolutionized direct marketing for promoting the sale of products and services to targeted audiences. Access to the World Wide Web provides users with services in four basic areas: information, entertainment, shopping, and individual and group communication. Many entrepreneurs opt to have informational website and lifestyle blogs to entice potential consumers to purchase. It also provides optimal market visibility to international retail partners.

Company Website

E-commerce is the buying and selling of products and services through an electronic medium. With the novelty of customizing websites and e-commerce storefronts channels, entrepreneurs can eliminate geographic considerations. Not only does this channel embody the optimal brand image and message, people around the world have the same access as the person across the street. Entrepreneurs who sell tangible goods through their own websites and ship their goods economically have tapped into an entirely new way to reach the ultimate consumer (Figure 9.4). Utilizing a corporate website as a direct market distribution tool can be more targeted, more flexible, more responsive, more affordable, and potentially more profitable in the long term. Building an e-commerce website and search engine optimization can be a costly endeavor, however, it can be far less expensive than incurring excessive overhead expenses such as leases or sales commissions. E-commerce has become a viable fit for direct marketing.

Another way to directly reach consumers without incurring the cost of building a website is to sell on consumer sites for a nominal fee, such as Etsy (Figure 9.5). This particular website is an online marketplace for crafters, artists, and collectors to sell their handmade creations, vintage items, and both handmade and non-handmade crafting supplies.

Social Media

Social media is a viable and powerful direct channel. Large companies and entrepreneurs use it to communicate exclusive offers, generate sales, and create a community of loyal brand advocates. Companies are still trying to figure out the best way to leverage social media to drive customer engagement and response. Opt-in emails are an integral part of social media, as it is relied upon to keep members informed about the latest

Figure 9.4 *d*irt's groundbreaking mission is to create beauty products with natural ingredients that nourish the body, exhilarate the senses, and harmonize the spirit. *Source: Erthe Beaute, LLC.*

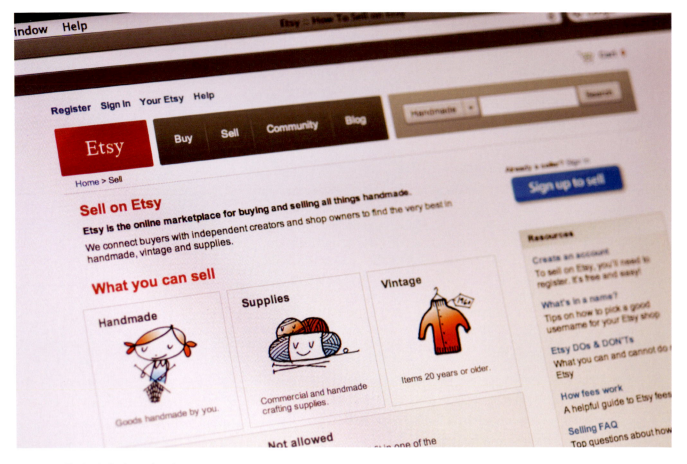

Figure 9.5 Etsy's mission is to reimagine commerce in ways that build a more fulfilling and lasting world. *Source: NetPhotos/Alamy.*

news and updates. The two channels allow entrepreneurs to get a more complete view of the customer, which is necessary for delivering relevant and effective communications. With the right tools, viral social media campaigns can be tracked, measured, and optimized to maximize reach and return on investment.

Kiosk

An emerging trend is the kiosk, which retailers are placing in their store environments. Customers can place an order from an iPad or computer, unlike vending machines that actually provide products. For example, AllSaints retail stores have technology stations where consumers can readily order product not available in store and purchase online. This is another form of a direct market channel that provides convenience at point-of-sale.

Tip 9.2 **Create-a-minute!**

I need to beat the streets? Could be fun! Street fairs are an opportunity to meet and greet potential consumers. The fair attendees must include your target market or else it will be all exposure and low to no sales.

Examples of kiosks range from computer terminals in stores so customers can order from the entire line of products that may not be available in the retail store to kiosks that are placed in airports for home and office delivery.

Direct Mail

Catalogs or look books are a common direct-selling communication tool. **Direct mail** involves featuring a variety of new products or specific seasonal trends that are desired by the target market in a printed form that is sent to the consumer. With the growth of e-tailing, all large mail-order companies have websites to supplement and support their direct mail campaigns. It is common for consumers to peruse and evaluate merchandise through catalogs and eventually purchase online. The convenience factor seems to outweigh the inability to feel the fabric or try on the product. In tandem, the liberal return policies of most retailers entice the consumer to shop online. Brand retailers, such as J.Crew and Pottery Barn, utilize catalogs to entice consumers and often feature products available exclusively through the catalog channel (Figure 9.6).

Street Fairs/Consumer Shows

Consumer shows and street fairs seek vendor participation and provide exceptional exposure for entrepreneurs. Supporting local businesses to generate city revenue and stimulate the economy has increasingly become a primary focus for many cities across the United States. Entrepreneurs can optimize their consumer reach and market visibility by participating in neighborhood fair and markets.

Street Fairs

Street fairs take place primarily during the summer, however many have indoor facilities to host fall/winter events. Vendor applications and participation fee structures vary by fair. For consistency and quality, many fairs have a juror who selects vendors on the basis of quality, presentation, and price point of the product. For example, Brooklyn Flea Market in New York has grown into one of New York City's top attractions, operating flea markets every weekend of the year (Figure 9.7). According to its website, the market "feature[s] hundreds of top vendors of antique and

Figure 9.6 J.Crew's presentation in The Studio at Lincoln Center. *Source: Fairchild Fashion Media.*

Figure 9.7 Brooklyn Flea Market has grown into one of New York's top attractions, open every weekend. People walk by a statue of a pink elephant on sale at Fort Greene Flea in Brooklyn, New York, September 22, 2012. *Source: Emmanuel Dunand/AFP/GettyImages.*

Figure 9.8 Shecky's mission is to create social experiences that empower and reward women in discovering and socializing with their girlfriends during a shopping event. *Source: John Parra/ Getty Images Entertainment/Getty Images.*

repurposed furniture, vintage clothing, collectibles and antiques, as well as a tightly curated selection of jewelry, art, and crafts by local artisans and designers, plus fresh food. *The New York Times* called the Flea, 'One of the great urban experiences in New York'; *Travel & Leisure, Country Living, Budget Travel,* and Fodor's have ranked the Flea one of the best markets or antiques shows in the United States and the world."

Another established market is The Randolph Street Market Festival in Chicago. This European-style, indoor-outdoor, urban antique market in the historic West Loop neighborhood features 200 select purveyors of high-quality, amazingly priced "finds," offering unlimited creative inspiration and hours of fun. Shoppers can find furnishings, vintage clothing, jewelry, collectibles, and other various merchandise. It has been touted in *Travel & Leisure,* the *New York Times,* and *Lucky Magazine.*

Consumer Shows

Consumer shows often have a broad spectrum of consumers. The target market segment may be among a varied consumer group. Entrepreneurs often select this type of direct market distribution channel as way to increase overall visibility in the marketplace. For a participation fee, a booth space can be obtained to display and sell products or services to attendees. A popular consumer show that travels to major U.S cities is Shecky's (Figure 9.8). Formed more than ten years ago, this Girls Night

Out social shopping experience has become a conduit to meet new consumers and introduce new brands across price segments.

Indirect Market Distribution

Indirect market distribution is the function of selling a product or service from business to business, commonly called B2B. An indirect marketing channel consists of businesses involved in the distribution process, each passing the product down until it finally reaches the target consumer. Although from a cost perspective the entrepreneur generates less revenue from selling to indirect channel partners, many prefer the fast track to market visibility and geographic coverage. For example, if an entrepreneur were to sell to his or her product(s) to Target, that would immediately amass simultaneous market coverage from a single retail entity for the product.

An indirect marketing channel can be as simple as using a retailer to get to the end consumer, or it might imply using both a wholesaler and a retailer or even using a complex system of a sales representative, a wholesaler, and a retailer. Intermediaries are generally classified as resellers. These resellers generally take ownership of the product upon sale. Resellers purchase or take ownership of products from the producing firm with the intention of selling them to others.

Indirect methods include:

- *Single-Party System:* The entrepreneur sells to a business who then sells and distributes directly to the target customer. This is most likely to occur when a product is sold to a retailer or to online retailer, in which case it is often referred to as a trade-selling system.
- *Multiple-Party System:* This indirect distribution system has the product passing through two or more distributors before reaching the target customer. The most likely scenario is when a wholesaler purchases from the entrepreneur and sells the product to retailers.

The most common categories are:

Retailers

Retailers sell product directly to target consumers. They purchase products from the producer at wholesale prices and sell it to the ultimate customer at the manufacturer's suggested retail price. Entrepreneurs generate a broader geographic reach in a short period of time by working with an intermediary. Retailers with multiple stores will purchase significant quantities to sell over a calendar season.

Entrepreneurs will strategically align with retailers based upon type and price classification. Price classifications are designer, bridge, contemporary, better, moderate, and budget. Entrepreneurs commonly will partner with varied types of retailers: department store, specialty store, boutique, mass merchants, discounters, off-price, category killers, and wholesale clubs.

Trade Shows

Entrepreneurs can participate in seasonal trade shows to introduce new products to retailers. **Trade shows** are places where producers of products or services sell to retailers or wholesalers. Trade shows can have an international focus, such as MAGIC hosted in Las Vegas. MAGIC is a well-known trade show where the international community of apparel, accessories, and footwear professionals' trade information, preview trends, build business, and shop fashion unlike anywhere else in the industry. According to its website, "Each February and August, tens of thousands of attendees from more than 80 countries meet more than 5,000 emerging-to-established brands to spark the strategic connections that become the relationship. Innovative initiatives and exclusive access to cutting-edge information come together in conveniently merchandised show areas" (Figure 9.9). There are also regional trade shows, such as Fashion Coterie in New York, and StyleMax in Chicago, which are also important venues for market synergy.

Wholesalers

Wholesalers purchase products from entrepreneur, and in turn sell it to other resellers, such as retailers or other wholesalers. Selling to a wholesaler is most common for low-cost, low-unit value products that are bought frequently.

Consignment

Entrepreneurs also can seek indirect channel relationships with consignment retailers. A **consignment**-based relationship is when the retailer

Figure 9.9 WWDMAGIC Trade Show in Las Vegas, Nevada. *Source: 911 Corbis.*

pays the producer only when the product is sold to the consumer. The retailer does not absorb the cost of the inventory, but takes a percentage of the sale once it is sold. The percentage amount is negotiated between both parties in the transaction upon acceptance of the product.

Internet

Online retailers have become a dominant force as consumer behavior has shifted toward Internet shopping. Entrepreneurs will often sell to retailers with both brick-and-mortar stores and Internet e-commerce. This double exposure tends to yield greater sales. For example, most retailers have physical stores and websites where products can be purchased. The benefit of selling to an indirect partner that has both would be the opportunity for a purchase order for stores and one to support the e-commerce distribution.

Merchandise Display/Floor Plans

Visual Displays

Indirect retail partners with brick-and-mortar physical space will allocate a fixed amount of square footage to each product or brand. The task of the entrepreneurs is to know the visual standards and guidelines of their retail partners and how to maximize visual opportunities. **Planograms** are a visual representation of a store's products or services and are considered a tool for visual merchandising. They are developed by the retailer or their corporate visual office. Floor plans are an overall view of the department. They diagram the positioning of fixtures, the cash wrap, aisle, and entry points to the department, as well as freestanding visuals. By viewing a retailer's floor plan, entrepreneurs can quickly assess the best product positioning during all phases of the product life cycle.

Fixtures

Many retailers have their own in-house fixture package to accommodate products and strict visual guideless for consistent product presentation. Although prestigious brands commonly offer branded fixtures, signage, or hangers to their retailer partners, approval is required. If allowed, the brand incurs the expense of all proprietary items for visual display. Branded fixtures should be a continuity of the company's brand image and support the aesthetics of the product. The type of fixture the product will be merchandised on will determine the number of units needed to stock the fixture. Entrepreneurs must become familiar with fixtures to confirm the estimated number of units a buyer purchases to fill each fixture. Depending on the price classification and merchandising strategy of the retailer, a racked fixture can be minimized or maximized. The usage of shelves, mannequin and windows can double expose product on the rack. On figure and off figure visual opportunities will increase visibility within the department.

Summary

Multichannel distribution strategies involve offering merchandise through more than one type of distribution channel. Two significant methods of placing product into the market for consumption are executed by direct or indirect market distribution strategies. Understanding these strategies and how they can best be implemented is essential to long-term success.

TRADE TERMS

direct market channel

direct selling

e-commerce

direct mail

indirect market distribution

retailers

trade shows

wholesalers

consignment

planograms

Online Resources

Electronic Retailing Association
www.retailing.org

Shop.org of the National Retail Federation
www.shop.org

Apparel News–Trade Show Calendar
http://www.apparelnews.net/events/

Activity 9.1 Direct and Indirect Market Channels

Select three direct and three indirect market channels that you would consider viable for your new product or service. Discuss the strategic alignment and how it facilitates your revenue goals to reach your targeted consumer.

Bibliography

Brooklyn Flea. "About." Accessed August 31, 2012. http://www.brooklynflea.com/about/

Businessdictionary.com s.v. "direct market channel." http://www.businessdictionary.com/definition/direct-marketing-channel.html

Businessdictionary.com, s.v. "indirect market channel." Accessed August 31, 2012. http://www.businessdictionary.com/definition/indirect-channel-of-distribution.html

DirectSelling411.com "What Is Direct Selling?" Accessed August 31, 2012. http://www.directselling411.com/about-direct-selling/

Investorword.com. s.v. "ecommerce." Accessed August 31, 2012. http://www.investorwords.com/1637/e_commerce.html#ixzz25FcXEgD4

J.Hilburn. "How it Works." Accessed August 31, 2012. http://www.jhilburn.com/why/how.aspx

Kerin, Roger, Eric Berkowitz, Steven Hartley, and William Rudelius. "Advertising, Sales Promotion and Public Relations, Using Social Media to Connect with Consumers, Personal Selling and Sales Management." *Marketing.* The Core 5th Ed. (New York, NY: McGraw-Hill, 2013), Ch. 15–17.

MagicOnline. "WWD MAGIC." Accessed August 31, 2012. http://www.magiconline.com/

MaryKay.com. "Employment at Mary Kay: Mission Possible." Accessed August 13, 2012. http://www.marykay.com/en-US/About-Mary-Kay/EmploymentMaryKay

Randolph Street Market. Accessed August 31, 2012. http://randolphstreetmarket.com/

Schecky's. "About." Accessed August 31, 2012. http://www.sheckys.com/events/

10

The Buyer's Mind

This chapter examines the role of a buyer and provides entrepreneurs with the tools to get their products into the right hands and offer the buyer the correct flow of information. Understanding what buyers are looking for and how to get the product in front of them will assist in launching a successful brand in stores and online. A relationship between a buyer and a vendor needs to be handled with respect and integrity to grow the relationship and business.

KEY CONCEPTS

+ Actively learn to communicate the most detailed information about the product.

+ Establish ways to build a strong and lasting relationship with a retailer.

+ Identify the competitors in the market and understand how to use this information to sell the product.

+ Prepare to make the sales call and learn how to proceed.

+ Recognize ways to approach the buyer to close the deal.

+ Understand how to negotiate terms, minimums, and shipping requirements.

Retail Partner Research

The key to a successful business venture is to make sure that the brand will fit the retailer. The way to determine this is to become a customer by going into the store or shopping online, depending on the business. The brand must fit into the environment of the retailer. Figure 10.1 shows a boutique and its atmosphere. As a customer, one must:

1. Look at the products being sold. Consider what type of product is being carried. Can the entrepreneur's brand fit in without disappearing? What are the various price points? What are the variations in quality?

2. Analyze where products in the same category are placed within the store. What types of fixtures are being used? Will the product display well?

3. Speak to the employees about the store and the products that are being sold. Often employees are not allowed to share proprietary information, but they are able to provide insight to product. What are the best sellers and why? What is not selling and why? What are customers asking for? Do the salespeople feel there is a void in the marketplace? Who are their competitors? Make sure to go in when the store in slow to be able to get the sales clerks' attention and time. Salespeople can be a wealth of knowledge. Attending a trade show will also assist the entrepreneur in

Figure 10.1 Every boutique has a consumer target market. Entrepreneurs must assess whether their brand fits that niche. *Source: amst/ Shutterstock.*

garnering information on the latest products. What booths look busy? Attend educational seminars to find out what the hottest trends are and what the customers and retailers are looking for to enhance and grow their business.

Large retailers can be difficult to sell into, so look beyond them. Large retailers may also ask for a **slotting fee,** which is a fee that is charged to the brand to house their product in a store. Boutiques are a great place to start, as are online-only retailers. A track record in smaller stores can be useful when it is time to approach the larger retailers, who want to know that the brand has been in operation and is running smoothly. Past sales will demonstrate that the entrepreneur can handle the business. The most important thing is to identify the best channel for the product.

Appropriate Internal Contact

Entrepreneurs must first decide whether they are able to sell the product on their own or if they would benefit from hiring a sales representative to sell the product. A **sales representative** is a person who sells the product for the brand for a fee, which is usually a percentage of the sales. Figure 10.2 is a sales representative showing a line to a buyer at WWDMAGIC, a trade show held twice a year in Las Vegas, Nevada, that shows women's apparel, accessories, and footwear. An entrepreneur may want to pursue selling her own product first. At times, a line that is just starting may get lost in the shuffle with a sales representative's existing

Figure 10.2 Sales representatives can be hired to sell an entrepreneur's brand. *Source: Bambu Productions/Collection/Getty Images.*

lines; the new brand may not get the attention that the entrepreneur would like. If an entrepreneur is going to sell the brand, then it is necessary to have confidence and product knowledge, which is essential when dealing with a buyer. The entrepreneur must prepare to find the appropriate contact and pitch the product.

Buyer Contact

The majority of entrepreneurs need to begin cold calling to get their product into stores or online retailers. The first step is to get the contact name for the buyer or category manager who is responsible for that category. Small boutiques usually have the owner buying the merchandise, so it simpler to reach them or find out who is doing the buying for the store. A larger retailer might be more difficult, since there is usually a corporate office that houses all the buyers. If this is the case, then one great source for identifying buyers is LinkedIn, the online professional network. Here are some pointers for using information that is available to registered users on LinkedIn.

1. Search for specific companies that the brand will be a good fit for.
2. Find the name of the buyer who handles the appropriate category. It is a small world, so one might find that the buyer and the entrepreneur have a connection through a mutual friend.
3. Contact the buyer outside of LinkedIn. Be aware: buyers do not appreciate constant soliciting and may ignore the request.

Other ways to use LinkedIn are to:

- Join LinkedIn groups that specialize in the brand's category.
- Follow several companies that are a good fit for the product.
- Network with people in the industry. One of the best ways to get the brand into a retailer is through a referral. People are more apt to listen to someone who has a personal or professional connection with them.

An open-call is an exciting way to get in front of the buyers to present the brand; but remember that they are seeing numerous products, so your brand needs to stand out.

A buyer can be hard to reach, so another key contact is the assistant buyer. The assistant buyer is often overlooked, but these individuals can be the key to getting one's foot in the door. An assistant can put the product in front of a buyer. The goal is to assist the buyer, so if assistants think that a brand is viable, they will want to show that brand to the buyer. Also, assistant buyers eventually will become buyers themselves. It is important to respect the role and position, as it can be a critical link to partnership. If they grow within the company, it is possible that they will add the brand to their assortment if the current buyer does not.

Other sources that can be used to contact buyers are paid services such as the Chain Store Guide or the Salesman Guide. Each of these guides provides company information, as well as a buyer's contact information. Paying for a service that breaks it down by industry will save the entrepreneur time, however this can eat into the start-up budget. The cost for these services can range from $200 to $1,000. Some local libraries carry these guides in their reference section, so it will be wise to find out and save money. The guide should not be more then a year old, since buyers may change positions or even companies.

Some buyers have monthly, quarterly, or annual open vendor dates. If that is the case, find out how much time is allotted for each vendor presentation; many buyers allot entrepreneurs 30 minutes to pitch their products. Figure 10.3 shows the retailer Henri Bendel, which offers its semi-annual "Open-See" event, giving up-and-coming designers the chance to present their merchandise to be selected for a trunk show or for sale at the Fifth Avenue store in New York City. Macy's offers a mentoring program to women and minority, which offers them a four and a half day intensive program on cultivating these entrepreneurs, so that they may one day become a vendor at Macy's.

Vendor Contact

An entrepreneur is sometimes fortunate enough that a buyer has seen their product and is reaching out to them. Buyers are continually looking for new and exciting products to add to their assortment. It is important to create a buzz for the brand through either a write-up in a magazine or online newsletter, such as *DailyCandy* or by a reputable blogger. Dirt products were featured in a *Daily Candy* national daily find, which prompted contacts from numerous buyers (Figure 10.4). A reputable blogger is one who is respected in the industry and has a large following. One well-known blogger in the fashion industry is Emily Schuman, who has a blog titled *Cupcakes and Cashmere.* She has blogged for Estée Lauder

CALLING ALL DESIGNERS!

WELCOME TO OPEN SEE®, BENDEL'S LEGENDARY DESIGNER CASTING CALL!

For more than 40 years, Henri Bendel has opened its doors to new and emerging talent from around the world. Open See® has launched the careers of countless young creators, including **Todd Oldham**, **Anna Sui**, **James Purcell**, **Pamela Dennis**, **Colette Malouf**, and many more. Held twice a year at Bendel's Fifth Avenue flagship, admission is open and on a first-come-first-seen basis.

Behind-the-Scenes >

Join the excitement at the next Open See® in October at 712 Fifth Avenue, New York, NY, 10019. Please be in line prior to 12pm in order to be seen. Our buyers will be viewing product for the Fall/Holiday season in the following categories:

- Cosmetics
- Skincare
- Fragrance
- Gifts
- Accessories (including but not limited to jewelry, handbags & small leather goods, belts, cold weather accessories, hats, & hair accessories)

Please note that Henri Bendel does not carry nor will our buyers be reviewing men's or women's apparel or shoes.

Email customercare@henribendel.com with any questions.

Figure 10.3 Henri Bendel has "open call" to give entrepreneurs an opportunity to show their products to the Henri Bendel retail buyers. *Source: Henri Bendel.*

and has collaborated with Coach. When searching for a reputable blogger, look for someone who has a high rank in popularity and an RSS subscribers. Newspapers and magazines also have bloggers, so find out who is blogging for them. When there is a buzz about the product, be prepared to get calls. Have a sales pitch ready, and be prepared to provide information about the product as well as samples.

Getting an Appointment

Different retailers prefer to be contacted in a specific ways, so it is important to know the appropriate way to do so. If it is a larger retailer, go online and determine whether a vendor application must be filed. Read the guidelines thoroughly to make sure that your product or brand meets all the requirements and that everything is complete. Once the application has been submitted, follow up with a phone call or email to the

Figure 10.4 (a) *Daily Candy* featured the brand *d*irt (b) and was seen by retailers and spa buyers throughout the country. It was the catalyst for a new partnership. *Source: DailyCandy.com.*

(a)

(b)

DAILYCANDY.   FASHION   BEAUTY   ENTERTAINMENT   FOOD & DRINK   HOME   KIDS

AUGUST 24, 2011 / BEAUTY

Exfoliate and Moisturize with Dirt Scrubs

A Dirty Shower Never Felt So Good

(Sung to the tune of the TLC classic)

9 SHARES

A scrub of this kind is hard to find,
It's also known as a buffer,
Always made of what's natural,
And just feels so luxurious.

So, no,
You can't borrow that Dirt scrub, no,
You'll just have to go online 'cause, no,
Nobody can make it better, no,
This stuff's one of a kind, whoa.

You must buy Dirt scrub,
It's locally made and smells good enough to eat,
Exfoliate and moisturize,
Your dry-ass thighs.
Pumice made of kiwi seeds,
Yeah, you want this scrub,
Ginger, lemongrass, and some vitamin E,
Throw in some corncob grit (that's some crazy $#!%),
Hell yeah, it's grease free.

You got your lemon leaf that's made with raspberry seeds,
Sea salt and some shea butter,
Vanilla sandalwood, ooh, what feels so good?
Ooh, baby, that's honey.

So, yo,
Baby, time to get some Dirt scrub, whoa,
Yeah, it's made for all skin types, no,
No one's gonna buy it for you, whoa,
Yeah, they will expand the line, ho,
Buy yourself some scrub,
That bod deserves to feel so fresh and clean,
Wash away that grit and grime,
That summer slime,
Ooh, that skin will gleam.

Available online at dirtbeaute.com, $45. DailyCandy readers enter code DCCHGO at checkout for 10 percent off through Friday.

Photo: Courtesy of Dirt

SEE MORE: **BEAUTY JUNKIES, LOCAL, NATURAL**

buyer who is responsible for buying that category. Figure 10.5 illustrates vendor requirements of the retailer JCPenney. If an application is not needed, the entrepreneur must be prepared to contact the buyer directly. It is important to find out who the correct key contact person is, so that the entrepreneur is not bounced around loses time getting the product information into the right hands.

Sales Call Preparation

Once the category buyer is established, contact the buyer to give a 30-second pitch on the product. It is crucial to get the buyer's attention to heighten their interest in the brand. Buyers are extremely busy and receive cold calls on a weekly basis, so do your homework. An ill-prepared entrepreneur could lose the chance of ever showing the product to that buyer. Before calling, the entrepreneur should be able to answer the following questions:

- What is the product's selling appeal and competitive edge?
- How will the retailer benefit from the brand's product?
- How can the brand help a buyer achieve their profit goal?
- How will the product fill a void in the in the retailer's merchandising assortment?

During the call, clearly explain the benefits and features of the brand. Offer to send the buyer information about the company and samples if

Figure 10.5 Retailers have different requirements for brand partnership. Entrepreneurs must discover the best conduit of communication to reach the retail buyer. *Source: Alamy.*

Talk to various people within your network and find out if they know any buyers or store owners. Use your network as a resource to connect with people in the industry.

it is possible. Tell the buyer that a follow-up call will occur in a couple of weeks after they have received and reviewed the package. Be persistent; do not let too much time go by without following up with the buyer. If the buyer expresses interest, then set up a date and time to meet to present the product in person.

Competition

Before meeting the buyer, the entrepreneur must be familiar with the brand's competition within the retail outlet as well the retailer's competition. Entrepreneurs who do not know what the retailer is carrying will hurt their chances from the beginning. Typically a buyer does not want products that directly compete or cannibalize sales of existing vendors, especially if the new product is priced the same or higher. Identify competitors in the market, and use that information to sell the product. A buyer is continually looking for the next best thing; it is up to the entrepreneur to demonstrate that your brand is the newest "hot" item or is a product that is missing from the retailer's assortment.

A buyer also wants to make sure that the retailer is carrying product that is different from the competitors' products. Case Study 10.1 is an interview with a buyer from a local boutique talking about what she looks for in a product. Research local competition and see what they are carrying. If many products are similar, it may be possible to show how the brand can differentiate them from the local competition. The more knowledge an entrepreneur has, the better prepared he or she will be to sell the product.

Buyer Presentation

Strong merchandise and an effective oral and written presentation is critical to engage a buyer. It is up to the entrepreneur to sell the product and showcase its benefits and value. Before the entrepreneur steps through the doors of a buyer meeting, thorough preparation is essential.

The buyer may want to know:

- How long has the company been in business? A buyer may be hesitant to take a chance on a start-up company unless the presentation has big brand appeal. It is important to be confident and well-versed on the product and its overall category
- Is the entrepreneur reliable? Will the brand deliver what they promise, and will the buyer receive exactly what has been described, not a substitute?
- Is there a steady source of supply? The buyer wants to make sure that the entrepreneur can handle the business. Can the vendor get product quickly if reorders are placed? Can the entrepreneur handle large sales volume?

The buyer may want to see:

An interview with boutique buyer and owner Heather Anderson from Muse located in Oak Park, IL

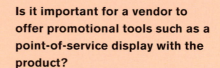

What do you look for in a brand when you are considering putting it into your store?

It is an aesthetic issue first and foremost. I need to fall in love with the product so that I feel passionate about it, and then my customers will feel the same. I also need to feel that the product is of good quality. Ideally, if the product is priced on the lower end of the price range, this will give the customer incentive to buy.

What makes a brand stand out?

If the aesthetic of the product fits our store and I love it, then I would want to be the first boutique to offer our customers that new and exciting designer or style. We want products that differentiate us from the many other stores that our customers can shop. I also want to know that we have exclusivity in our zip code in exchange for placing an order.

How do you decide if a product is successful?

These are the questions we ask after having the product in store:

1. What was the quality of material used to make this product, and how well was it put together?
2. Does the price range of this product make my customers want to stay loyal to this product?
3. Are my customers talking about this product? Do they want more?
4. Review of my numbers on my POS program. How many sales did I have on his line of products? And what was my margin on this product?
5. What was the customer service like from this vendor?

What are the main considerations when selecting a vendor?

We need to know that if we commit to introducing a new brand to our customers, the brand will be there for the long run. The fashion industry is pretty small, and we talk about which brands are selling well and shipping on time and which brands are not. We look to see that a brand is consistent, because we not only want to find the latest styles, but which brands we can add to our store on a long-term basis.

Is it important for a vendor to offer promotional tools such as a point-of-service display with the product?

I personally don't want promotional tools: I feel like they are "canned," and we want to look unique as a store.

What is the process for a new vendor?

Know that we have very limited budgets for the entire season, and at least 80 percent of it will go to brands we've already bought from in the past, so there's only a small budget left for new brands. So they need to stand out—style, quality, and service. Also know our buying season. The big sales seasons are spring and fall. Boutiques buy for spring from mid-August to late-October and for fall from mid-January until late March. Be sure to meet with boutiques in those periods, otherwise even if we like your line we won't be able to buy it.

What can a vendor do to make them stand out over the competition?

A search for the best boutique for your product starts with you browsing stores for a similar aesthetic. Spend some time in the boutiques that you would want to see your product in. Picture where in the store your product would sit on the shelf, and keep that in mind when it comes time to approach the store's buyer and make your presentation.

As your company requires sales to survive, doing trade shows is an important way to grow your brand, but since shows are very expensive and time consuming, I suggest you also try to get showrooms at the same time. A showroom will sell for you; you can then reach a larger amount of stores this way. At the trade shows, you will be able to connect with buyers and get direct feedback about your new collection, check out or maybe network with your competitors, and hopefully meet with fashion editors and bloggers.

What does the vendor need to do to maintain a good relationship with the buyer?

The success of your business is partly dependent upon service, quality, pricing, value,

muse.

a boutique for inspired living

and satisfaction from your boutiques. Your success is their success. Well-selected, consistent boutiques with proven records of high performance certainly can help you succeed with your business, but you, in turn, must put effort into building a solid working relationship with your boutiques, a relationship that should develop beyond the simple services rendered and into a true business partnership. The ultimate partnership is based on communication, trust, and information sharing, and, for both parties, should be based on long-term success.

How is a vendor evaluated when it comes to performance?

Prices:

- The prices paid should be comparable to those of vendors providing similar product and services.

- Prices should be reasonably stable over time but sensitive to costs. The vendor should demonstrate respect for the customer's bottom line and show an understanding of its needs.

- Are vendor invoices accurate? The average length of time to receive credit memos should be reasonable. Effective vendor bills are timely and easy to read and understand.

Quality factors:

You need to comply with terms and conditions as stated in the purchase order. Does your product quality match the samples your customer saw when they placed the order?

- *Reliability of repairs.* Will they repair and rework items that have fit issues?

- *Replacement or credit.* The length and provisions of replacement protection offered should be reasonable. Are quality problems resolved in a timely manner?

- *Durability.* Will this product last a reasonable amount of time?

- *Support.* Is quality support available from the vendor? Immediate response to and resolution of problems is desirable.

- *Modern, cutting-edge product.* Do you offer products that are consistent with the industry's current style? The vendor should consistently refresh product life by adding enhancements.

Delivery:

- *Time.* Does the vendor deliver products and services on time; is the actual receipt date on or close to the promised date? Does the promised date correspond to the vendor's published lead times? Also, are requests swiftly answered? Is the average time for delivery comparable to that of other vendors for similar products and services?

- *Quantity.* Does the vendor deliver the correct items or services in the contracted quantity? Does this match the sample product?

- *Packaging.* Packaging should be sturdy, suitable, properly marked, and undamaged.

- *Documentation.* Does the vendor furnish proper documents (packing slips, invoices, technical manual, etc.) with correct material codes and proper purchase order numbers?

- *Emergency delivery.* Does the vendor demonstrate extra effort to meet requirements when an emergency delivery is requested?

Service factors to consider:

Good vendor representatives have a sincere desire to serve. Representatives should be courteous, professional, approachable, and handle complaints effectively. They also should display knowledge of customer inquiries involving order confirmation, shipping schedules, shipping discrepancies, and invoice errors. The vendor should also provide up-to-date look books, line sheets and price information.

The vendor should respond in a timely manner to resolve problems. An excellent vendor provides follow-up on status of problem correction.

What advice would you give to an entrepreneur that is trying to sell to a boutique?

Get to know your ideal prospect—a boutique that can't live without your product. Get real feedback from your target prospect. Start with social media or a survey to find out their thoughts on your product—what do they like or not like about your product? Then test your idea with a product customer survey. You'll get a road map that shows exactly what they want, how they want it delivered, even what they'll pay! You need to be passionate about your product and how you would work together with the stores. Also very, very important—wear and be seen in that product.

Always have samples and product information on hand. A buyer might see the brand and want info on it ASAP.

- A sample of the product and what the packaging will look like. Many times, the packaging is what sells a new product. It is important for the buyer to see that the brand has a visual appeal.
- A brochure with information to assist the buyer in understanding the product.
- A line sheet, which should include: product name and description, product flat or image, style numbers, size range, wholesale and suggested retail price, color and fabric information, delivery dates and order cut-off dates, order minimums by item and/or total dollar, company and/or sales rep contact information.
- Any marketing and promotional plans that will help in promoting the brand. Some ideas are hosting a trunk show or offering point-of-purchase displays. Buyers want to make sure that there is a partnership between the brand and the retailer.

Typically, an entrepreneur has one chance to make a lasting impression. Table 10.1 shows a schedule of a buying season. Use this to make sure that the buyer is looking at product during the buying season. The product that is being pitched must meet the customer's current needs, as well as generate a profit for the buyer and vendor.

The Follow-Up

When following up with a buyer, make sure, as shown in Figure 10.6, that emails and phone messages are clear and concise. The follow-up will

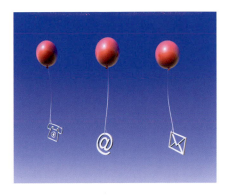

Figure 10.6 An entrepreneur must determine the most efficient method to contact or follow up with a buyer, whether it be email or telephone. *Source: eholdingEye/iStockphoto.*

TABLE 10.1

SEASON	SELLING DATES	DELIVERY DATES
Spring I	End of August–end of October	1/30, 2/28, 3/30 deliveries
Spring II	October–January	3/30, 4/30, 5/30 deliveries
Fall I	End of January–March	7/15, 8/30 deliveries
Fall II	March–April	9/30 deliveries
Holiday	May–June	10/15, 10/30 deliveries
Resort	June–August	11/30, 12/30, 1/15 deliveries

An entrepreneur must be aware of a buyer's buying and selling season. One does not want to make a bad impression by trying to sell a fall product when the buyer is currently looking for spring merchandise.

show the buyer that you are vested in the buyer/seller relationship. The conversation or email should state:

1. It was a pleasure meeting the person and thanking the person for taking the time to meet with you.
2. The commitment on your end to service the business and assist in marketing the product.
3. If the buyer is not ready to make a decision, promise to follow up again in a couple of weeks.

Mondays tend to be the busiest day for boutique owners and buyers. Avoid that day and follow up on Tuesdays, when things slow down. If the buyer is not available, then try again later in the week, but do not hound the buyer. A buyer's job is fast-paced, and the buyer wants to quickly get to the point to continue with all their other buying tasks. The buyer does not want the communication between them and the vendor to drag out. If the buyer likes the product, then they will consider placing the brand.

If a retailer decides not to sell the brand to the store, use that information to improve one's sales pitch and product. Rejections should not be viewed as discouraging, but rather as opportunities to gain valuable knowledge. It is important to listen to what the buyer is saying and why she might feel that the product is not a good fit.

The Negotiation

The relationship between a vendor and a buyer is important and must be built on trust, open communication, and common goals. The relationship and the outcome of the product placement will benefit the buyer as well as the vendor. It is important to keep this in mind when negotiations begin.

The buyer will assume that the entrepreneur has an understanding of the industry and is familiar with specific terms that are used to negotiate the sale. When entering into negotiations, the buyer usually has an idea of how much he or she is willing to spend on the product. It is important to remember that profit should never be compromised just to get the brand into a store. Understanding and agreeing on the conditions of sales will facilitate a smooth ordering process. **Conditions of sales** are arrangements for a sale that are agreed upon by a buyer and seller, which may include the net terms, how the goods will be shipped, and so on. The entrepreneur must allow a cushion for any added costs, such as co-op allowance, sometimes known as an **advertising allowance.** A **co-op allowance** is a fee, usually shown as a percentage, to help a retailer with the cost of advertising the brand. The co-op can usually be anywhere from 1 to 10 percent but should be mutually agreed upon if the entrepreneur partakes in this fee.

An entrepreneur must be conscious of:

- What allowances are needed from the buyer before a firm cost is agreed upon? It is hard to negotiate if a cost is given and the buyer comes back with various demands that do not leave the entrepreneur with room to negotiate.
- Negotiation is a two-way street and should not be solely led by the buyer, as shown in Figure 10.7. An entrepreneur needs to ask questions

Figure 10.7 A brand designer, or manufacturer must effectively negotiate with the retail buyer to reach a mutual agreement. *Source: wavebreakmedia/Shutterstock.*

and be prepared to stand firm to make a profit. Do not be tempted to sell the product at a loss.

- Take caution when agreeing to concessions that may not be profitable for the entrepreneur. For example, a buyer may ask for a guaranteed sale. A **guaranteed sale** is when a retailer does not sell through the product and wants the brand to take it back after a season. If the product is a fashion-forward apparel piece, then the entrepreneur will be stuck with product that is out of season and cannot be sold to another account.

Once there a mutual agreement has been reached, a buyer may ask for a vendor agreement to be executed. The entrepreneur must look over the agreement to make sure that all the requirements of the agreement can be met. A retailer may ask for chargeback allowances if the entrepreneur does not comply with the rules. **Chargeback allowance** is when a retailer deducts money for not following the specifics of vendor requirements, from shipping on time, packaging product correctly, or more or less anything that causes an interruption in the process. Larger companies use **electronic data interchange (EDI)** to place their orders and reorders. EDI is a real-time online system used by retailers to handle most communications with a vendor, including issuing orders, reorders, and handling returns. It can be a costly investment, so start-ups tend to delay in purchasing the software until the business warrants the system. Large companies will request small vendors to become EDI-compliant prior to partnership. Entrepreneurs can outsource their EDI demands to a third party.

An entrepreneur must understand that negotiations are part of the job. Confidence and knowledge is key to starting the negotiating process. If negotiating is not an entrepreneur's forte, then hiring a sales representative with experience is a good option. If hiring a sale representative is not an option due to financial constraints, then the entrepreneur should work on improving these skills. An entrepreneur can take a negotiation class at a local community college or talk to people who have strong negotiation skills and ask for some tips.

TRADE TERMS

slotting fee

sales representative

conditions of sales

co-op or advertising allowance

guaranteed sale

chargeback allowance

electronic data interchange (EDI)

Summary

One of the entrepreneur's most important relationships is with a potential buyer. It is imperative to build a long-lasting and strategic relationship with a buyer. An entrepreneur must first establish what retail outlets the brand should be in and who is the key contact person to get the brand into the hands of the decision maker. Successful entrepreneurs often prospect smaller retail environments to sell to and build a sales track record and then shift to larger retailers later. Once the contact has been made, the goal is to engage and excite the buyer about the product. The presentation is where the entrepreneur needs to make sure that the buyer understands the brand concept and knows that the entrepreneur is looking to build the relationship and not just make a quick sale. Once the buyer has decided to place the brand in the store, then a buyer must understand the terms used within the industry in order to be prepared to negotiate. A vendor and buyer relationship must be viewed as a long-term commitment where both parties are mutually invested in beneficial opportunities.

Online Resources

RetailSales Connect

An online source listing corporations in the United States and Canada, which features company profiles with contacts, titles, merchandise, sales volume, price points, number of stores, and store type for a fee.
www.retailsalesconnect.com

Buyer at Large

Buyer At Large is an online source where new and unique products are presented to retail store buyers.
www.buyeratlarge.com

Buyerly

Buyerly allows entrepreneurs to get feedback on their products by leading retail buyers.
http://buyerly.com/

Activity 10.1

Research three retailers where you would like to see your product placed. Explain why the brand would be best suited for these three retailers.

Bibliography

Cambridge Dictionaries Online. s.v. "Conditions of Sales." Accessed Jun. 25, 2012. http://dictionary.cambridge.org/dictionary/business-english/conditions-of-sale

Debetta, Jim. 2009. "Playing Hardball: Making Deals and Turning Profits Requires Smart Negotiating Skills." *Inventors Digest.* Accessed July 5, 2012. http://www.inventorsdigest.com/archives/2279

Kruse, Jon. 2010. "Getting Your Line into Boutiques/Shops." *How to Start a Clothing Company,* Sept. 30. Accessed Oct. 11, 2011. http://www.howtostartaclothingcompany.com/getting-your-line-into-boutiques-shops/

Waksman, Karen. "Selling Your Products to Retailers: How To Get Access to a Retail Buyer's Name and Contact Information." *About.com.* Accessed Nov. 27, 2012. http://wholesalers.about.com/od/Sellproductstomajorretail/a/How-Do-I-Get-Access-To-A-Retail-Buyers-Name-And-Contact-Information.htm

11

Untangling the Web

An entrepreneur needs an understanding of all the diverse Internet opportunities. An understanding of where to begin with creating the content that a site should contain is crucial to the success of the business. The online portion consists of the analytics, online sales applications, and ways to persuasively market product to induce sales. An entrepreneur must understand the importance of search engine optimization for improving the visibility of a website or a web page in search engines via non-paid and paid forms. Furthermore, exploring social media and blogging as avenues to get started right away in the online world will help build the success of the brand and its business.

Internet Visibility

"Brands are changing the way they are handling their business. In the past, the main focus has been on product, promotion, and price. This focus is still important, but emphasis is now being given to commerce content, connection, community, and conversation,"[1] according to Karen Murray of VF Corp. The retail environment is quickly changing with the advancement of technology, so a brand needs to be able to evolve with what is happening around us. Customers are connected 24 hours a day, 7 days a week through the Internet. It is important for a business to have a website so customers can have access to them and give them maximum exposure. It is the job of the entrepreneur to make sure that one has a website and that it is eye-catching to be able to promote and sell the brand if an e-commerce site is created. E-commerce is the most common form, but there is a higher cost to this format. **E-commerce** is the selling and buying of goods on the Internet. Yet, it is up to the entrepreneur to determine the type of website to use, based on the financial budget. An e-commerce site can cost anywhere from $5,000 to more than $100,000, so it is important for entrepreneurs to have goals that fit within their website budgets. An e-commerce site can be simple or elaborate. A pre-made template or design will usually cost the entrepreneur much less than a custom design, which will entail many hours of work (Figure 11.1).

KEY CONCEPTS

+ Recognize the importance of 24–7 Internet visibility.

+ Establish an informational website and understand the benefits for a brand.

+ Exploring e-commerce websites as a selling tool.

+ Discover m-commerce and its numerous benefits.

+ Grasp the significance of keywords and search engine optimization.

+ Discuss the importance of connecting to customers with social media and blogging.

Figure 11.1 An e-commerce site is an important tool for businesses to connect with customers by offering an array of services. *Source: Top left: © iStockphoto.com/4x6; bottom left: © iStockphoto.com/Gubcio; right: © iStockphoto.com/ClarkandCompany.*

Starting the Process

The Internet provides the consumer the opportunity to purchase products online. Launching a website can be overwhelming if the entrepreneur does not have any experience and does not know where to begin. Creating a plan that entails creative direction, layout, and product presentation will facilitate the planning process. The focus and plan for a website should be brand focused. The website is a reflection of the brand. Before a website can be started, several steps need to be taken.

Domain Name

A **domain name** is an identification string of characters that enables people to find your site on the web using an address bar. A domain name should be short, simple, and memorable. A short domain name is easier to remember than a long one. A domain should:

1. Have the name of your brand in it. This is the best way to reinforce and market the brand's name.
2. The name should be short and simple. Two is the minimum number of characters that can be used, and the maximum is 63. People become tired of typing out a long and complicated domain name every time they visit a brand's website.
3. Do not use numbers or hyphens if possible. This goes back to making the domain name easy for the customer. If a hyphen is in place, customers might not remember that and become frustrated when they continually get the wrong website.
4. There are various extensions that can be used for a domain name, such as .com, .org, .biz, and .info. The most commonly used and recognized extension is .com. If possible the brand should use .com as an extension. If the brand's name is taken, try shortening the name or adding a word to the domain name. Figure 11.2 and Table 11.1 show a list of extensions and their usage. Currently, the Internet Corporation for Assigned Names and Numbers, also known as ICANN, will start letting companies apply for new top level domain names. Apple has an application in to sponsor the

Figure 11.2 Entrepreneurs should become familiar with and understand the meanings of various domain extensions.

TABLE 11.1 MOST POPULAR TOP-LEVEL DOMAIN NAME EXTENSIONS

EXTENSION	TYPE	INTENDED
.COM	Commercial	Short for commercial. The most common form. Could be purchased by individuals or businesses.
.NET	Network	Network intended use, now used in place of .com if it is not available.
.ORG	Organization	Nonprofit or trade organizations
.BIZ	Business	A website as a business entity
.US	United States	U.S.-based companies
.INFO	Informational	An informational site
.MOBI	Mobile	Mobile devices
.TV	Television	Used for media
.NAME	Name	Personal use

Source: enom. "TLD Overview." *Enom.com.* Accessed Aug. 25, 2013. http://www.enom.com/help/faq-tlds.aspx

extension .apple, which may join the generic names currently uses such as .com. The amount to register for a top-level domain will be $185,000, with an annual fee of $25,000. The change is to lessen the shortage of dot-com web addresses. Unfortunately, this will put smaller brands at a disadvantage, since they may not be able to afford this, and will have to use the current generic terms.

5. The domain name should be memorable and unique. Making a name memorable and unique will help ensure that customers remember the brand domain name. A brand wants a customer to be able to type in the brand's domain without it taking them to a different website, which could be the brand's competitor.

Once the domain name has been determined, the entrepreneur needs to check to make sure that the name is not already in use and is available for purchase. To check whether a domain name is taken, visit a site such as GoDaddy.com or checkdomain.com, as shown in Figure 11.3, to see if the domain name is available. GoDaddy.com is one of the world's leading domain name registrars and web hosting sources. The site will facilitate finding a domain name that is available, as well as offering website builders, hosting, and other e-commerce tools. A domain name can run between $10 and $30 a year. If the preferred name is already taken, it may be possible to buy back the name. Domain names are continually going up for auction, so one should place a backorder on a domain name to become aware of the sale of the name. Backordering a name can be done through a site such as GoDaddy. Placing a backorder does not guarantee that one will be able to purchase the name, but it is worth a try if the entrepreneur feels strongly about the name. The cost will vary depending on what the seller is asking for, which could go up to thousands of dollars.

Internet Provider
The next step is to find a provider that will host the website. The choice of host provider will depend on what the entrepreneur needs, such as a merchant account for processing payments, a shopping cart, and security

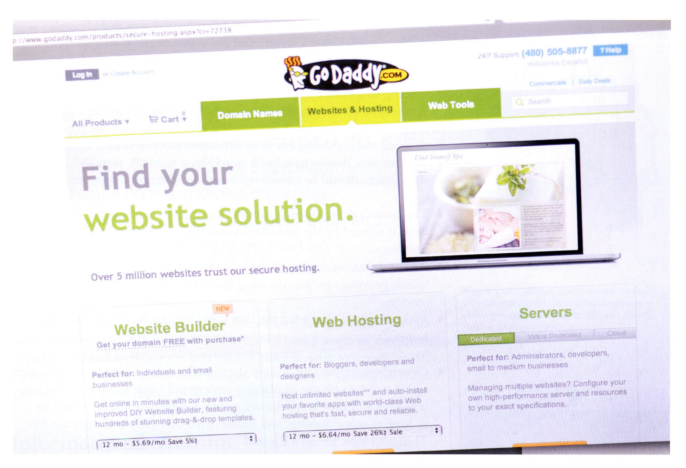

Figure 11.3 GoDaddy is a site used to purchase a domain name, create a website, and host it. *Source: NetPhotos/Alamy.*

systems. There are many Internet providers, so research should be done to see who meets the needs of the brand.

A website provider is important when it comes to housing the brand's website. A **host provider** maintains a connection to the Internet. An external host should be used to house the brand's website. Three basic kids of web host are shared, dedicated, and cloud as shown in Figure 11.4. A shared web host will host the brand's website with other websites. This is the most economical way of hosting the site, but if there is heavy traffic

Figure 11.4 Entrepreneurs must choose their hosting partners for website development. *Source: sheelamohanachandran2010/ Shutterstock.*

Starting the Process 165

An informational site is very basic, but still requires creativity and information to capture the target audience. The site should contain the following basic information:

- A home page should quickly explain what the brand is.
- A product description for each product. A customer cannot feel or touch the product, so give a strong description of what the product is.
- An "About Us" page that tells the audience about the brand and what it stands for.
- A contact page that has a contact phone number and email.
- A press page where any write-ups about the brand can be listed. This is the perfect page to let others know that the brand is being noticed.
- The company's privacy policy, which explains the brand's policies regarding the collection, use, and disclosure of information on or through the website.
- The options to email product information to a friend via Facebook, follow the brand on Twitter, or post the brand's product on Pinterest.

E-Commerce Website

An e-commerce site is a way to be able to sell directly to the consumer. When starting out the brand business, the product will go into a few retailers and hopefully continue to grow. An e-commerce site will allow the entrepreneur to reach out to new and expanding markets as well as numerous consumers who may not be near a store that the brand is in. An e-commerce site should contain the same basic information as an informational site, as well as a shopping cart.

Online payment service is a part of the e-commerce business that allows the customer to complete a secure sales transaction and facilitates payment to the entrepreneur. PayPal is one of the most common world-wide payment systems as shown in Figure 11.8. Many people are familiar with PayPal and may feel more comfortable making a payment through this vehicle, since PayPal does not share the buyer's credit card details.

In the past, online retailers were only required to collect tax in states in which they had a physical presence. "The Marketplace Fairness Act grants states the authority to compel online and catalog retailers ["remote sellers"], no matter where they are located, to collect sales tax at the time of a transaction—exactly like local retailers are already required to do. However, there is a caveat: States are only granted this authority *after* they have simplified their sales tax laws."[2] Currently,

Figure 11.8 PayPal is a simplistic and efficient way to collect money from customers on an e-commerce website. *Source: tumpikuja/ iStockphoto.*

any small business doing sales over the Internet that does not exceed remotely more than $1,000,000 in sales annually will not need to follow this new act. The term "remotely" in this context means not having a physical presence in a state.

Online Security

When customers shop online, they want to be sure that their transaction is secured. It is imperative that the brand's website maintains physical, electronic, and procedural safeguards to protect customers' personal information. A website should let the customer know that:

- The company uses industry-standard secure sockets layer (SSL) authentication for online transactions made on the site. SSL authentication and encryption of any information that is sent over through the Internet is protected from third party inceptions.
- A customer's credit card information is never used for anything other than for charges placed on one's website to issue a refund. Never request that a customer's credit card number be emailed to the company.
- A customer's credit card number is displayed once it has been entered. Only the last four digits can be revealed for verification purposes.
- The customer's credit card information is never stored once it has been processed.

Tip 11.3 **Create-a-minute!**

The most popular e-tail website is amazon.com. Take a look at successful sites and analyze why they are successful. This will help in building your brand's website.

It is imperative that the entrepreneur attempts to protect their customer as much a possible when it comes to online security. Unfortunately, no system is 100 percent secure, so it is important that if there is a security breach, the company has a plan in place to inform all customers who may have been affected in a timely fashion, as well as the credit card companies.

Customers should always be given the option to opt in or out of receiving emails from the company. An opportunity must be given to the customer to elect whether to receive promotional correspondence from the company or share their personal information with third parties for marketing purposes.

E-Commerce as a Wholesaler

An e-commerce site also can allow you to sell directly to the retailer. Once the retailer has set up an account on your site, it is easy to facilitate selling and collecting payments directly. The retailer can go online to place new orders and reorders, as well as pay for the cost of goods. An order can be placed and paid for at any time, since the website is available to all, 24 hours a day, 7 days a week. When setting up this option a site should include:

- A retail account password that only the retailer can use. The wholesale page should only be available to retailers, so that customers cannot log onto the page and see the wholesale cost.
- A list of product, with any pertinent information such as backorder dates and quantity on hand. This helps to avoid frustration by letting the retailer know immediately what is available and when there may be delays in fulfillment.
- The option to pay online with a credit card, debit card, or cash on delivery (COD). An open account should not be started with a retailer until a relationship has been developed and the retailer is continually ordering product.

The entrepreneur's website should not be a substitute for human interaction. It is still important to follow up with a retailer and to continue to build a rapport. If one forgets about the retailer, then the retailer might not make the brand a priority if it is not the best-selling brand that it is carrying. Yet, selling over the inventory should be used as a way to enhance the business and relationship.

M-Commerce

M-commerce, or mobile commerce, is becoming widespread and relevant in today's markets as customers increasingly rely on smartphones for a variety of everyday needs. Creating an m-commerce site gives a business a competitive edge; yet entrepreneurs need to understand the benefits and what is involved in a successful m-commerce application. **M-commerce** refers to customers making purchases through their smartphone as shown in Figure 11.9. Here are some tips for have a successful m-commerce app:

- Keep the app simple and easy to use. Customers are using the app on a smartphone and tablet, but if they are only viewing the app on a smartphone, the size of the screen will limit what can be seen.

Figure 11.9 L.K. Bennett is a luxury British brand that uses m-commerce as a viable avenue to sell their product. *Source: Christopher Griffin/Alamy.*

- Vary the information that is on the brand's website and m-commerce application. Use an app to offer deals or a special promotion to keep customers excited about the app.
- Use a web payment system that is compatible for a mobile device. The checkout process should also be made simple and fast, so that a customer can easily complete the transaction. According to Chris Mason from Branding Brand, data shows that "clients with fewer steps in their checkout process experience significantly higher funnel conversion rates." A **conversion rate** is the ratio of people who take a preferred action. It is measured by how many people buy a product, fill out a form, such as joining a mailing list, or whatever intended goal is set in place.

M-commerce should be a part of the long-term plan, but it is more crucial for a brand to have a web presence. It's best to wait until the brand is up and running before making an investment in an m-commerce application.

Search Engine Optimization and Key Words

A website is only as good as its search engine optimization. **Search engine optimization (SEO)** is the process of getting traffic from the "free," "organic," "editorial" or "natural" listings on search engines.[3] SEO is an excellent way to direct traffic to the brand's website. According to

While consumers have been able to purchase fashion online for years, they have only more recently become comfortable enough to significantly increase their smartphone shopping. Perhaps that is because 47 percent, or 110 million shoppers, own a smartphone, according to comScore. And the number of tablet users will reach 117 million by 2013, according to a report from the Online Publishers Association.

To be sure, of those who shop for apparel online, more than half agree (57 percent) that they do so because it gives them a chance to shop at retailers and brands that are not located near them, according to the Cotton Incorporated *Lifestyle Monitor* Survey.

Total online apparel shopping, including purchases made on smartphones, tablets, or computers, increased 11 percent to $19 billion from September 2011 to August 2012, up from $17 billion from the same period a year before, according to NPD's Consumer Tracking Service.

More than 8 of 10 consumers (85 percent) browse the Internet for apparel, and 72 percent buy clothes online, the *Monitor* shows. Those aged 13 to 34 are significantly more likely than older shoppers to both browse and buy apparel online.

Lori Schafer, executive advisor at SAS Institute and author of *Branded!: How Retailers Engage Consumers with Social Media and Mobility,* says today's retailers, whether a national chain or a mom-and-pop store, are looking at the Web as a growth engine.

"Stores have more opportunities than ever before, even small retailers," Schafer says. "Ten years ago, people said they didn't have a chance because big retail had taken over. But it's totally opposite of that now. Because of the technology available today, they can do better than ever."

Whether a mobile app, a mobile web site, or a hybrid of the two, m-commerce has cemented its place as an integral piece of retail's future.

Source: Cotton Incorporated. 2012. "Screen Time: Mobile Devices Become Increasingly Essential to Retail." *WWD,* Nov. 15. http://www.wwd.com/markets-news/textiles/screen-time-mobile-devices-become-increasingly-essential-to-retail-6475259/print-preview/

VeriSign, more than 1 million new website addresses are registered every month—that's over 40,000 per day.[4] All SEOs search the web for frequently used terms, store all searches in an index, and allow a user to use the web to search for the index. Search engines use software called a "spider" to look for all pages that are on the web. A spider copies all the information found on each page and stores it in its own database, called an "index," that is later used to find sites for the person doing the searching. It is important for the entrepreneur to add metatags. Meta-tags are a summary of the company, which is used so that spiders can easily find certain words that are not visible to people viewing the website. A web designer will assist in adding appropriate metatags, but with the assistance of the entrepreneur who will need to provide the keywords. Once a spider has finished searching a page, the search engine will prioritize site by:

1. How many times and where a keyword or phrase appears on the site.
2. How many people view the page? This will reveal the popularity of the page.
3. How old or new the page is. Older pages have more of an importance than newer ones.
4. The number of pages that are linked to the site.

All of this information combined will produce a list of URLs when a user is searching for a keyword term. The URL should also be simple to understand and convey. A URL should not have a cluster of numbers and letters, but rather descriptive words of the brand.

Just because a website is built does not mean people will come to the site. Many websites are found due to the popularity of their brand and not through a search engine. Popular well-known search engine sites are Google, Yahoo, and Bing. The entrepreneur must make sure that the website content employs keywords that will bring customers to the brand's site. A customer will not look at page after page to find the brand.

- Key descriptive words should be used on the home page as well as each page that the site contains. What is on the title page is what those will view in the search engine.
- Key phrases should be used throughout the site rather than just key words. An example would be if the entrepreneur were selling earrings made of recycled goods, then the description should be specific— "earrings made from recycled materials" as opposed to just "earrings." Many customers usually are looking for something specific when searching the Internet.

When thinking of keywords and phrases, look at other websites to gain ideas. Looking at other sites should only be used as a guide, since specific content must not be plagiarized. Trademark and copyright names should not be used unless permission has been granted by the company in writing. An entrepreneur can also pay a search engine marketing service, such as Google, to advertise the brand's website. The paid advertising will appear on the top of the page, on the side, or on mobile phones when a customer is searching for a product that contains some of the brand's website keywords. Google offers cost-per-click, which allows the entrepreneur to control how much they spend. When someone clicks on the link, the company is charged a set amount. According to Google, an example of what they charge is:

Daily budget: $10

Maximum cost-per-click bid: $0.50

Average actual cost-per-click: $0.40

Approximate number of clicks per day: 25

A good way to gauge whether visitors are coming to the brand's site is to implement a statistical tracking tool. Google Analytics is a free statistical tracking tool that will assist in understanding how viewers visit the brand's website. Statistical analytic tools allow users to view data that provides information on how people are using their sites. Figure 11.10 shows an enterprise-class web analytic tool.

An affiliate program can also help bring customers to your site as well as bring customers to someone else's website. An **affiliate program** is a marketing tool that connects businesses that are selling products online with other websites that sell products that are similar. There are several affiliate programs to join that are related to the product. Brands and websites such as Amazon have affiliate programs. The brand and website should be established before joining affiliate programs and sending visitors from one site to another.

Figure 11.10 Google's analytic tool provides data that allows the user to measure and understand how people are using their site. *Source: RuslanDashinsky/iStockphoto.*

Social Media and Blogging

Social media and blogging are beneficial ways to connect with the customer. Brands around the world are doing it, so there is a good chance that your brand's competition probably is tapping into social media and blogging. Social media offers a way to find out what customers are saying and what they are looking for, so it is important to be aware of consumer wants and needs. Consumers Internet at their fingertips, so it is imperative that the brand tells the consumer who the brand is and gives them a sense of ease about the brand, so that they can learn everything about it.

Social Media

Social media allows entrepreneurs to get more personal, find out customers' wants and needs, and get feedback to be more flexible. **Social media** is defined as forms of electronic communication (i.e., websites for social networking and microblogging) through which users create online communities to share information, ideas, personal messages, and other content (e.g., videos).[5] Time is being wasted if you have any set goals on how the brand will utilize social media. Three goals that can be considered for a social media presence are:

1. Increase brand awareness and let people know about the brand.
2. Create a rapport with customers to build brand loyalty.
3. Augment sales by using social media to market and advertise.

Social media is successful when one goal is targeted at a time. When a brand is first being introduced, the first priority is creating brand awareness. *d*irt used Facebook to increase brand awareness by holding a contest asking people to "like" the *d*irt page and tell their friends to do so as well. Once they reached 2,000 likes, five random winners were chosen to win a body scrub. Figure 11.11 shows *d*irt's efforts to increase its fan base. An entrepreneur must understand, however, that numerous followers do not equate to higher sales.

The use of social media is important to reach a broad spectrum of customers, especially customers that are influencers. Figure 11.12 shows that

Figure 11.11 *dirt* utilizes social media tools such as Facebook to increase brand awareness. *Source: Erthe Beaute, LLC.*

consumers who use social media have a stronger connection to the brand, according to Motista, a web-based company that offers Fortune 1000 companies marketing tools to connect with consumers via their marketing programs and operations. These are key people that other people tend to watch and follow to see what they are purchasing. These people are key to the success of building the business. Many of these customers can be found using social media. The top three social media sites for retailers are:

- Facebook, a social networking site that is used worldwide. Facebook gives entrepreneurs the opportunity to promote the brand and garner followers as shown in Figure 11.12.
- Pinterest is a social media website that allows people to bookmark or upload images that can be found on the web, their own images, or browse images on other users' boards for ideas and inspiration. A brand could incorporate Pinterest by embedding a piece of code on their website that connects directly to the customer's personal Pinterest page. Pinterest could help build a brand's visibility, increase followers, and stimulate excitement regarding the product. Like Facebook, if people begin to pin the entrepreneur's brand, then it could go viral. "In the last 6 months, the retail deal site ideeli.com has seen a 446 percent increase in web traffic from Pinterest, and sales resulting from those visits have increased five-fold."[6]
- Twitter is a social media tool that allows users to connect with each other by sharing the latest stories, ideas, opinions, and news. Its users can send short text-based, messages (known as tweets) that are limited to 140 characters. Twitter users also can "follow" others to get real-time information and updates.

Figure 11.12 Designer Jason Wu uses Facebook as a way to create brand awareness. *Source: Fairchild Photo Service/Condé Nast/ Corbis.*

Figure 11.13 Tory Burch uses a blog to inform and excite consumers in a relaxed tone. *Source: ZUMAPRESS.com/Alamy.*

When using social media networks, it is imperative that an entrepreneur's personal account and business account are kept separate. Customers want to know about the brand and not what you did the night before.

Blogging

Blogging is a form of giving a voice to the brand as shown in Figure 11.13. A **blog** is a lesser version of a content site and usually lists its content in a chronological order. It is also a collection of reflections, experiences, observations, comments, and suggestions from one person or brand's perspective. Many companies are blogging to promote their brands, and not blogging would put a brand at a disadvantage. Blogs are becoming more relevant than their counterpart content websites. They are also a simple and inexpensive way to promote the brand. Common blog sites that are free are Blogger.com, Tumblr.com, and WordPress.com. Blogs give the entrepreneur an advertising vehicle that can save money over traditional marketing, yet blogging should not be a sole substitute. A blog is an easy way to continually update the brand's content with new and exciting information.

Blogging will help with:

- Providing information that will make the consumer want to visit the site on a continual basis.
- Making the most of relevant keywords and improving search engine ranking.
- Showcasing information, such as video advertising and pod casting that will help increase the conversion rate.

According to Neil Patel, who is an entrepreneur from Quick Sprout, blogs should:

- Let your audience think for you. Listen to what people are saying about the brand. People many times will use blogs to discuss what they do and do not like.
- Lead from the top by being intimate. Blog with the brand's audience. People like to believe that they are being heard.
- Create a niche blog by building brand awareness. Connect with the reader through various topics. If the brand is a green product, then talk about the green movement or other topics that the reader can connect with.
- Market, not sell. The brand must be talked up on the blog. This vehicle should be used to talk up the brand.
- Never abandon your blog for Facebook. Blogging should be intimate and be another platform to be able to talk about the product.

Another method of getting the brand's name out there is to get the product on bloggers' sites. Many bloggers discuss specific brands and products, and they have a loyal following. Figure 11.14 shows a blogger in the fashion industry and who writes their thoughts on fashion brands. A blogger can increase the chance of the brand getting more public awareness, and the blog's comment feature is a way for customers to give feedback that can be used to better the brand and its reputation. Also, online influencers may talk about the brand and spread the word about the product. If a blogger talks about the brand in a positive light, then the blogger's link should be posted on the brand's website under publicity.

Figure 11.14 A fashion blogger may write and visually present the latest styles and brands. *Source: Michael Patrick O'Leary/Corbis.*

Social media and blogging are changing the ways we advertise a brand. Social media has started a wave of getting the product out there through word of mouth. People are posting on social media sites such as Facebook about brands they love (or dislike) in ways that reach out to hundreds and sometimes thousands of their Facebook friends. Brands are also being discovered through these vehicles. However, social media can also be used to bad-mouth a brand, so it is important to offer exceptional customer service and continually keep the customer wanting more. Updating the brand's social media site and blog is imperative to make an impact and keep customers following the brand. An entrepreneur needs to blog often and make sure that sharp, high-quality pictures are used.

Summary

Choosing what type of website should be used to represent your brand or product will depend on available resources. A website should be utilized as a way to market and sell the brand through 24 hours, 7 days a week visibility. The amount of time and resources will dictate whether a site will be an informational site that covers the basic information or an e-commerce site that actually sells the product. Once the brand is up and running, then m-commerce can come into play to enhance and market the brand. Social media and blogging are other ways to let people know about the brand and is always a work in progress. Social media can be powerful tools to get the customer excited about the product.

Online Resources

Big Cartel
A website that allows designers to sell their products by using its shopping cart system.
www.bigcartel.com

Search Engine Watch
Offers information and tips regarding searching the web, the search engine industry, and the ability to improve one's ability to be found through search engines.
www.searchenginewatch.com

Host My Site
A website that offers to host a site through different hosting plans.
www.hostmysite.com

TRADE TERMS

e-commerce

domain name

host provider

informational site

landing page

m-commerce

conversion rate

search engine optimization (SEO)

affiliate program

social media

blog

Activity 11.1

Use a search engine, such as GoDaddy, and check to see if your brand name is available. If not, list various options for names that can be used. Also, list the cost the register a domain name as well as the cost of hosting an e-commerce site.

Activity 11.2

Find three websites that would be considered competitors for your brand. Fill out the online competitor analysis for the three different websites.

Activity 11.3

Create an informational website using a word document. List the different links that you would use. Create a page for each link and include what information each page would have.

Notes

1. David Lipke. 2012. "VF Corp.'s Karen Murray on Brand Evolution." *WWD*, Apr. 04. Accessed Aug. 13, 2012. http://www.wwd.com/menswear-news/retail-business/vf-corps-karen-murray-on-brand-evolution-5843651.

2. Taxcloud.net. "Marketplace Fairness Act Compliance." Accessed Aug. 16, 2013. http://www.marketplacefairness.org/compliance.

3. Searchengineland.com. "What Is SEO / Search Engine Optimization?" *Search Engine Land.* Accessed June 3, 2012. http://searchengineland.com/guide/what-is-seo.

4. WSI Retail Group. "Organic Search Marketing—Search Engine Optimization." *WSI.* Accessed Aug. 13, 2012. wsiretailgroup.com/search-engine-optimization.

5. Merriam-Webster. "social media." *Merriam-Webster dictionary online.* Accessed Jul. 11, 2012. www.merriam-webster.com/dictionary/social media.

6. Jason Falls. 2012. "How Pinterest Is Becoming the Next Big Thing in Social Media for Dusiness." *Entrepreneur,* Jul. 20, 2012. www.entrepreneur.com/article/222740.

Bibliography

Get Smarter. "Using Search Engines." *Internet Super User Textbook.* Accessed Dec. 12, 2012. http://www.internetsuperuser.com/textbook/using-search-engines/getting-the-most-out-of-google.

Google. "How it Works." *Google Ad Words.* Accessed Dec. 15, 2012. http://www.google.com/adwords/how-it-works/ads-on-google.html

Ira, Garrett. 2012. "The Most Important Social Media Influencer For Retailers." *Windmill Marketing,* Apr. 20. Accessed Aug. 13, 2012. http://windmillnetworking.com/2012/04/20/the-most-important-social-media-influencer-for-retailers/.

Kats, Rimma. 2012. "Top Do's and Don'ts of Mobile Commerce." *Mobile Commerce Daily,* Aug. 14. http://www.mobilecommerce daily.com/top-do%E2%80%99s-and-don%E2%80%99ts-of-mobile-commerce

Krynin, Jennifer. "Affiliate Program." *About.com.* Accessed Dec. 20, 2012. http://webdesign.about.com/od/affiliateprograms/g/affiliate_program.htm.

Magids, Scott. 2012. "How Do We Prove the Value of Facebook and Twitter to Our Business?." *Motista,* Apr. 12. Accessed July 13, 2012. http://www.motista.com/blog/2012/04/how-do-we-prove-the-value-of-facebook-and-twitter-to-our-business/.

McCorvey, J.J. 2010. "How to Start a Website." *Inc.,* Mar. 17. Accessed Aug. 14, 2012. http://www.inc.com/guides/make-a-website-for-business.html.

Nazarian, Birgit. 2012. "Pinterest the Best Social Networking Site for Retailers." *Enterprise Efficiency,* Feb. 29 Accessed Jul. 20, 2012. http://www.enterpriseefficiency.com/author.asp?section_id=1195&doc_id=239878

Patel, Neil. 2011. "5 Lessons Fortune 500 Companies Can Teach You About Blogging." *Quick Sprout,* Dec.28. Accessed Aug. 13, 2012. http://www.quicksprout.com/2011/12/28/5-lessons-fortune-500-companies-can-teach-you-about-blogging.

Zumwalt Law Group. "Is Dot-Com Gone?" *Forward Thinking.* Accessed Dec. 9, 2012. http://www.zumwaltlawgroup.com/forwardthinking.

PART IV

THE PROCESS

In this age of burgeoning brands, brand extensions, co-labeling, and brand collaborations, every fashion entrepreneur needs a solid business skill set. Successful fashion entrepreneurs are respected for their creativity but admonished if they lack tactical business skills. Building a fashion business is an ongoing process that is governed by a plan. Fashion entrepreneurs must cultivate a comprehensive business plan to build organizational infrastructure. In lieu of seizing opportunities or spontaneity, an entrepreneur must steer from a well-devised business plan that informs our decision-making ability at the crux of an opportunity or challenge. Within the overarching plan, the marketing components—the product, pricing, placement, and promotional plan—must be attuned. The marketing plan reinforces the branding strategy and distribution plan. Whether the entrepreneur is a single entity or has team of executives, the business plan is also the first reference tool for growth or expansion. We explore fundamental business practices and protecting intellectual property. We close with the posture every fashion entrepreneur hopes to face—growth. Timing is everything—knowing when to expand or exit the business is a dynamic decision that can yield exponential success—THE PROCESS.

12

The Marketing Plan

A corporate marketing plan provides cohesive information about a company's marketing objectives for the firm's overall business strategy. For an entrepreneur, it is an internal tool to develop and set objectives, strategies, and tactic for new and existing products. A marketing plan is generally developed by the entrepreneur. It introduces the company, identifies the goals, explores the marketing strategies and tactics, and finishes with a budget and defined timeline for execution. An entrepreneur can readily engage the marketing environment with a well-defined plan. The marketing plan must reinforce the branding strategy and distribution plan. The marketing plan becomes the "glue" that creates consumer attachment and loyalty. In totality, it is the communication conduit. For the sake of clarity and continuity, Coach will be used as a core example.

The Marketing Plan

Executive Summary

The **executive summary** outlines the who, what, where, when, how, and why of the marketing plan. It states the intended purpose of the plan and the company's interest in introducing new products, extending product lines, and exploring any new opportunities, such as online sales. Many entrepreneurs will develop the executive summary last, although it is positioned as the first page of a marketing plan.

Company Description

The **company description** provides detailed information about the organization. It gives in-depth insight to how the company was formed and by whom. It comprises information about the product and why it is unique. It "sells" the reader on the growth possibilities. It also reinforces the company's tagline and brand strategy and references the brand's message, consumer demographic and geographic sales growth, and social responsibility.

KEY CONCEPTS

+ Develop major components of a marketing plan.

+ Understand the marketing objective, strategy, and tactic.

+ Examine and determine the marketing mix.

+ Discuss the marketing budget.

+ Create the media kit.

Mission and Goals

It is important to clearly define the company's mission and goals, including financial and nonfinancial goals. Understanding the purpose of the company steers the marketing plan. It enables a clear path to set marketing goals and objectives to support the overall business strategy.

Financial Goals

1. Obtain financing through equity partner relationships.
2. Increase revenues by a specific percentage with new product introductions.
3. Donate a specific amount a year to social responsibility and/or charitable organizations.

Nonfinancial Goals

1. Create a new product collection or brand extension.
2. Enter new markets and distribution channel outlets.
3. Develop successful social media campaigns while maintaining strong relationships with retailers

For example, Coach launched a brand extension collection called "Poppy" to delve into a more youthful market segment. The collection encapsulates a vibrant product assortment for a younger spirited demographic. This consumer also desired this accessible luxury Coach brand (Figure 12.1).

Core Competencies

Entrepreneurs can highlight their **core competencies** as their competitive edge. This section of the marketing plan serves as a reminder to internal members as well as those external the company and also includes how the company plans to achieve a sustainable competitive advantage over the competition.

For example,

- Exceptional high-quality products;
- Creating brand loyalty and community through a social media relationships; and
- Credibility based upon manufacturing and on-time shipments.

Coach has a core mission to be the leading brand of quality lifestyle accessories with classic, modern American styling. They also have a list of values that serve as foundational competencies for the company (Box 12.1).

Situation Analysis

A **SWOT analysis** provides an outline of the marketing environment. A SWOT analysis identifies a company's strengths, weaknesses, opportunities, and threats (Figure 12.2). An entrepreneur must conduct industry and market research to determine the proper positioning for the product. They must consistently focus on the core competencies that create their competitive advantage and remain competitively astute. The SWOT analysis presents a crosshair of the company's position in the marketplace.

The marketing environment in the fashion industry has overwhelming opportunities. It also contains challenges of product saturation.

Figure 12.1 The Poppy Collection is distinguished by bright colors and fun fabrics. The youthful spirited fragrance is brightly scented with cucumber, juicy mandarin, and freesia buds. *Source: Cherry Blossom/Alamy.*

BOX 12.1 Coach Mission Statement

Coach seeks to be the leading brand of quality lifestyle accessories offering classic, modern American styling.

VALUES:

The Brand is Our Touchstone.

The Coach brand represents a unique synthesis of magic and logic that stands for quality, authenticity, value and a truly aspirational, distinctive American style. Everything we make, advocate or engage in reflects the attributes of the brand.

Customer Satisfaction is Paramount.

Our responsibility to our internal and external customers calls for impeccable service to ensure that their needs are always met. By treating customers like guests in our own home, we seek to establish long-term relationships based on trust and satisfaction.

Integrity is Our Way of Life.

Our success is rooted in uncompromising devotion to honesty and fairness where our people, our business and our community are concerned. We stand behind our products, staking our name and reputation on everything that we make.

Innovation Drives Winning Performance.

We constantly challenge ourselves to be the very best we can in every aspect of our business. We strive to be a nimble and flexible organization committed to increasing consumer and shareholder value.

Our Success Depends on Collaboration.

Our brand flourishes through our people. Coach brings together strong, collaborative people in a dynamic culture of mutual respect, support and passion for our brand and product. Our team bands together in the face of adversity and celebrates our victories.

Source: Fairchild Fashion Media.

Source: Coach.com. "About Coach." *Coach.* www.coach.com/online/handbags/genWCM-10551-10051-en-/Coach_US/CompanyInformation/InvestorRelations/MissionStatement

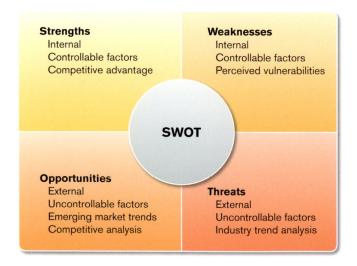

Figure 12.2 SWOT analysis.

BOX 12.2 Competitors in the Industry Segment

Finding Value in Coach

Coach Inc. is one of the most recognized brands in the luxury goods industry. It is a leading marketer of fine handbags and accessories for women and men.

Coach markets its products as "accessible luxury." Its pricing strategy for a handbag ranges from $298 to $1,000, which means that its product reaches a larger consumer demographic than other high-priced competitors, such as Louis Vuitton and Prada, which focus on the very wealthy. The strategy of targeting the higher- and upper-middle-income shoppers differentiates Coach from its competitors and also helps to establish it as the poster child of tapping into the global trend of consumers wanting to trade up in the quality and style of what they buy. Coach Inc. has a narrow moat and a competitive advantage. It has a strong brand presence in the luxury market, not easily eroded by other competitors. New competitors in the luxury brand industry would have to spend a large amount of money and resources to build up competitive brand awareness and image. Coach also has consumer loyalty as it has been delivering high-quality products that are simple and reliable, with a perceived value.

To further grow the business, Coach has outlined its strategy as:

1. Raising its brand awareness and market share in the under-penetrated Asian market, with China being the top targeted market

Source: Fairchild Fashion Media

2. Growing its women's business in the North American and European markets

3. Increasing its men's business in North America and Asia

4. Maximizing e-commerce sales

Source: Gurufocus. 2013. "Finding Value in Coach." *NASDAQ,* May 04. http://www.nasdaq.com/article/finding-value-in-coach-coh-cm243653

Image Source: http://www.cpp-luxury.com/wp-content/uploads/2013/02/Coach.jpg

To overcome the challenges, an entrepreneur must find and exploit an underserved niche. For example, Coach has maintained a leading position as one of the most recognizable brands in the luxury goods industry. In the saturation of premium handbags, Coach touts itself as the "accessible luxury" handbag brand (Box 12.2).

Marketing Objectives, Strategies, and Tactics

A successful entrepreneur has an objective, strategy and tactic for implementation of his or her marketing plan. An **objective** is a goal that can be achieved within a set and expected timeframe with resources. It fundamentally explains the goal. A **strategy** draws from market research and includes the product mix plan to achieve maximum profit potential. It fundamentally explains the plan of how the goal will be met. A **tactic** is the advantageous action to meet the goals of a plan. It explains what detailed activities will achieve the goal. For example, in the beauty and fragrance industry, complimentary samples are a critical tactic for consumer experience and sell-through:

- Objective—Increase sales by 20 percent for Q2 ending April
- Strategy—Social Media Partnership
- Tactic—Implement a free sampling program exclusively for industry bloggers.
- Work with social media beauty bloggers. Offer an opt-in "brand expert" membership that includes ongoing product samples and a discount code for press partnership on all full-size product. To generate buzz, blog members will also receive a limited-time, nominal discount on a single purchase to boost sales on full-sized product during the second quarter. The viral power of social media will induce sales from the blogger's community of followers.

The Marketing Mix

Entrepreneurs must develop their marketing mix. It facilitates putting the right product in the right place, at the right price, at the right time, and with the right promotion. The **marketing mix** is a marketing tool to satisfy customers and company objectives. It is a general phrase used to describe the different kinds of choices organizations have to make in the whole process of bringing a product or service to market. It involves product, price, promotions, product placement, and traditional and nontraditional marketing strategies, such as events and organizing activities that support the brand strategy. Entrepreneurs must review the marketing mix regularly, as components will evolve as the product or service, and its market, grow, mature and adapt in its competitive environment. The four Ps of the marketing mix:

- Product (or Service)
- Place
- Price
- Promotion

Product Strategy

The product is the tangible good; a service is an intangible good for consumer consumption. Entrepreneurs can ask themselves a myriad of questions to ensure they are offering the "right" product.

1. What does your target customer want from your new product or service?
2. What want, need, or void does it satisfy and how?
3. How will customers experience the product or service?
4. What would you need to do to differentiate your product from the competition?

Price Strategy

Entrepreneurs must have a competitive price structure in their market. Price strategies range from setting the retail at the high, prestigious, and luxury price setting at the high point to skimming the market with

Sales force vs. Me: I need to grow the business with a team approach. As an entrepreneur, I must make smart decisions and relinquish my product into the hands of those who will multiply it!

low prices by selling high quantities of products. Value pricing is also a common strategy to introduce a sense of consumer satisfaction in an industry flooded with brand and product saturation. Here are questions to ensure the product is offered at the "right" price:

1. How does the price compare with your competitors'?
2. Are there established price points industrywide?
3. What is the perceived value of the product or service?
4. Is the customer price sensitive or value driven?
5. Will a decrease in price gain extra market share? Or will a small increase be indiscernible to a better profit margin?
6. What trade discounts or allowance should be made to accounts/customers?

Placement Strategy

Distribution is a critical factor to the marketing mix. It is imperative that the consumer has access to the product through a direct or indirect channel. In the example of Coach, the merchandise is sold through Coach stores, factory outlets, department and specialty stores, duty-free locations in airports, and online. Coach has two business segments, direct-to-consumer and indirect. Over 85 percent of the company's sales are generated by its direct-to-consumer segment with sales being generated from handbags and accessories.

Entrepreneurs must ensure the market coverage.

1. Where can customers purchase competitive products or services?
2. Department store, specialty store or boutique, or both? Online retailer?
3. What are the "best" distribution channels?
4. Is a sales force needed? Should you attend trade fairs? Make online submissions? Send samples to bloggers or web-based companies?

Promotional Strategy

Entrepreneurs must develop a cohesive plan to communicate with consumers and retailers about its products in numerous ways. The company's promotional brand message seeks to differentiate its products from those of its competitors and demonstrate the products' unique qualities. It will also build relationships. The voice of the brand must be loud and clear—it must speak to the targeted consumer in a brand-oriented tone and use language that builds immediate relationships.

Despite heavy competition and amid an economic slowdown, Coach became the third best-selling brand in the Chinese market [in 2012]. While several other luxury brands slowed, Coach boasted a turnover of $300 million in the first half of [2012] and expected that number to exceed $400 million by [2013]. With an annualized sales growth of 60 percent in China, Coach hoped to get 10 percent of China's high-end handbags and accessories market.

Currently at 96 stores on the mainland, Coach plans to add 30 new stores annually, particularly in second- and third-tier cities. Coach's success in China can be attributed to three key factors: its strategic market position, its focus on the men's category, and its multichannel distribution strategy.

Coach positions itself as an accessible luxury brand, which means its prices are 50 percent to 75 percent lower than, and thus avoids direct competition with, the top luxury brands. "We are good and affordable, something which can withstand the risk of the economic

Source: Fairchild Fashion Media

downturn. As has been proved, the consumption of luxury goods tends to be more rational too," explains Jonathan Seliger, Coach's president and CEO for China. Furthermore, the accessible luxury strategy captures the large emerging Chinese middle-class consumers and also provides a broader reach into the second- and third-tier cities.

Source: Red Luxury. 2012. "Why Coach Is Succeeding in China." *Red Luxury*, Dec. 12. http://red-luxury.com/brands-retail/why-coach-is-succeeding-in-china

Viable questions are:

1. What is the dominant marketing message to your target market?
2. Where can you reach your targeted consumer? Social media? Direct marketing? Outdoor media?
3. How do competitors promote their products? And how will this influence your choice of promotional activity?

Promotional strategies must be carefully executed for the product exposure or impressions to reach the targeted consumer. Following the competition isn't always an indicator of the right strategy. Tapping into innovative ways to build relationships with the consumer are often more productive strategies that yield sales and loyalty. For example, Coach showcased a line of their high price point items through a mobile advertising campaign that encouraged shoppers to shop from their mobile devices. "The number of visitors engaging with our brand via mobile device has grown exponentially over the last year, a trend that we still continuing," stated David Duplantis, executive vice president of global digital media and customer engagement at Coach, New York. He further said, "Historically, mobile visitors were accessing our store locator, and today the primary purpose of a mobile visit is commerce or to browse an item that they intend on purchasing in a store," he said. "It is important that we offer the most compelling brand experience across all devices."

Traditional Strategies

Small businesses will often have a restrictive promotional budget. Hiring a public relations firm or developing direct mail pieces and print advertising can be cost prohibitive for a new company. Many entrepreneurs will self-manage promotions by submitting their press releases to magazine editors and bloggers for editorial press. Entrepreneurs must conduct market research to acquaint themselves with appropriate and credible blogs and print/online magazines relevant to their target consumer. Most will have an email address to send new product information for editorial coverage. Entrepreneurs will also engage nonprofit organizations in social responsibility endeavors to support the initiative and gain visibility in the marketplace.

Nontraditional Strategies

In tandem with traditional strategies, nontraditional marketing methods can require minimal funding and a wealth of creativity for a profitable outcome for the entrepreneur. Interactive social media, blogs, and email blasts are market-driven opportunities to promote the brand and garner brand loyalty with the target consumer. For example, a small business can easily implement cooperative partnerships, such as distributing samples or product discount cards in gift bags at appropriate events that its target market attends. Entrepreneurs also can take advantage of a retail partner's website by requesting product visibility on the static page during the launch period.

Press Kit

A **press kit,** is a comprehensive packet of information in electronic and print form that is created for use by the press. With a limited start-up budget, entrepreneurs often will compile and write their press kits. Most of the core information is populated from the company's mission and vision statement as well as the product philosophy. Editors are on a tight deadline to execute and complete stories, they need the most efficient way to get the information (Box 12.3). The press kit consists of promotional material, most commonly:

- Press release(s)
- Product collection overview
- Product images with retail prices
- Designer/brand biography

Tip 12.2 **Create-a-minute!**

I'm socially conscious, so why not exhibit social responsibility with my brand! It will help the community and certainly shape my company's brand image. Consumers are increasingly aware of companies who give ... and those who don't!

BOX 12.3 Media Kit

A media kit includes key information to inform and acquaint the press with the product assortment and it's point of difference. The core content of a media kit includes detailed product descriptions, images, the manufacturer's suggested retail price, the press release, recent press, the creator's biography and other relevant facts. An updated electronic media kit is often the 'go-to' file for the entrepreneur.

Source: Courtesy of *d*irt, Erthe Beaute LLC

Press Release

A press release functions as an announcement and should answer who, what, when, where, and how facts. It should be written with critical information in the first paragraph of the document and should include the mission statement and other pertinent information about the product launch and business.

Products/Services

A line sheet or list of the products and services and the benefits of each are fundamental components of the media kit. An editor or external source should be able to ascertain fast facts in just a few minutes. This format should be brief and to the point. Retail prices should be stated on the line sheets.

Bios

Biographies of corporate leaders in the organization are a common enclosure in a media kit. Images/headshots are usually included. With the advancement of technology, images can be inexpensive. Brief facts and industry-related experience is a sharper presentation than a resume. Add pertinent anecdotes, quotes, and other unique criteria that establish credibility. Include recognition, awards, and any other vital facts to engage media members.

Current Press

By searching the World Wide Web, many entrepreneurs discover their positive product reviews from bloggers. If applicable, recent press should be included in the media kit. This provides insight to current news, events, and supports the press–worthy stance of the company. Inserts or published press, upcoming dates about personal appearances along with product images and your logo will aid editors in generating an article.

Marketing Budget

Percentage of Sale Approach

Many small businesses allocate a percentage of actual or projected gross revenues. Seasonal marketing budgets are often established in tandem with sales projections, hence they fuel one another. The common range is 1 to 10 percent of sales revenue for start-up marketing. The higher the volume of sales a business does, the lower the percentage of sales they can expect to spend.

Entrepreneurs should have margins in the range of 10 to 12 percent after covering other expenses, including marketing. In such a competitive industry, the marketing budget should never be based on just what's left-over once all your other business expenses are covered. It costs more to market new products than it costs to market existing products. Therefore, if a business is launching a new product or product line, the percentage of annual sales revenue they will need to budget for marketing will be closer to 10 percent.

To avoid overprojecting or overspending, the simplest way of determining the value of a marketing budget is by deciding to spend a certain percentage of each month's revenue on advertising and marketing.

Budget Allocation

Budget allocation depends on several factors: the industry, the size of your business, and its growth stage. This budget should be split between:

- Brand development costs that include all the channels, such as your website, blogs, and sales collateral.
- Brand promotion, which includes the business campaigns, advertising, and events.

Brand Awareness

A significant percent of marketing funds are going toward building brand awareness. Companies that have established a strong brand in their given markets have a competitive edge when it comes to how much they will have to spend to maintain their brand awareness. If a company's target market is not familiar with either the company itself or the brand of products or services that company offers, the percentage of sales revenue budgeted for marketing will need to be higher.

Marketing Evaluation

To evaluate the effectiveness of the marketing budget, you must be able to gauge how much revenue or how many unit sales you received per dollar of each type of advertising or marketing. Differentiated sales channels make tracking such numbers relatively easy when determining online versus offline advertising. Analytics and metrics are useful in denoting website traffic. Many advertising campaigns can be highly customized to determine the source of the sale. For example, Victoria's Secret's direct mail program that provides a free, in-store gift is still an effective tool to bring consumers into the store to shop.

TRADE TERMS

executive summary

company description

core competencies

SWOT analysis

objective

strategy

tactic

marketing mix

press kit

Summary

Entrepreneurs are the inherent executers of the marketing plan. A marketing plan is a vital tool in steering the product image in the marketplace. Knowing the core competencies of the company is the backbone of the plan. The marketing mix defines the marketing elements for successfully positioning the product or service. A new product launch must have multichannel synergy that stems from the marketing plan. They have the creative vision, branding strategy, and product knowledge and development from conception to now navigate and develop the plan to market to the ultimate customer.

Online Resources

"How to Write a Marketing Plan" *Entrepreneur.com*
http://www.entrepreneur.com/article/43018
Information on the fundamentals of writing a business plan.

Marketing Plan Pro Software
Step-by-step software to aid in developing a business plan.
http://www4.paloalto.com/sales_and_marketing_pro/?gclid=CKid_52rmrICFahaMg
odJ28AGA&

Activity 12.1

Once the marketing mix has been developed, answer the questions below:

1. Does the product meet the customer's needs or wants? How?

2. Where will they purchase the product? What percentage will be online versus at a brick-and-mortar location?

3. Is the price competitive? What brand is the price leader?

4. What social media channels are being used for product introductions?

Activity 12.2

Now that you've planned your sales and floor plans, now it is time to set strategy to market your product to the ultimate customer. Create at least one objective, strategy, and tactic per phase of business for your marketing plan. The tactic must be detailed.

Bibliography

Businessdictionary.com s.v. "marketing strategy." http://www.businessdictionary.com/definition/marketing-strategy.html#ixzz25RdwHdsp

—— s.v. "objective." Accessed August 31, 2012. http://www.businessdictionary.com/definition/objective.html#ixzz25ReMoISn

Donnelly, Tim. "How to Put Together a Press Kit." *Inc.com*. Updated Sept. 10, 2010. Accessed August 31, 2012. http://www.inc.com/guides/2010/09/how-to-put-together-a-press-kit.html

GuruFocus. 2013. "Finding Value in Coach." *Nasdaq,* May 4. Accessed May 4, 2013. http://www.nasdaq.com/article/finding-value-in-coach-coh-cm243653#ixzz2bo4HSClM

Hellomarketing.biz. "How to Choose Marketing Plan Objectives." Accessed August 31, 2012. http://www.hellomarketing.biz/planning-strategy/marketing-plan-objectives.php

HuffingtonPost.com. 2012. "L'Oreal Tops Beauty Industry 2011 with $28.33 Million in Sales." Accessed August 31, 2012. http://www.huffingtonpost.com/2012/08/09/loreal-beauty-industry-2833-billion_n_1761412.html

Johnson, Lauren. 2012. "Coach Spurs mcommerce Sales via Interactive Ad Campaign." *Mobile Commerce Daily,* Sept. 27. Accessed August 13, 2013. http://www.mobilecommercedaily.com/coach-spurs-mcommerce-sales-via-interactive-ad-campaign

Kerin, Roger, Eric Berkowitz, Steven Hartley, and William Rudelius. "Advertising, Sales Promotion and Public Relations, Using Social Media to Connect with Consumers, Personal Selling and Sales Management ." *IMarketing The Core.* 5th Ed. (New York, NY: McGraw-Hill, 2013), Ch. 15–17.

Mindtools.com. "Marketing Plan." *Mindtools.* Accessed August 31, 2012. http://www.mindtools.com/

Startupnation.com. "Marketing Plan." *Startup Nation.* Accessed August 31, 2012. www.startupnation.com

13

The Action Plan

Entrepreneurs need a business plan as a fundamental guide to drive their business. It is an essential road map to navigate the business from the start-up phase and beyond. The perceived value of creating the plan dwells within the research and viewing the business in a systematic way. A well-devised business plan informs an entrepreneur's decision-making ability at the crux of an opportunity or challenge. Ideas are more often viewed from a critical perspective than from an impulsive one. Once solidified, a business plan will keep the business true to its purpose, mission, and vision. This document sets the trajectory three to five years ahead and outlines the route a company intends to take to reach, maintain, and grow revenues. For the sake of consistency, we've utilized lululemon athletica to convey concept examples throughout the chapter.

The Business Plan

Although business plans can vary in style and length, there are key components that are considered static: an executive summary, a description of the business, the market analysis, competition, management, marketing, sales, and financial projections.

Business Plan Executive Summary

An executive summary often is considered the most important part of a business plan. It is an at-a-glance synopsis of the company. For ease of execution, an executive summary is often written at the completion of the business plan. Entrepreneurs must explain the vital components of the company that make it relevant, needed, or desired in the industry and how it will forge ahead to become successful. The summary should be comprehensive enough to map the infrastructure of the company with an expressed outcome. Potential financial investors often review the executive summary as the barometer of their interest.

Figure 13.1 The mission statement of Canadian-based lululemon athletica is a "manifesto" of ideas and life philosophies. *Source: Corbis.*

Although it appears first in the business plan document, the summary is usually written last since it highlights the strengths of the overall plan. Existing companies include pivotal insights for the reader of their executive summary by including:

- Mission statement—explains the purpose of the company. It can be brief or comprehensive in scope. It can be direct or embody a concept. For example, the lululemon althletica mission is a manifesto of 31 ideas and life philosophies for healthy and positive living. It creates a definitive culture for employees in the workplace and thus a unique way of doing business and interacting with their consumers (Figure 13.1).
- Company information—identifies the name, formation, founders, roles, number of employees, and geographic location.
- Growth—examples of market movement, highlights, and gains.
- Product/Service—describes the product or service in detail.
- Financials—includes current statements of profitability.
- Goals—future plans that inform the stability of the plan.

For a newly established business, the executive summary should consist of an entrepreneur's experience and fundamental decisions that led to the start-up. The perspective must be shaped from a concise demonstration of market analysis—a need, along with a plan of how the business will resolve it. Identifying the business as a fulfillment of a void in the marketplace will pinpoint the niche. A niche is to have specific appeal that is under-served (Box 13.1). Entrepreneurs must consider the following:

- Well-established competition
- Voids in the marketplace
- Untapped opportunities

Market Analysis

The market analysis is part of the business plan that reflects the entrepreneur's knowledge of the respective industry. It illustrates research, findings, and ultimately the market profile. The analysis explores the industry at large—its size, growth rate, trends, and dominant consumer characteristics. The analysis should reveal specifics about the target market. Entrepreneurs must know their consumers—their needs and wants—purchasing trends, price caps, and their geographic and demographic matrices. By knowing the industry, market segment, and the consumer, an entrepreneur can project the anticipated market share. This information must be laced throughout the market analysis.

For example, lululemon has shown itself to be an inventive retailer, focusing on innovative and functional products as well as innovative business practices. Unlike most clothing retailers, lululemon does not just penetrate a new market and open a retail store. The company first sets up a showroom in the market, goes out into the community, attends local yoga classes, and engages with the practitioners in the community. The dedicated sales team for the hopeful market guides athletes and yoga enthusiasts toward the lululemon website (Figure 13.2). Once the team establishes a feel for the community, gains acceptance, and sees follow-through from online sales, they decide whehter the market is ready for a full-scale retail store. The typical lululemon store is roughly 2,500 square feet. Bigger stores might push 3,500 square feet.

After 20 years in the surf, skate, and snowboard business, founder of lululemon, Chip Wilson took the first commercial yoga class offered in Vancouver and found the result exhilarating. The post-yoga feeling was so close to surfing and snowboarding that it seemed obvious that yoga was an ideology whose time had come (again).

Cotton clothing was being used for sweaty, stretchy power yoga, and seemed completely inappropriate to Chip, whose passion lay in technical athletic fabrics. From this, a design studio was born that became a yoga studio at night to pay the rent. Clothing was offered for sale, and an underground yoga clothing movement was born. The success of the clothing was dependent on the feedback from yoga instructors who were asked to wear the products and provide their insights.

Source: Lululemon.com

Competitive Analysis

Within the market analysis is a competitive component. It identifies the leaders in the segment and product lines that an entrepreneur perceives as direct competition. The competitive landscape assessment should include:

- Market shares
- Strengths and weaknesses
- Barriers to market entry
- Competition across the segment and price tiers

Figure 13.2 lululemon has shown itself to be an inventive retailer, focusing on innovative and functional products as well as innovative business practices. They have an inclusive work environment that embraces the company's manifesto. *Source: Corbis.*

When lululemon athletica Inc opened its first U.S. shop in 2003, its form-fitting yoga pants, free classes, and Pacific Northwest vibe were a revelation to its new American customers. But time has caught up with the Vancouver-based retailer. lululemon, closely watched by investors because of its meteoric rise, now faces a cluster of competitors whose stores and products bear a striking resemblance to its own.

Montreal-based Lolë, Gap Inc's Athleta, and others are expanding aggressively in the United States. They could threaten lululemon's stellar growth and robust brand, especially by competing on price. Conversely, lululemon could reap more growth from the expanding market for premium fitness wear, building on its 10 years of dominance in North America and its aggressive push into European and Asian markets. Lululemon shareholders have had a very good run so far. The stock is up more than seven-fold since its 2007 debut, and fitness-minded women have developed a fierce loyalty to the brand.

The copycats can, however, be viewed as a positive development for lululemon, suggesting the niche it

defined is not a passing fad. Chic, feminine apparel specifically designed for yoga and other fitness activities has entered the fashion mainstream. In that respect, the rise of yoga wear is not unlike the ascendance of blue jeans in the 1970s, said Bernard Mariette, chief executive of Coalision Inc, the closely held Montreal company behind the Lolë concept. "I really believe that, especially for women, both fashion and technical are merging," Mariette said. "You cannot have technical clothing for ladies [that] is not feminine and beautiful."

Source: Allison Martel. 2012 "lululemon Is Suddenly Facing Competition from Every Direction." *Business Insider,* Dec. 11. http://www.businessinsider.com/lululemon-is-suddenly-facing-competition-from-every-direction-2012-12

Image Source: Corbis

Regulatory Restrictions

This section should include any consumer or governmental regulatory requirements and compliance. In tandem, cite the cost of compliance process.

Company Description

Entrepreneurs are experts on describing their core business. The company description is a critical review of the nature of the business and the different facets of the business. It allows the reader to understand what the company does and why it exists. This section allows the entrepreneur to passionately dissect each piece of the business and present it as a unique idea or service that is needed in the marketplace. Include in the description:

- Nature of the business—satisfaction of a need/want
- Differentiation—unique attributes of the company
- Competitive advantage—value of company
- Social responsibility—community involvement

What makes lululemon athletic wear so unique and charge such lofty prices for yoga pants is quite simple—the company puts focuses on the form, fit, and function of its products. They focus on innovative materials that provide the consumer with a multilayered and multifunctional garment. Much of the company's expenditures go directly into the production of these highly sought-after garments. Scarcity is also a tool the company uses, as it does not mass-market its product line nor does the company offer a wide variety of lesser quality items. When testing new products, lululemon offers the products in capsules or small runs; this is basically an industry definition of limited supply or quantities. Think of the capsules as testing sites in much the way showrooms are for eventual stores. The feedback through sales or direct consumer feedback is what is used by the company to go forward with the products as a full run. This system of capsule releases to the marketplace is unique to lululemon. Another competitive advantage is that lululemon offers yoga classes in the store environment to reinforce its brand and lifestyle mantra.

Organization/Management

The structure of the company and the roles and responsibilities of each person involved must be clearly defined. Entrepreneurs typically have a small, one- to three-person operation during start-up. Each person may have several key cross-functional duties. A finite explanation of the divisions within a company is also needed. This section of the business plan details the structure from ownership to profiles of the management team and board of directors or advisory board.

Organizational Structure

For large organizations, an organizational chart is a visual outline of the corporate divisions and managerial structure (Figure 13.3). Along with

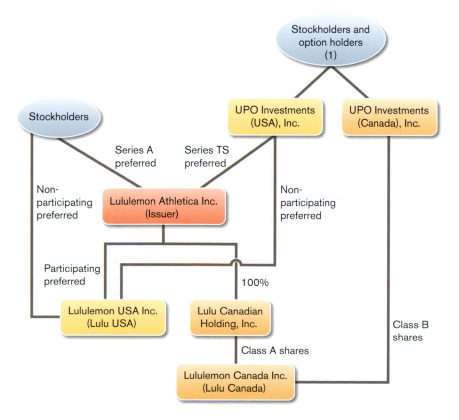

Figure 13.3 This organizational chart is a visual outline of the corporate divisions and managerial structure.

the chart is a brief narrative of the functional duties within each part of the company. Often this part of the plan will reinforce the comprehensive synergy of the company. Although the chart may be limited for entrepreneurs, it is still a viable part of the plan for future investors and employees.

Ownership Information

The legal structure of the business is important. The corporate entity reveals the ownership formation and boundaries of entry or dissolvent. According to the Small Business Administration, the following ownership information should be incorporated into a business plan includes:

1. Names of owners
2. Percentage ownership
3. Extent of involvement with the company
4. Forms of ownership
5. Outstanding equity equivalents
6. Common stock (i.e., authorized or issued)
7. Management profiles
8. Industry recognition
9. Community involvement
10. Compensation basis and levels

Entrepreneurs should highlight how each owner or manager within the organization will bring value. That person's overall skill set and contribution to the company should be highlighted as a link to the intended success of the organization.

Board of Directors' Qualifications

A board of directors or advisory board is an unpaid group of experts that provide direction and industry insights that could otherwise not be afforded by the organization. The board comprises well-known, credible people who can influence direction and enhance the perception of the company. The board's knowledge base should vary in order to generate diversity in the decision-making process.

Within the business plan, the qualifications of the board will lend strength to the managerial status of the company. It is an extension of the management profile and should include the following information:

- Names
- Positions on the board
- Extent of involvement with company

- Background
- Historical and future contribution to the company's success

Marketing and Sales Strategy

The marketing strategy is the lifeline to the targeted consumer who will generate sales for the company. In this section of the business plan the market penetration should be carefully explained—the marketing plan will dictate and duplicate this section of the business plan. Although a marketing and sales strategy is always evolving and being evaluated, articulating the way the company is going to drive sales and maintain customer loyalty must be conveyed in the plan.

According to the Small Business Administration, an overall marketing strategy should include four different strategies:

1. *Growth strategies:* An internal strategy, such as how to increase your human resources; an acquisition strategy, such as buying another business; a franchise strategy for branching out; a horizontal strategy, in which you would provide the same type of products to different users; or a vertical strategy in which you would continue providing the same products but would offer them at different levels of the distribution chain.
2. *Channels of distribution strategy:* Choices for distribution channels could include an internal sales force, distributors, or retailers.
3. *Communication strategy:* A combination of the following tactics—promotions, advertising, public relations, personal selling, and printed materials, such as brochures, catalogs, flyers, and so on.
4. *Sales strategy:* A sales force strategy and a sales activity strategy can be denoted. If a sales force will be used, the business plan must stipulate whether an internal sales force or independent contractors will be hired. Also, the compensation structure must be clearly outlined. For sales activities, an entrepreneur must identify and prioritize prospects. Once identified, the sales projection per targeted channel partner must be listed. Next, determine the average number of sales calls that will be needed to yield the sale projections—the average dollar size per sale and the average dollar size per channel partner.

lululemon is an example of an effective marketing and sale strategy, as shown in Box 13.2.

Product/Service Description

The product or service is the heart of the business plan. This part of the plan includes information about the product or service. It clearly defines the features, benefits, and attributes of the product or service. It also high-lights the company's ability to meet the needs and satisfy the wants of the target market. The competitive advantage or edge is a fundamental premise of why the product will be a success in the marketplace.

Product's Life Cycle

The product life cycle should be introduced to provide the life span of the product. This will also provide the reader with insight to repeat sales, seasonal peaks, and obsolescence.

BOX 13.2 lululemon athletica's Strategic Sales

At lululemon, we've made it our vision to elevate the world from mediocrity to greatness. We realize that to do this we need to partner with great people. Our Strategic Sales team partner with local entrepreneurs and athletes who are passionate about elevating their communities. We value quality over quantity, our partners are people who get up every morning for something bigger than themselves and inspire others with their enthusiasm and achievements.

Under the Strategic Sales umbrella there are three programs designed to spread the yoga love and help raise the level of health in our communities.

■ Wholesale program—we select leading fitness and yoga studios and work with them so they can provide their guests with technical gear to sweat in
■ Yoga hard goods program—we offer studios (and their guests) essentials like yoga mats, blocks and straps
■ Team sales program—we help teams get into technical athletic gear so they can focus on sweating hard and inspiring their communities.

Source: *lululemon.* http://www.lululemon.com/about/stratsales?mnid=ftr;strategic_sales

Intellectual Property

If there are any pending, existing, or anticipated copyright or patent filings, they must be listed. Any trade secrets or formulations or work-for-hire or nondisclosures or noncompete agreements also must be document in this section of the business plan. For example, lululemon have created a signature fabric under the registered trademark name Luon. Their famously sought-after signature black yoga pant is made with Luon fabric. It is moisture wicking, breathable, soft, and has a four-way stretch. This particular high-performance fabric is used for different silhouettes every season—tanks, pants, bras, and jackets (Figure 13.4). Although consumers have become loyal to this best-selling product, in March 2013, all Luon pants were pulled from the stores for being too sheer. The company suffered a decrease in sales and revenue loss, however consumers remained brand loyal in spite of the production challenge. As anticipated, the signature Luon fabric pants were placed back on shelves a few months later, and sales reflected a welcomed return.

Tip 13.2 **Create-a-minute!**

Hmm … Money matters! How much will I need to maintain a solid cash flow and grow my business?

Research and Development (R&D) Activities

Entrepreneurs should include any information that relates to new product developments in this section of the business plan. Outline any R&D activities that you are involved in or are planning. What results of future R&D activities do you expect? Be sure to analyze the R&D efforts of not only your own business, but also of others in your industry.

Financials

Entrepreneurs experience periods of growth and development, whereas a firm financial plan within the business plan is necessary. Financials need to be current and reveal the profits and losses incurred to date. Many entrepreneurs plan for a funding request. A funding request is when a company seeks money to expand or reprieve the business in some facet. If applicable, this type of information is needed in the business plan. According to the Small Business Administration, a funding request should include the following information:

- The current funding requirement/amount.
- Type of funding and terms—equity/debit.
- Any future funding requirements over the next five years.
- Use of funds: Is the funding request for capital expenditures? Working capital? Debt retirement? Acquisitions? Whatever it is, be sure to list it in this section.
- Any strategic financial situational plans for the future, such as: a buyout, being acquired, debt repayment plan, or selling your business. These areas are extremely important to a future creditor, since they will directly affect the company's ability to repay a loan.

Financial Statements

Regardless of whether funding is needed, financial projections are a critical closing of the business plan. The financial data should include historical information that relates to performance, income statements, balance sheets, and cash flow statements for each year in business. The following is a list of the critical financial statements to include in the business plan.

Prospective Financial Statements

Prospective financial data is important as well. This will reveal the expectations for the financial performance of the company. Most of the time, creditors will want to see the expected financials for the next five years. This would include forecasted income statements, balance sheets, cash flow statements, and capital expenditure budgets. It can be divided into monthly or quarterly projections and annual projections for later years. It is imperative that the projections match any funding requests; creditors will be alerted by any inconsistencies. Finally, include a short analysis of your financial information. Include a ratio and trend analysis for all of your financial statements—both historical and prospective. Since visuals have impact, graphs and charts are effective for positive trend analysis and reinforcement.

Exit Strategy

The evolution of a brand and its product matrix is limitless. However, an exit strategy is also included in business plans. An exit strategy is often considered when the company has a strong valuation and has achieved a predetermined revenue goal or as a way of escape for a business that is underperforming. Including the exit strategy in a business plan will reinforce a well-devised plan to the reader.

Lastly, an appendix can be included in a business plan. It can include any ancillary information such as résumés, industry recognition, or other noted items within the business plan.

Summary

Entrepreneurs need a business plan. They steer the direction of the company and must update the plan on an ongoing basis. The business plan keeps the business on a defined path to ensure the intended success. It starts with an executive summary and includes the company's description, ownership, management team, structure, sales, marketing, and financials. A well-devised business plan is the blueprint to construct success, plan extension, and reveal deterioration in all facets of the business. This document sets the trajectory three to five years ahead and outlines the route a company intends to take to reach, maintain, and grow revenues.

Online Resources

"Free Sample Business Plans." Bplans
www.bplans.com/sample_business_plans.cfm

"Build Your Business Plan." U.S. Small Business Administration
web.sba.gov/busplantemplate/BizPlanStart.cfm

Activity 13.1 Business Plan

1. What is the optimal business structure for an entrepreneur and why?

2. Name five people you would select to be on your advisory board. What are their attributes and professional skill sets?

3. Define/describe your company and analyze the competition. What are the distinguishing differences? What is your company's competitive edge?

4. When is the right "financial" time to end a business entity?

Bibliography

Entrepreneur.com. "Your Business Plan Guide." Accessed August 31, 2012. http://www.entrepreneur.com/businessplan/index.html

Golden, Seth. 2012. "Lululemon Continues to Grow." *Seeking Alpha,* Oct. 2. http://seekingalpha.com/article/899491-lululemon-continues-to-grow$

Lululemon.com. http://shop.lululemon.com/home.jsp

Martell, Allison. 2012. "Lululemon Is Suddenly Facing Competition From Every Direction." *Business Insider,* Dec. 11. http://www.businessinsider.com/lululemon-is-suddenly-facing-competition-from-every-direction-2012-12

U.S. Small Business Association. "Starting & Managing a Business." *SBA.gov.* Accessed August 31, 2012. http://www.sba.gov/category/navigation-structure/starting-managing-business

Wasserman, Elizabeth. 2010. "How to Write a Great Business Plan." *Inc.com,* Feb. 1. Accessed August 31, 2012. http://www.inc.com/guides/write-a-great-business-plan.html

14

Trade Tools

Establishing the tools of the trade with key materials is needed to effectively manage the administrative functions of a business. The business needs to institute itself as a business entity—sole proprietorships (sometimes known as sole props), partnerships, limited liability corporations (LLCs), and corporations. Understanding the basics of establishing a business entity and how to set up basic accounting practices will assist the entrepreneur in launching the brand and its business. A business will need to project start-up capital to cover variable and nonvariable expenses and how to manage the financial basics prior to retaining professional contractors. The entrepreneurs must build the fundamentals of labeling requirements for products and what components of a product can be protected—from brand name to tagline. Finally, entrepreneurs must garner an understanding of trademarks and the process of registering for a trademark to protect their ideas.

Business Structure

Once the market has been researched and the product niche has been developed, the next step is building the foundation of the business. Businesses can be formed in different business entities: alone, with a partner, or with multiple partners. When beginning a business, the form of the business entity needs to be established. The business entity will determine which type of income tax return to file. The most common forms of business are the sole proprietorship, partnership, corporation, and S corporation. A limited liability company (LLC) is a fairly new business formation allowed by state decree.

The form of business entity that is chosen will determine on:

- Liability
- Taxation
- Recordkeeping

KEY CONCEPTS

+ Establish a business entity.

+ Prepare the company's start-up capital.

+ Understand start-up financial basics.

+ Examine trademark(s) and protecting one's work.

+ Identify the various labeling requirements.

Sole Proprietorship

A **sole proprietorship** is the most common form of business organization for entrepreneurs. There is only one owner, which gives the entrepreneur complete freedom to run the business. In addition, the sole proprietor is personally responsible for all financial obligations and debts of the business. The company must operate as a business and cannot be an investment or hobby. A sole proprietor must:

- Maintain adequate records to act in accordance with federal tax requirements regarding business recordkeeping.
- File Schedule C or C-EZ (Profit or Loss from Business), with Form 1040.
- Pay self-employment tax on the net income reported.
- Make quarterly estimated tax payments if the business is expected to make a profit, since taxes are not withheld.

Partnership

A **partnership** is when two or more people unite to have ownership of the business shown in Figure 14.1. Each partner contributes money, property, labor and/or skill(s), and anticipates sharing in the profits (or losses) of the business.

- Income taxes are not paid at the partnership level.
- Self-employment tax must be paid on the net earnings.
- If a profit is expected, then generally quarterly estimated taxes should be paid.
- Taxes are not withheld from any distributions.
- Partners report their individual share of income or losses on their personal tax returns.

BizStats.com states that 72 percent of small businesses are started up as a sole proprietorship, and only 6 percent are established as a partnership. Starting a business single-handedly can be lonely, but if the entrepreneur opts to start a business venture with one or more partners, the following factors should be considered:

- *Visions and goals:* Each partner must be on the same page concerning how they would like to see the business evolve. If one person is planning on building the business as a sideline and the other person is looking to make the business a sole priority, then the visions of each entrepreneur are not the same. Each partner must agree on the same visions and goals.
- *Define roles:* Each partner brings strength to the business venture, so those strengths should be capitalized on. One partner may be creative, yet lacking in business experience, or vice versa. Both partners should not try to lead or be everything. Discuss each other's strengths and decide who will handle the different aspects of the business.
- *Hold meetings:* Each month the partners must get together to discuss the business. The meeting should be held to discuss any issues, each other's roles, offer constructive criticism, and brainstorm. Do not use these meetings to attack each other, as this will only injure the partnership and business.

Figure 14.1 Italian designers Domenico Dolce and Stefano Gabbana started the company Dolce & Gabbana more than 20 years ago; clearly a successful partnership. *Source: Jacopo Raule/Getty Images.*

- *Create a legal partnership agreement:* Many friends go into business together and unfortunately end up as enemies. Legal documents are not required to form a partnership, but for the sake of the business, a partnership agreement should be drawn up. According to the Small Business Administration (SBA), the agreement should include the following:
  - Who will make which business decisions?
  - How will profits and losses be shared?
  - How will disputes be handled?
  - What happens if a new partner is brought on board?
  - How will the partnership dissolve in case of death or if a partner wants to leave?
  - How will buying out an existing partner work?
  - How much will each partner invest?
  - What will each partner's role in the business be?
  - What will each partner's compensation be?

A partnership can be rewarding and can alleviate the pressures of starting a business alone. However, do not choose a partner just because of a friendship. Choose a partner based on passion, drive, and vision.

Corporation

Corporations are subject to more regulations and tax requirements than a sole proprietorship or a partnership. Each state has its own laws governing corporations and how they are formed.

- The **corporation** is an entity that manages the everyday jobs of the business.
- A corporation is generally liable for the debts of the business, not the person or people who own the business. (Exceptions may exist under state law.)
- A separate tax-paying entity can be formed.

Subchapter S Corporation

A variation of a corporation is a **subchapter S corporation** or **S corporation.** This type of corporation is similar to a partnership in which income or losses are passed through to individual tax returns. An S corporation has the same corporate makeup as a standard corporation. State laws charter an S corporation separately from its shareholders and officers. Generally, there is limited liability for corporate shareholders. Taxes for this entity are not paid at the corporate level. Income that is received is streamed through the shareholders' individual returns.

Limited Liability Company

A **limited liability company (LLC)** has two or more members, and each partner reports his or her share of the earnings and losses.

- An LLC provides ownership flexibility and the advantage of pass-through taxation.
- LLC owners are called members.

A lawyer will benefit the entrepreneur greatly when deciding how to establish a business. Table 14.1 is a quick-reference guide to the pros and cons of each business entity. One form is not better than another, so one

TABLE 14.1 **TYPES OF BUSINESS ENTITIES**

	PRO	CON
Sole Proprietorship	• Simplest structure • Expenses and income are included in your personal income tax return • Full control of the business	• Personally responsible for your company's liabilities • Your assets are at risk • Financing is difficult
Partnership	• Shared responsibility • Company does not pay tax on its income • Partner can act on behalf of the partnership • Can share the work based on the partners' skills	• Each partner reports his or her share of income and loss on tax form • Partners are personally liable for their partners' business actions • More expensive to form because of more legal work
Corporation	• Independent legal entity that is separate from its owners • Personal liability protection	• Most complex and expensive to form • Double taxation: the corporation pays taxes on its income and the shareholder pays taxes on dividends.
S Corporation	• Shareholders have personal limited liability • Income or losses can be passed through to individual tax returns • Separate legal entity	• Follow same requirements as corporations • Higher legal and tax service costs
LLC	• Owners have limited personal liability for the debts and actions of the LLC • Can choose to be taxed like a partnership or a corporation.	• Active members are subject to self-employment tax for Social Security and Medicare. • Relatively new business form and the laws are still changing

This quick guide shows the pros and cons of the various business entities.

must assess one's own needs. Table 14.2 shows the types of legal entities and the forms that are used.

Start-Up Capital

The need for start-up capital will vary according to what the entrepreneur is trying to accomplish and the requirements of the business. Costs for starting a business depend on many factors, such as whether equipment will be bought to create the product, if a manufacturer will be used, whether a designer will be hired, whether to rent space to run the business, and whether it is necessary to have a sales representative, an other such questions.

TABLE 14.2 **TYPES OF LEGAL ENTITIES AND TAX FORMS**

TYPE OF LEGAL ENTITY	TAX FORM
Sole Proprietorship	1040
Partnership	1065
Corporation	1120 or 1120-A
S Corporation	1120-S
LLC	1065, 1120, or 1120-A

This table lists the types of legal entities, which need to be filed with the appropriate tax forms.

Source: Fred S. Steingold, 2008. *Legal Guide for Starting and Running a Small Business.* Berkeley, California: Nolo Publishing

Tip 14.1 **Create-a-minute!**

An LLC is the most common form of business entity when starting a company, due to the fact that people have limited liability for the debts.

Obtaining Money to Fund the Business

Before a brand can be executed and launched, funds need to be obtained.. Borrowing money is one of the most common ways to obtain those funds. There are various places to look for funding, including using an entrepreneur's own savings. Most businesses will find funding through various mediums. Friends and family are can be a great source to obtain funding, but this can sometimes be a delicate situation. It is important to separate business and personal relationships when accepting money from a family member or friend, so a contract must be written up between the two. It is also important to keep in mind that if the business does not succeed, it could also put a strain on current relationships.

A **venture capitalist** is someone who will invest in the business for a percentage of the ownership. Many times, a venture capitalist will dictate where the money should be invested. A venture capitalist will assess the business plan, if there is an opportunity within the market, and any indicators that the company is a viable business venture. Venture capitalists look for high-growth prospects. Another type of investor is an angel investor, who has a high net worth and will invest her own money in a company. An angel investor takes an equity share of the business. Many times, an angel investor will invest in start-ups that are in their region. Angel investors will usually require that the entrepreneur do due diligence and be ready to launch a product. Figure 14.2 lists the top 10 angel investor groups according to Entrepenuer.com.

Credit cards can be used to assist with starting the business, which is considered unsecured credit. It is important to look for cards that do not carry a high-interest rate or steep fees. Many credit cards offer cash back or rewards, which can be beneficial to the business. A credit card should be used with caution to pay for things, making sure that there is money available to pay the credit card monthly. Entrepreneurs also can take money from the company's line of credit. A bank may extend a line of credit to its qualified customers and will do so for short-term financing. Secured short-term credit can be found through commercial banks, commercial finance companies, and U.S. Small Business Administration (SBA), which will not make direct loans, but a "guaranteed" loan could be obtained through a private lending institution.

When applying for a loan, an entrepreneur must be prepared to answer the following questions:

- Will the business be able to pay back the loan?
- If the business fails, will the business be able to come up with money to repay?
- Does the business pay its bills in a timely manner?

Ohio TechAngel Funds, Columbus, Ohio
Number of angels: 282
Who it helps: Supports early-stage Ohio-based information technology, advanced materials, and medical technology companies.

Investors' Circle, San Francisco
Number of angels: 225
Who it helps: Uses private capital to promote businesses that address social and environmental issues.

Golden Seeds LLC, New York City
Number of angels: 190
Who it helps: Members invest directly, or through a managed fund, in companies that are founded by or led by women. Sectors include consumer products, technology, software and life sciences.

North Coast Angel Fund, Cleveland, Ohio
Number of angels: 180
Who it helps: Invests in Ohio-based technology startups.

Band of Angels, Menlo Park, Calif.
Number of angels: 136
Who it helps: Group of former and current high-tech executives that has invested almost $200 million in early-stage technology companies.

Hyde Park Angel Network, Chicago
Number of angels: 133
Who it helps: Members invest in seed and early stage businesses, primarily located in the Midwest. Industries include: information technology, business services, industrial technology, financial services, consumer or industrial products and healthcare services.

Alliance of Angels, Seattle
Number of angels: 100
Who it helps: Early-stage investors in startups based in the Northwest region of the country.

Pasadena Angels, Altadena, Calif.
Number of angels: 100
Who it helps: Provides up to $750,000 in early-stage and seed financing to startups in southern California.

New York Angels Inc, New York City
Number of angels: 99
Who it helps: Made up of entrepreneurs, CEOs, venture capitalists and other business leaders, the group invests between $250,000 and $750,000 in early-stage technology companies generally located in the Northeast.

Figure 14.2 A list according to Entrepreneur.com of the top ten angel investor groups. *Source: http://www.entrepreneur.com/article/220149#*

- Are the owners committed to the business and have their own money invested into the business?
- Is the business growing in sales?
- What does the future of that industry look like?
- Who are the competitors of the brand?

Answers to all of these questions and more should be a part of the business plan.

Financial Basics

A financial plan is one of the most important tools of a business. It shows the probability of making a profit for the business. The three fundamental financial statements are the cash flow statement, income statement,

Figure 14.3 QuickBooks is an effective accounting tool many entrepreneurs prefer to use to help run their business. *Source: Photosebia/ Shutterstock.*

and balance sheet. All of these components are needed to understand the financial impact of the business. An accountant should be a part of the brand venture. Not every entrepreneur is strong with numbers, so an accountant will be able to assist in running the business effectively. There are many facets to a business, and it can become overwhelming for an entrepreneur to do it all successfully. Once a financial plan needs to be put together, it can be created manually or using a budgeting function that comes with most bookkeeping software packages, such as QuickBooks, as shown in Figure 14.3, Bookkeeper, or Sage Peachtree Complete. According to *TopTenREVIEWS,* Sage Peachtree Complete, a brand of Tech Media network, ranked top three in accounting software for 2012 for its ease of help and customer support. Various accounting software can facilitate in managing the business, such as, reports, account receivables, payables, inventory, payroll, invoicing, banking, time billing, and job-costing modules.

When preparing a financial plan, assumptions about the business need to be made. Some questions that will help the entrepreneur in preparing the plan are:

- What sales figures are expected for the year?
- How will sales grow or decline from month to month?
- What are the price points for the brand?
- Will there be any employers or contractors used? If so, how many hours will they work and what will their pay be?
- What salaries will the entrepreneur and partners, if any, draw for the year?
- How much will it cost to manufacture the product along with its packaging?
- What type of facilities will be used? A list of expenses should be formulated, such as rent, utilities, and other recurring upkeep fees.
- How much money is needed to run the business? What will be the interest rate on loans?

Once these questions have been answered and listed, then it is time to create the financial statements.

Cash Flow Statement

The **cash flow statement** summarizes the money that is entering and exiting a business and is important in assessing the availability of funds, as shown in Figure 14.4. The cash flow will show how much cash is coming

Tip 14.2 **Create-a-minute!**

An accountant can be detrimental to the business if accounting is not the entrepreneur's forte. Yet, an entrepreneur should be aware of what is happening with the finances at all times and not rely solely on an accountant.

	[MONTH]	[MONTH]	[MONTH]	[MONTH]	[MONTH]	[MONTH]	[MONTH]	[MONTH]	[MONTH]	[MONTH]	[MONTH]	[MONTH]	TOTAL
Beginning Cash Balance													$0
Cash Inflows (Income):													$0
Accts. Rec. Collections													$0
Sales & Receipts													$0
Equity Received													$0
Loan Received													$0
Other:													$0
Total Cash Inflows													$0
Available Cash Balance													$0
Cash Outflows (Expenses):													$0
Advertising													$0
Bank Service Charges													$0
Shipping and Delivery													$0
Inventory Purchases													$0
Miscellaneous													$0
Office													$0
Payroll													$0
Payroll Taxes													$0
Professional Fees													$0
Rent													$0
Subscriptions & Dues													$0
Supplies													$0
Taxes & Licenses													$0
Utilities & Telephone													$0
Production Expense													$0
Marketing and Promotion													$0
Web and Security Services													$0
Tradeshow													$0
Other:													$0
Subtotal													$0
Other Cash Out Flows:													$0
Capital Purchases													$0
Owner's Draw													$0
Other:													$0
Subtotal													$0
Total Cash Outflows													$0
Ending Cash Balance													$0

Figure 14.4 A sample of a pro forma cash flow statement for a company. *Source: http://www. entrepreneur.com/formnet/form/939*

compared with how much is being spent month to month. The entrepreneur and investors are able to see where the cash is going and if more or less is going out in a specific month. The statement also will show how cash is coming in per month either through sales, accounts receivables, equity, loans, or any other sources of income. This statement will help in pinpointing any problems that may arise with cash flow.

For example, a business can show that it is making a profit, but if an account is late on a payment or defaults on a payment, then the entrepreneur can look at the statement and see where the company can cut costs. It is imperative to investigate your company's cash flow, such as where money is coming from and going and what particular changes can be made to avoid a loss. The fundamentals of a cash flow are:

- How much cash the entrepreneur has at the beginning of each month
- Cash that is going into the business
- Cash that is going out of the business
- Ending balance for each month

When it comes to managing the financials of the business, an entrepreneur must be meticulous in daily record keeping.

Income Statement

The **income statement,** also known as the profit and loss statement or revenue and expense statement, measures a company's revenues, as shown in Figure 14.5. The income statement captures the company's financial performance over an accounting period. The statement reviews the revenues and expenses that are acquired through operating and nonoperating activities. A net profit and loss is shown in the statement as well. The income statement is separated into the revenues section, which includes the sales of the brand throughout the year, and the expense section, which illustrates all expenses that have been incurred throughout the year.

Balance Sheet

The **balance sheet** represents the company's assets, liabilities, and equity at a specific point in time as shown in Figure 14.6. The balance sheet is based on the following financial structure:

Assets = Liabilities + Shareholders' Equity

The assets are resources that the business owns at a given point in time. These resources can include cash, inventory, equipment, and buildings. Current assets are assets that develop within a year. The total of current assets include cash, accounts receivable, inventory, notes receivable, and any other current assets in the business. Fixed assets are any equipment or building purchased that is a year or older.

The liabilities are based on the company's legal debts or obligations at a given time. Current liabilities are debts and obligations that must be paid within a year. Current liabilities consist of accounts payable, accrued expenses, notes payable, and current fraction on long-term debt. Non-current liabilities are debt that is paid after the year. Shareholders' equity constitutes funds that have been contributed by the shareholders plus any retained earnings (or minus any losses). The two sides of the balance sheet must be equal as illustrated in the above formula.

YEAR-END INCOME STATEMENT <COMPANY NAME>
JANUARY 1, 2014 ENDING DECEMBER 31, 2014 PROJECTED

Sales Revenue	
Product/Service 1	
Product/Service 2	
Product/Service 3	
Product/Service 4	
Total Net Sales [A]	0
Cost of Sales	
Product/Service 1	
Product/Service 2	
Product/Service 3	
Product/Service 4	
Total Cost of Goods Sold [B]	0
Gross Income [C = A – B]	**0**
Operating Expenses	
Sales and Marketing	
Advertising	
Direct marketing	
Other expenses (specify)	
Other expenses (specify)	
Total Sales and Marketing Expenses [D]	0
Research and Development	
Technology licenses	
Patents	
Other expenses (specify)	
Other expenses (specify)	
Total Research and Development Expenses [E]	0
General and Adminstrative	
Wages and salaries	
Outside services	
Supplies	
Meals and entertainment	
Rent	
Telephone	
Utilities	
Depreciation	
Insurance	
Repairs and maintenance	
Other expenses (specify)	
Other expenses (specify)	
Total General and Administrative Expenses [F]	0
Total Operating Expenses [G = D + E + F]	0
Income from Operations [H = C – G]	**0**
Other Income [I]	
Taxes	
Income taxes	
Payroll taxes	
Real estate taxes	
Other taxes (specify)	
Other taxes (specify)	
Total Taxes [J]	0
Net Income [K = H + I – J]	**0**

Figure 14.5 A sample of an income statement for a company. *Source: http://www. entrepreneur.com/formnet/form/939*

COMPANY NAME
YEAR-END BALANCE SHEET (PROJECTED)

	2014
Assets	
Non-current assets	
Intangible assets	
Property, plant and equipment	
Less: accumulated depreciation	
Non-current other assets	
	$ [A]
Current assets	
Cash and cash equivalents	
Accounts receivable	
Inventories	
Security deposit	
Current other assets	
	$ [B]
Total assets	$ [C = A − B]
Liabilities and equity	
Non-current liabilities	
Loans	
Mortgages	
Non-current other liabilities	
Total non-current liabilities	$ [D]
Current liabilities	
Accounts payable	
Line of credit	
Other current liabilities	
Total current liabilities	$ [E]
Total non-current and current liabilities	$ [F = D = E]
Equity	
Equity investments	
Retained earnings	
Less: Owner's and investor's draw	
Total equity	$ [G]
Total liabilities and equity	$ [H = F + G]

Figure 14.6 A sample of a balance sheet statement for a company. *Source: http://www. entrepreneur.com/formnet/form/939*

Key-Operating Ratios

The key-operating ratio is a snapshot of the comparison of two or more entries from the financial statement. An investor will look at the key-operating ratios to see how the company is performing to help decide whether to invest. Ratios can illustrate any trends or issues that a business is having and will assist in comparing with others within the industry in publications, such as key business ratios published by Dun & Bradstreet. The key-operating ratios can be viewed as:

- Operating financial ratios show how a company manages its operations while making use of its capital. An example would be inventory control.

  Formula for inventory turnover ratio = costs of goods sold/average inventory balance

  Example: 85,000/42,000 = 2.02 times

- Profitability financial ratios look at how proficient the company is being executed. A company that works on higher gross profit margins puts itself in a better situation when analyzing the business.

  Formula for gross margin ratio: gross profit/net sales

  Example: 43,000/124,000 =34.7%

- Leverage financial ratios are any ratios that show how the business is using borrowed money.

  Formula: net debt/equity

  Example: 89,000/160,000 = 0.05

- Solvency financial ratios take a look at whether a company can pay its long-term debts and the interest on those debts.

  Formula: Total debt/total asset

  Example: 48,000/98,000 = 49%

- Liquidity financial ratios show whether a business can pay its current debt.

  Formula: current ratio = current assets/current liabilities

  Example: 64,000/24,000 = 2.66:1

Financial Plan

All three statements go hand in hand; each one provides information that is needed to complete the other. Together the three statements are the foundation of the determining whether the business can be profitable. The plan needs to be reviewed often to see if any problems have arisen and if there is enough cash coming in to sustain the business. The main goal of starting up a brand is to make sure that there is a profit. The first year this may not happen, but the goal is to make sure that the brand breaks even and is not losing money, which would make the business unsustainable. The **break-even point** is where revenue equals expenses during a specific time period shown in Figure 14.7. The formula for the break-even point is:

Break-even point = fixed expenses/gross margin percentage

COMPANY NAME

BREAK-EVEN ANALYSIS

	2014
Sales	$ [A]
Less Variable Expenses	
Materials	
Labor	
Variable overhead	
Other	
Contribution Margin	$ [B]
Contribution Margin Ratio	$ [C = B / A]
Fixed Expenses	
Salaries and wages	
Employee benefits	
Payroll taxes	
Rent	
Utilities	
Repairs and maintenance	
Insurance	
Travel	
Telephone	
Postage	
Office supplies	
Advertising	
Marketing/promotion	
Professional fees	
Training and development	
Bank charges	
Depreciation	
Interest Expense	
Other	
Total Fixed Expenses	$ [E]
Total Fixed Expenses Ratio	$ [F = E / A]
Break-Even Sales	$ {I = A * H]
Break-Even %	$ [H = (E / (E + G))]
Operating Profit	$ [G = A − B + E]

Figure 14.7 A sample of a break-even analysis for a company. *Source: http://www. entrepreneur.com/formnet/form/939*

An example would be: if the monthly expenses for the brand are $15,000 and the gross margin percentage is 50 percent, then one would divide $15,000 by 50 percent to get a break-even number of $30,000, which is the amount the brand would need to sell to break even. An accountant should be used or at least consulted when working on the financial plan.

Intellectual Property Rights

A great idea can many times be taken and copied. Because of this risk, an entrepreneur should look into protecting the brand's intellectual property. **Intellectual property** is the original ideas of an individual or a company, which are protected under the Intellectual Property Law. The purpose of IP laws is to encourage ideas and the creation of new services and products to stimulate economic growth. There are three main methods of protecting one's work in the United States: using copyrights, patents, and trademarks.

- Copyright, shown in Figure 14.8, is a form of protection provided by the laws of the United States (Title 17, U.S. *Code*) to the authors of "original works of authorship. This protection is available to both published and unpublished works.[1] Ideas cannot be protected, but how they are articulated can be. To officially protect one's expressive art, it should be registered with the U.S. Copyright Office. Copyrights include[2]:
    - Literary works
    - Musical works, including any accompanying words
    - Dramatic works, including any accompanying music
    - Pantomimes and choreographic works
    - Pictorial, graphic, and sculptural works
    - Motion pictures and other audiovisual works
    - Sound recordings
    - Architectural works
- Patents protect companies and individuals from having their inventions made, sold, or used by someone else during a certain period. Patents are usually good for about twenty years in the United States. Patents should be registered with the U.S. Patent and Trademark Office. Due to the complexity of the process and time to apply for a patent and get approval, an intellectual property attorney should be used.
- A **trademark** as shown is Figure 14.9 is a word, phrase, symbol, design, or a combination of these elements, that identifies and differentiates the source of the goods. A trademark will protect the name and logo of a brand, but not the design. A **service mark** is a word, phrase, symbol, design, or a combination of these, that identifies and differentiates the source of a service rather than goods. A mark does not need to be registered, but it has its benefits:
    - Public acknowledgment of ownership of the mark
    - Exclusive rights to the mark
    - The ability to take action in court if there is infringement on the mark
    - The right to use the federal registration symbol ®
    - A record in the online database for the United States Patent and Trademark Office

Figure 14.8 The copyright logo is used to let people know that all rights are reserved to the authorship. *Source: "All About Copyrights." Commerce.Gov: United States Department of Commerce. N.p., n.d. Web. 14 July 2012. http://www.uspto.gov/smallbusiness/copy rights/faq.html.*

Figure 14.9 The following brands are trademarked to protect the brands' logos. Hugo Boss Sign Soho Manhattan. *Source: wdstock/ iStockphoto.*

Both Christian Louboutin SA and Yves Saint Laurent America Inc. are claiming victory in the appellate court's decision Wednesday to uphold the former's protection for its red-sole shoes, although the court modified the decision to exclude instances when the upper of the footwear is also red.

William Borchard, partner at intellectual property law firm Cowan Liebowitz & Latman, said, "Louboutin may have lost this particular battle against YSL [over the monochromatic shoes], but he won the war against everyone else. It was unfortunate that they decided to sue YSL on an all-red shoe–that's what started [them] off down a wrong track. But the color of a sole can't stand on its own without the shoe. The court reached the right conclusion that the red sole did have secondary meaning."

The appellate court is, in effect, modifying Louboutin's red sole trademark. It wrote in its decision that the secondary meaning of the mark held by the designer "extends only to the use of a lacquered red outsole that contrasts with the adjoining portion of the shoe."

The court added, "We modify the red sole mark … insofar as it is sought to be applied to any shoe bearing the same color 'upper' as the outsole. We therefore instruct the Director of the Patent and Trade Office to

limit the registration of the red sole mark to only those situations in which the red lacquered outsole contrasts in color with the adjoining 'upper' of the shoe. We therefore affirm the denial of the preliminary injunction insofar as Louboutin could not have shown a likelihood of success on the merits in the absence of an infringing use of the red sole mark by YSL."

Source: Michelle Tay. 2012. "Coury Upholds, Modifies Louboutin Trademark." *WWD*, Sept. 5. www.wwd.com/footwear-news/business/court-upholds-modifies-louboutin-trademark-6226489

Image Source: Brian Jannsen/Alamy

A business can use "TM" (trademark) or "SM" (service mark) to let people know that there is a claim of ownership to the mark, but the ® symbol cannot be used unless the product or service has been registered with United States Patent and Trademark Office (USPTO). In the United States, an application can be filed to the U.S. Copyright Office, which handles all copyright registration. An entrepreneur must perfom due diligence, and hiring a lawyer will assist in this when it comes time to defend intellectual property. An intellectual property attorney should perform the search and assess whether the entrepreneur can apply for ownership to a trademark or service mark. The current average fee to file for a trademark is between $275.00 and $375.00.

Tip 14.3 Create-a-minute!

When creating a brand, make sure that the name has not been trademarked. A search can be done with the United States Patent and Trademark Office.

Summary

The business entity is what is needed to actually start the business and incorporate it. The form that is chosen will affect the liability, taxation, and record-keeping obligations of the business. A lawyer will be beneficial in establishing the business entity of the business. When starting the brand, capital will need to be raised to get the business up and running. There are various ways to find funding such as one's own money, bank loans, funds from an investor, or from friends and family. Anyone loaning money will want to know when they might see a return on investment. The financial plan, which is the backbone of the business, will show that it is a profitable endeavor. The three primary financial statements (balance sheet, income statement, and cash flow statement) will show where the money is going and how much revenue is coming in. Once this is set in place, it is important to protect the entrepreneur's idea by trademarking the brand.

Online Resources

U.S. Patent and Trademark Office
The USPTO is a federal agency that grants patents and trademarks.
www.uspto.gov

U.S. Small Business Administration
Offers assistance to small businesses.
www.sba.gov

Internal Revenue Service (IRS)
The IRS provides America's taxpayers with information for understanding and meeting their tax responsibilities.
www.irs.gov

Activity 14.1

Use Figures 14.4 through 14.7 to create a financial plan for the brand. List the start-up funding and expenditure assumptions. The instructor will provide you with a loan for the start-up company.

Activity 14.2

Research and find out if the intended brand's name is taken by searching the United States Patent and Trademark Office. If it is taken, then list the serial number and trademark term. Come up with other forms that are available and list the new name.

Notes

1. U.S. Copyright Office. "Copyright Basics." *Copyright: United States Copyright Office.* Accessed July 27, 2012. http://www.copyright.gov/

2. "All About Copyrights." *Commerce.Gov: United States Department of Commerce.* N.p., n.d. Web. 14 July 2012. http://www.stopfakes.gov/faqs

TRADE TERMS

sole proprietorship

partnership

corporation

subchapter S corporation

S corporation

limited liability corporation (LLC)

venture capitalist

cash flow statement

income statement

balance sheet

break-even point

intellectual property

trademark

service mark

Bibliography

Entrepreneur.com. "Building A Financial Budget." Accessed Aug. 28, 2012. http://www.entrepreneur.com/article/21942.

Entrepreneur.com. "Business Structure Basics." Accessed Dec. 21, 2011. http://www.entrepreneur.com/article/75118

Internal Revenue Service. "Business Structures." Accessed Dec. 21, 2011. http://www.irs.gov/businesses/small/article/0,,id=98359,00.html

Investopedia. "Cash Flow Statement." Accessed July 6, 2012. http://www.investopedia.com/terms/c/cashflowstatement.asp

Investopedia. "Ratios." Accessed Jan. 17, 2013. http://www.investopedia.com/search/allresults.aspx?q=ratios&title=Definitions§ion=definitions

Longenecker, Justin G., Carlo W. Moore, J. William Petty, and Leslie E. Palich. 2007. *Small Business Management: Launching and Growing Entrepreneur Ventures.* Mason, Ohio: South-Western College.

TopTenReviews. "2013 Best Accounting Software Comparisons and Reviews." Accessed Jan. 10, 2013. http://accounting-software-review.toptenreviews.com/

U.S. Small Business Administration. "Borrowing Money." *SBA.gov.* Accessed Aug. 14, 2012. http://www.sba.gov/content/borrowing-money

15

Strategic Growth

Strategic growth is essential to understanding the dynamic timing of the business—knowing when to expand or exit the business. As sales begin to climb, the natural progression is seemingly to multiply what is fundamentally successful in a business, whether it is new product or physical space; entrepreneurs often face junctures of growth. Growth can be a detriment or success to a business. An entrepreneur should have the insight to understand the various strategies that provide stability for profitability. Entrepreneurs ought to learn how to utilize virtual options that cut cost and build virtual teams that enhance efficiency. Entrepreneurs must also have an understanding regarding the exit strategies that yield accelerated growth for the brand.

Work Space

Home Office

Many small businesses start out in the entrepreneur's home as shown in Figure 15.1. When a business is home-based, the cost is minimal compared with a leased or owned space, which can save the entrepreneur money. Entrepreneurs working at home can work as early or late as they want without having to leave the comfort of one's own home. A pitfall that can arise is a lack of discipline. It is easy to engage one's attention elsewhere or get distracted, especially if one does not live alone.

The business also can start to take over one's personal space. It is critical to treat the home office environment as one would a regular office space. The entrepreneur should set specific work hours each day, have a dedicated space in the house for the office, have a dedicated phone line separate from a home phone or cell number, minimize breaks that are taken, and avoid any distraction such as television or doing household chores.

Money may be an issue when starting a brand; so working from home may be the best option for now. If that is the case, make sure that there is

KEY CONCEPTS

+ Determine home office space versus virtual space versus studio space.

+ Define hiring versus contracting versus utilizing interns.

+ Examine brand/product expansion.

+ Understand expansion and viable exit strategies.

Figure 15.1 Working from home is most often cost effective. Organization and prioritization of time are important. *Source: Richard Cartwright/ Disney ABC Television Group/ABC/Getty Images.*

enough space to work. A rented storage space can alleviate some of the same space issues and is a cost-effective way to store the product. The entrepreneur should have a dedicated space and not let the business take over the home. A key to running a successful branded business is to be organized and tidy. At the end of each workday, organize and get ready for the next day. A to-do list is always helpful to make sure all things listed have been done, and if not, carry those to-do items for the next days list. When one is ready to work the next day, the office space should not be left in disarray, so that time the following day is productively spent. Working from home is still an expense to the entrepreneur. If leasing an apartment, the lease should be reviewed to make sure that the landlord has not made any stipulations about running a business from the rented premises.

Virtual Office

A virtual space is a good option when office space and business services are needed, as shown in Figure 15.2. Working from home can be a challenge, and virtual space offers an option that can alleviate some of those challenges. There are companies that charge a weekly or monthly fee, and an office space can be rented when needed. An entrepreneur can still work from home; a virtual office will give the company a professional way to conduct business for the brand. Once the business continues to grow, then virtual services can be added onto the business.

A virtual space can offer:

1. Office space and a conference room. Meeting at a coffee shop or at an entrepreneur's home might not be the best setting. A virtual office will allow the entrepreneur space to meet in a professional setting.

2. A virtual office receptionist service. A virtual receptionist will answer all calls with a personalized greeting and will screen calls, which will be forwarded to the entrepreneur's direct line. This service takes the place of hiring an actual receptionist. Knowing that a business call is coming through will ensure that one is prepared and can walk into a quiet room where a child or pet might not be making noise.

Figure 15.2 A virtual office provides full support without significant overhead. Virtual Office offers various services and pricing. *Source: Stacy Barnett/Shutterstock.*

3. An attended mailing address. It can be an advantage to have mail and packages sent to the virtual office location. Sometimes it is necessary to sign for packages, and it can be time consuming to track down missed deliveries. A virtual office can solve that issue by accepting the company's packages.

CASE STUDY 15.1 **Calling the Spades: Kate and Andy Spade Look Back**

The day after [the 2013] presidential inauguration turned out to be the perfect time to interview Kate and Andy Spade on the 20th anniversary of the company they founded in 1993. For the ceremonial occasion of her dad's incumbency, Sasha Obama had appeared on the mall in a purple coat by Kate Spade, thus handing a reporter an icebreaker on a silver platter—except Kate Spade beat her to the punch.

"So, I read that Sasha was wearing Kate Spade!" she said at the outset of the interview. She cannot take credit for the actual design, as she, her husband, Andy, and their two partners cashed out of the company that bears her name seven years ago to the tune of $59 million.

It must be pretty weird to hear your own name in such a public yet disassociated way.

"Oddly not," said Kate. "I get asked that all the time. I always felt there was me and there was the company. It was obviously very personal, but I didn't confuse a bill not getting paid by Kate Spade as me not paying it."

Before they were Kate Spade the brand, the Spades were college sweethearts from the Midwest, she from Kansas City and he from Arizona. They came to New York after graduation to pursue fashion and advertising. She worked as an accessories editor at *Mademoiselle,* and he was in advertising at TBWA/Chiat/Day.

Neither grew up fantasizing about being fashion designers, but they shared an entrepreneurial itch.

"I thought we'd start our own ad agency," said Andy. "We kind of wanted to do our own thing." One night over dinner at their favorite Mexican restaurant on the Upper West Side, they were talking business ideas and "Andy said, 'Why don't you do handbags? You love handbags, accessories,'" recalled Kate. "And I said, 'It's not like you can just start a handbag company.' And he's like, 'Well, why not?'"

The Spades, who were not yet legally the Spades—Kate Spade had a better ring to it than Kate Brosnahan, her maiden name—did not have a formal business plan, but they did see the proverbial void in the bag market, which had yet to explode for the traditional ready-to-wear designer houses. There was Coach, there were the Europeans, and there was a lot of leather and hardware going on. Kate knew what she wanted: simple, straightforward totes and shoppers. Her original samples were done in linen and burlap, since the only fabric resource willing to sell to a no-name designer with

(continues)

no track record and no minimums turned out to be a potato sack company.

Eventually the bags evolved into the more durable nylon for which she became famous. Spade had 10 black and 10 navy made up for her first trade show at the Jacob K. Javits Convention Center in New York. They didn't write a ton of orders, but they got the right attention, from Judy Collinson at Barneys and Candy Pratts Price of *Vogue*, who featured Kate Spade bags in *Vogue*'s Last Look.

For the first few years the operation was "scrappy." Kate as designer and Andy as creative director worked out of their apartment, took no salaries, and Andy always had one foot out the door, mostly for financial reasons but also because they weren't sure. At one point he and Kate moved to Los Angeles for six months when he accepted a job as creative director at Saatchi & Saatchi. They thought about bailing on Kate Spade altogether, but their partners, Kate's best friends Elyce Arons and Pamela Bell, pleaded—if they [had] quit [then], everyone [would've lost] everything.

"We never thought about starting a company. We just said, 'Let's make some bags and see what happens.' And people ask us now, 'How do I start a company?' It's daunting," said Andy. "You don't start a company; a company is what you become if you are successful, right?"

A big part of what the Spades think made it resonate was their outsider, Midwestern sensibility. "Straightforward," "optimistic," "earnest," "friendly," and "not pretentious" are words they used to describe their vision. Kate is the first to say she was never a trained designer.

"I wasn't always sketching on top of some mountain overlooking the glistening sea in Belize," she said. "The real truth of it is that I was crudely drawing and taking it to a patternmaker I found in the back of *Women's Wear Daily*."

At first, being the girl from Kansas gave Kate a bit of a complex. She recalled how Linda Wells introduced her for her CFDA award, using the word "sensible" to describe the Spade aesthetic. "I remember at first going, 'It's sensible? So are running shoes.' Now I look at [the original bags] and it's true and I like that."

In 1999, the Neiman Marcus Group acquired 56 percent of the company for $33.6 million in cash. "That was kind of a sigh of relief," said Kate. "We could get a little bit lifted off our shoulders financially."

They continued on, market upon market, season after season, building the brand until, in 2006, they walked away. Kate and Andy, along with Arons and Bell, sold the remaining 44 percent of the company to Neiman Marcus, which in turn sold the whole thing to Liz Claiborne Inc. (now Fifth & Pacific Cos. Inc.).

There are no regrets. Judging from their Park Avenue apartment, decorated in an eclectically stylish mix of the modern, classic, and earthy, their front door sweetly covered in artwork by their eight-year-old daughter, Bea, things are pretty rosy in the Kate Spade afterlife.

Kate is a full-time mom, one of her primary reasons for letting go of her business. "Having waited to have a baby as long as I did, which was 42, I wanted to be there," she said. "I felt like it was a luxury I couldn't pass up."

"I think we both loved inventing things and creating things," said Andy. "We created [Kate Spade], and I felt like 15 years was probably five years longer than we thought we would actually go. We're really lucky that it actually worked … I felt like creatively it was complete."

The couple still pays attention to the company, but with a healthy distance. "It's like watching a stock," said Andy. "Exactly," said Kate. "I think they've done a great job, shepherding the brand. That was something we kind of jokingly said as we left, 'Don't make us afraid of our own name!' And we're not."

Source: Jessica Iredale. 2013. "Calling the Spades: Kate and Andy Look Back." *WWD*, Feb. 4. http://www.wwd.com/fashion-news/fashion-features/calling-the-spades-kate-and-andy-spade-look-back-6686321?full=true

Image source: Brian Ach/WireImage/Getty Images

Studio Space

Working away from home can often help in conducting the business efficiently, as shown in Figure 15.3. Coulisse is a window treatment design studio that has an office space where it finds the latest trends and creates fashionable window treatments. A leased studio space, however, should only be considered once the business is growing. Some entrepreneurs jump into this process only to turn around and close shop after a couple of months. A landlord may require a one- to three-year lease. When searching for an office space, make a list of what requirements are needed. Make sure to be thorough and look around; don't jump into the first space that one sees. When the entrepreneur has narrowed down the choice to a couple of spaces, make sure to check out the location during the day and at night.

Things to consider when looking for are spaces are:

- *Location:* the space should be located near clients and suppliers if possible. This will facilitate reaching them as quickly as possible when needed. The location's safety also should be a factor. Studios that are more affordable may not be situated in the safest neighborhoods.
- *Size:* The space should be conservative in size. Once the business grows, then the entrepreneur can look into finding a larger space to work.
- *Cost:* The entrepreneur needs to be conservative when it comes to the cost of leasing the space. It is easy for an entrepreneur to want to lease a space that is brand new and has many amenities, but when starting out it is best to focus on the basics. Also, consider the cost of the day-to-day business, such as utilities, insurance, and maintenance.

Figure 15.3 A studio is an added space in which to run the business more efficiently. Designer Christian Dior working on a new collection in his studio, Paris, France, 1957. *Source: Loomis Dean/Time Life Pictures/Getty Images.*

When comparing rent for a space to run the business, one must factor any build-outs or modifications that need to be made to the space.

Hiring Help

The business will consume much of the entrepreneur's time. Once the business has grown to the extent that the entrepreneur can no longer handle all of its demands, a decision must be reached about whether to hire one or more employees or contract work out to independent providers. The type of work needed will dictate what type of help is required. There are different scenarios to consider, such as whether an employee will be brought on as a payrolled employee, contracted, or interning for the company. These options will depend on how the business is doing overall and how much help is needed.

Employees

Hiring an employee is a significant step in growing the business. An employee should be hired if staff is factored in the budget or if the brand is prospering and needs assistance to remain competitive. Hiring an employee adds legal obligations, liabilities, and expenses. To find out what legal obligations are required in one's state, visit the Secretary of State's website and check the information pages for small businesses. Table 15.1 shows a list of federal laws applicable when hiring an employee. According to Beth Laurence, J.D., writing for *Nolo,* an Internet-based provider of legal information, an entrepreneur must take these steps before an employee is hired:

- Attain an employer identification number (EIN). This number is used for tax purposes. The form can be found on www.irs.gov.
- Register with the state's labor department. State unemployment compensation taxes must be paid (where applicable).
- Obtain workers' compensation insurance. This will protect the entrepreneur if any employee injuries occur on the job.

TABLE 15.1 **FEDERAL EMPLOYMENT LAWS**

LAW	PROHIBITED ACTION/PROTECTION GRANTED
Title VII of the Civil Rights Act of 1964	Discrimination based on race, religion, sex, or creed
The Age Discrimination in Employment Act of 1967	Discrimination against individuals who are 40 years of age or older
The Americans with Disabilities Act of 1990	Discrimination based on disability
The Family Medical Leave Act of 1993	Allows for unpaid leave under certain circumstances

Source: Entrepreneur.com. "Hiring Your First Employee." http://www.entrepreneur.com/article/83774-2

- Set up a payroll system so that taxes, Social Security, and Medicare withholding can be deposited with the IRS.
- Fill out the Employment Eligibility Verification (I-9) form to show that the employee is eligible to work in the United States.
- Report new employee hires to the state's new-hire reporting agency. This report is used to find parents who owe child support.
- Post any workplace notices in a visible spot for an employee to see. The Department of Labor requires that certain notices be posted regarding workers' rights. Visit www.dol.gov/elaws/posters.htm for a list of posters that are required. Figure 15.4 illustrates a poster for labor wages and hours in Illinois.
- Keep a file for each employee. The file should contain any IRS forms, evaluations, and the job application.

Once the entrepreneur has decided that an employee is needed, it is time to search for the right employee. An employee should possess experience and qualifications that can help build the business and increase profits. A referral source is often the best way to recruit an employee. Many people who refer employee candidates are usually confident with the people they refer, since the competence of the prospective employee is a reflection on them. Before the interview process can begin, create a job description that details the role and responsibility of the position. Interview various people and know what questions can be legally asked. Be mindful; the new employee is to aid with the workload and generate revenue for the company. Make sure to conduct reference checks on all employee candidates as fundamental part of the interview process.

Independent Contractor

An independent contractor is different from an employee. The contractor is hired with an agreed-upon contract that states the pay rate, the duration, and the duties for a specific job. Hiring a contractor often can be a savings of time and expenses for the company.

The benefits of hiring an independent contractor are:

1. Payroll taxes, benefits, and insurance are not paid when hiring an independent contractor.
2. An independent contractor's contract can be terminated once the contract ends.
3. Independent contractors can be hired to do work only when needed. This avoids having to terminate an employee if business slows during specific seasons.
4. Specialized work can be obtained through an independent contractor.

The risks to hiring an independent contractor are:

1. There is less control over the job that is being done. A contractor's work is not often conducted under the entrepreneur's direct supervision.
2. Contractors work under contract. Early termination can be considered a breach of contract that can result in potential legal action.

BASIC INFORMATION

current as of June 2012

The U.S. Department of Labor's Wage and Hour Division (WHD) is responsible for administering and enforcing laws that establish minimally acceptable standards for wages and working conditions in this country, regardless of immigration status.

FAIR LABOR STANDARDS ACT

The Fair Labor Standards Act (FLSA) affects most private and public employment. The FLSA requires employers to pay covered non-exempt employees at least the federal minimum wage and overtime pay for all hours worked over 40 in a work week.

Covered employees must be paid for all hours worked in a workweek. In general, compensable hours worked include all time an employee is on duty or at a prescribed place of work and any time that an employee is suffered or permitted to work. This would generally include work performed at home, travel time, waiting time, training, and probationary periods.

• Federal Minimum Wage:
  $7.25 per hour effective July 24, 2009

• Tipped employees may be paid $2.13 per hour; if an employee's tips combined with cash wage does not equal the applicable minimum wage, the employer must make up the difference

• Overtime after 40 hours in a week = 1 ½ times an employee's regular rate of pay

CHILD LABOR

The FLSA also regulates the employment of youth.

Jobs Youth Can Do:
• 13 or younger: baby-sit, deliver newspapers, or work as an actor or performer
• Ages 14-15: certain permitted in such establishments as office work, grocery store, retail store, restaurant, movie theater, and amusement parks
• Age 16-17: Any job not declared hazardous
• Age 18: No restrictions

Hours Youth Ages 14 and 15 Can Work:
• After 7 am and until 7 pm
  (Hours are extended to 9 pm June 1–Labor Day)
• Up to 3 hours, including Fridays
  on a school day
• Up to 18 hours
  in a school week
• Up to 8 hours
  on a non-school day
• Up to 40 hours
  in a non-school week

Note: *Different rules apply to youth employed in agriculture. States also regulate the hours that youth under age 18 may work. To find more information on federal or state rules, log on to www.youthrules.dol.gov.*

FAMILY AND MEDICAL LEAVE ACT

The Family Medical and Leave Act (FMLA) applies to employers who employ 50 or more employees, public agencies, and elementary and secondary schools. Eligible employees are entitled to take unpaid, job-protected leave with continuation of group health insurance coverage for up to 12 workweeks in a 12-month period for:

• the birth and care of a newborn child;
• the placement and care of an child for adoption or foster care;
• for the serious health condition of the employee or the employee's spouse, child, or parent;
• for qualifying exigencies arising out of a covered military member's covered active duty status.

And 26 workweeks of leave during a single 12-month period to care for a covered servicemember with a serious injury or illness.

MIGRANT AND SEASONAL AGRICULTURAL WORKER PROTECTION ACT

The Migrant and Seasonal Agricultural Worker Protection Act (MSPA) requires farm labor contractors, agricultural employers, and agricultural associations who "employ" workers to:

• Pay workers the wages owed when due
• Comply with federal and state safety and health standards if they provide housing for migrant workers
• Ensure that vehicles that they use to transport workers are properly insured, operated by licensed drivers and meet federal and state safety standards
• Provide written disclosure of the terms and conditions of employment

---

CONTACT US:
1-866-4US-WAGE

MORE INFORMATION AVAILABLE AT:
YOUTHRULES!: *WWW.YOUTHRULES.DOL.GOV*   ELAWS: *WWW.DOL.GOV/ELAWS*
WHD WEBSITE: *WWW.WAGEHOUR.DOL.GOV*   DOL WEBSITE: *WWW.DOL.GOV*

Figure 15.4 The U.S. Department of Labor requires that specific posters be posted in a visible spot for employees to see. This is an example for the State of Illinois regarding wages and hours. *Source: U.S. Department of Labor.*

When hiring a contractor, make sure to get referrals from local suppliers as well as your network. It is important to find someone who is qualified.

3. If a contractor is injured while performing work for the employer, he or she can sue the employer. Independent contractors are not covered by workers' compensation insurance.

4. Work executed by an independent contractor might not be able to be copyrighted by the entrepreneur. In contrast, the employer can copyright work that is created by an employee.

Interns

Internships can bring value to the brand as well as providing a great learning experience for the intern. Colleges and universities are excellent sources when seeking an intern, as shown in Figure 15.5. Many higher learning institutions offer credits for an internship, and some require the completion of an internship for graduation. Benefits to hiring an intern are:

1. Interns bring fresh and new ideas. Interns are generally excited about working in a business and are eager to learn. An intern enrolled in school is learning all about the industry and may be able to bring a fresh perspective to the business.

2. Interns are generally well acquainted with technology. Social media tends to be a significant part of their lives as well as computers, smartphones, and tablets. An intern's social media connections and know-how can be extremely valuable.

3. An internship lasts for a fixed period of time. If an intern is not grasping the business, then it is easy to terminate the business

Figure 15.5 Interns are most often beneficial to an entrepreneur. The entrepreneur can teach an intern the many facets of starting a business and acquire new ideas and perspective on launching the brand. *Source: Robert Kneschke/ Shutterstock.*

relationship when the internship comes to an end. If the intern is doing an amazing job, if the budget allows, the intern can be hired.

4. An intern can expand brand awareness. If the intern is having a good experience and is enjoying the job, then he or she is more likely to tell others about the company and the brand.

Some of the pitfalls to hiring an intern are:

1. Training: The investment of time it takes to train an intern, albeit for a short-term relationship.
2. Time: The business demands the entrepreneur's time that there isn't enough time to mentor and teach the intern.
3. Undefined goals: Entrepreneurs can get overwhelmed but do not know what help is needed. Goals should be set prior to

A question that is often brought up for an entrepreneur is to whether or not to pay the intern. The Fair Labor Standards Act states that an intern at a for-profit company must be paid minimum wage if he or she is working 40-plus hours in a work week. Under some circumstances, an employer does not need to pay an intern if the following criteria are met:

- The job done by an intern is similar to what is done in an educational setting.
- The internship should benefit the intern and not solely the employer.
- The intern does not replace another employee, but is supervised by the existing personnel.
- Training that is given to the intern is not done to immediately benefit the entrepreneur.
- A position with the company does not need to be given to the intern at the end of their internship.
- There is an agreement between both the intern and employer that there is no compensation involved.

An intern can be a valuable asset but should never be looked at as free labor. An entrepreneur must follow the Fair Labor Standards Act guidelines. There should be clear and concise goals set in place for the internship. The purpose is to help an intern achieve the goals of understanding and learning the business. In the process, an intern can bring fresh ideas and assist with building the brand.

Brand/Product Expansion

As business growth accelerates and brand loyalty is engaged, many entrepreneurs start to consider ways to diversify the product offering in their category of business. The purpose of expanding the brand's market presence and product selection is to generate an increase in market visibility that will yield greater profits. Much like a product launch, expansion must be strategic and time sensitive to market trends. There are four strategies entrepreneur's commonly used for product diversification and expansion.

New Product

Product expansion brings renewed consumer interest. New product introductions are the lifeline to revenue growth for many small businesses. Although an industry segment can be saturated with competitive products, consumers are eager to experience newness. With apparel, accessories, and footwear, seasonal changes demand new product launches. In most categories of business the expansion can be simplistic and cost effective. The product matrix can be expanded by the differentiation of a new size, flavor, scent, color, or fabric. For example, for a handbag company, such as Rebecca Minkoff, the silhouette of a bag can remain the same, however the fabric may change or the product may be offered in a larger size. Minkoff's signature Morning-After Bag, first introduced in 2005, has skyrocketed Minkoff's career and business (Figure 15.6). It does not need to be a completely new product to constitute growth opportunity.

New Markets

Many companies seek new ways to tap into new market segments with existing products. Entrepreneurs can often target new market segments if the product has cross-functional appeal. Products can be repurposed to serve a new audience. This is quite common for athletic brands. Many sportswear companies create high-performance clothing or footwear for athletes but learn a percentage of the purchasers are wearing the product for the aesthetic or status benefit, not the performance. Fashion influences, such as unique color combinations, will stimulate interest of a shared market (Figure 15.7).

Brand Collaborations

Collaboration has become a successful growth strategy in the fashion industry. Many designers are comingling with brand retailers to create limited-edition collections. Greek fashion designer Mary Katrantzou collaborated with Italian clothing brand Moncler to create a stunning new Moncler M Capsule Collection. The well-received capsule collections from the talented designer brought elegance to the Moncler collection with feminine cuts, bold prints, and a beautiful mix of old-fashioned and contemporary accents (Figure 15.8). Retailers are also tapping into this revenue-generating trend by offering assortments that reach dual consumer groups at varied price classifications. Be mindful that not all collaborations yield the expected outcome, they can be risky and not revenue generating. In 2013, Neiman Marcus and Target partnered to offer a limited edition collection of designer apparel, jewelry, footwear, and home

Figure 15.6 Handbag designer Rebecca Minkoff. *Source: Fairchild Fashion Media.*

Figure 15.7 Vibram Five Fingers running shoe is frequently worn by the non-athlete as well as the athlete. *Source: Solent News/REX USA Ltd.*

Figure 15.8 Fall 2013 brand collaboration between Moncler and Mary Katrantzou. *Source: Left: Getty Images. Right: Corbis.*

goods that were distributed simultaneously at both retailers (Figure 15.9). The monumental partnership gained mass popularity, however the products did not trend well at the register. Products were almost immediately markdown to clearance to get rid of excess inventory. Collaborating with another brand or brand retailer to co-label, co-design, or co-join ingenuity will often ignite a new consumer group; expand market visibility and generated additional revenue.

Figure 15.9 In 2012, Neiman Marcus and Target Corporation brand partnered for a limited-edition collection of designer apparel, accessories, and home goods. *Source: Fairchild Fashion Media.*

New Demographic

Entrepreneurs often penetrate the market by placing product in a niche market. One way to expand the brand's reach is to increase the demographic segment. Products can be appealing to another untapped market segment. This is often the case with beauty products. Often, highlighting an existing ingredient can trigger a new demographic to emerge. For example, in the beauty industry a significant product shift are those with anti-aging ingredients (Figure 15.10). These products are not solely pitched to the mature consumer, but also to youthful consumers as a preventative product to retain their youth. Eye cream was once targeted to middle-aged women; now young women are purchasing nutrient-rich eye creams to prevent wrinkles in the eye area and prevent the need for cosmetic enhancement. A strategic alignment with the new demographic segment can yield significant growth to the business.

International Partnerships

With the Internet, many entrepreneurs have the luxury of exposing their brands to an international consumer market. There are a plethora of online retailers that have an international client base. This type of partnership will enable a brand extension that benefits the brand image and notoriety abroad. For example, although the grassroots Canadian retailer lululemon athletica is sold domestically, the company has extended its international reach beyond the United States to engage new international markets (Figure 15.11). They test market in international showrooms to ensure viability in the market. In 2013, key market tests were performed in London, Singapore, Netherlands, Germany, and China.

Figure 15.10 Anti-aging beauty products are targeted to youthful consumers. *Source: Science & Society Picture Library/SSPL/Getty Images.*

Figure 15.11 lululemon has extended its international reach beyond the United States to engage new international markets. *Source: Wolffy/Alamy.*

Exit Strategies

In this day, time, and age, the evolution of a brand and its product matrix is limitless. Parallel to the liveliness of a business plan, entrepreneurs often will have a strategy or plan in place to exit the business. This voluntary plan often is considered when the company has a strong valuation and has achieved a predetermined revenue goal or as a way of escape for a business that is underperforming. Entrepreneurs do not view exit strategies with remorse but a sense of achievement in the face of success or a positive way to mitigate failure in a challenged business.

The timeline for getting out of a business is determined by the complexity of the business and the decision underlying the reason for the exit. Unless the business is going through an initial public offering (IPO) or being bought out by a larger company, the exit process will involve:

- An agreement and authorization from owners to dissolve
- Designating an Exit leader
- Onboard professional experts, such as an attorney and accountant
- Preparing a list of assets
- Performing a valuation of the business
- Developing a schedule for implementation
- Releasing announcements and notices
- Concluding or transferring contract obligations
- Closing operations
- Disposing or transferring assets
- Preparing final financial documents
- Filing article of dissolution
- Closing bank accounts
- Storing business records

The goal is to exit the business by maximizing the value of the company during every stage of the business and before converting it to cash. The exit strategy and process is unique to every business entity. Many companies involve legal counsel to escort them through the exit from beginning to end.

Summary

Growth is natural progression. Entrepreneurs have to make tough choices to protect the bottom line of the business. The discipline and maturity needed to have a home office must be equivalent to the level of desire you might associate with being a corporate climber. The virtual space provides a professional setting for phone conferences and meetings. To maintain financial stability during growth, entrepreneurs may choose to bring on interns or contractors in lieu of hiring full- or part-time employees. Entrepreneurs must decide how to expand the brand's exposure or product matrix and when to employ exit strategies.

Online Resources

U.S. Department of Labor
The U.S. Department of Labor (DOL) looks after and promotes the well-being of job seekers, wage earners, and retirees of the United States.
www.dol.gov

NOLO Law for All
A website to help answer legal and business questions for consumers and small businesses.
www.nolo.com

Biz Office
A website offering advice for small business owners.
www.bizoffice.com

Activity 15.1

What method of product expansion is most appropriate for your brand/product? How would you expand your market reach? Discuss.

Bibliography

Fishman, Steven. "Pros and Cons of Hiring Independent Contractors." *NOLO Law for All.* Accessed Aug. 15, 2012. http://www.nolo.com/legal-encyclopedia/pros-cons-hiring-independent-contractors-30053.html

Meadows, Toby. 2010. *How To Set Up And Run A Fashion Label.* London: Laurence King Publishers.

Small Business Notes. "Exit Strategies" Accessed September, 2012. http://www.smallbusinessnotes.com/managing-your-business/exit-strategies.html

U.S. Department of Labor. "Wage and Hour Division (WHD): Fact Sheet #71 Internship Programs Under The Fair Labor Standards Act." Accessed Aug. 15, 2012. http://www.dol.gov/whd/regs/compliance/whdfs71.htm

YEC Women. 2011. "5 Reasons You Should Hire an Intern and 3 Reasons You Shouldn't." Forbes.com, Dec. 6. Accessed Aug. 15, 2012. http://www.forbes.com/sites/yec/2011/12/06/5-reasons-you-should-hire-an-intern-and-3-reasons-you-shouldnt/

Glossary

absolute quota: no more than the amount allotted can be allowed entry during a quota period.

African Growth and Opportunity Act (AGOA): created to expand U.S. trade and investment with sub-Saharan Africa, to stimulate economic growth, to encourage economic integration, and to facilitate sub-Saharan Africa's integration into the global economy.

Andean Trade Preference Act (ATPA)/Andean Trade Promotion and Drug Eradication Act (ATPDEA): created to help the Andean countries (Bolivia, Colombia, Ecuador, and Peru) in their fight against drug production and trafficking by expanding their economic alternatives and providing duty-free treatment for certain products.

artisanship entrepreneur: a person with primarily technical skills and little business knowledge who starts a business.

balanced assortment: a well-planned variety of products that appeals to a specific market.

balance sheet: represents the company's assets, liabilities, and equity at a specific point in time.

behavioral segmentation: classifying customers by comparable purchasing intentions and behavior.

best seller: a high sales volume item that is considered the best performing.

blog: a lesser version of a content site, usually lists its content in a chronological order.

brand: a distinct entity with a name, sign, or set of perceptions intended to create an identity and differentiation among likeness. It represents a product, idea, or service.

brand analysis: sizing up the industry, evaluating the competition, and creating a strategic plan.

brand equity: the value of a brand.

brand extensions: product lines marketed under the same general brand as a previous item or items.

brand identity: the personality of a product. It is a set of distinct characteristics that provides identity cues to the consumer.

branding: the process of attaching a name, image, or reputation to a product, idea, or service. It is a vital strategy laced within brand development.

brand loyalty: when a consumer buys the same manufacturer-originated product or service repeatedly over time rather than buying from competition within the category.

brand name: a symbol, word, logo, or set of perceptions intended to identify or represent a product or service.

brand positioning: a company's intended posture and image of the brand in the mind of the consumer. It highlights the brand's differentiation among the competition and its advantage in the price classification.

brand statement: defines the company's brand message and promise. It is a touchstone to communicate the intrinsic value of the brand as well as provide direction for where the brand is going in the market.

brand story: generates brand power through an emotional connection with consumers, whereas the brand is perceived as an extension of their personality and lifestyle.

break-even point: when revenue equals expenses during a specific time period, i.e., the point when sales cover all direct and indirect expenses.

Caribbean Basin Initiative (CBI) and the Caribbean Basin Economic Recovery Act (CBERA): intended to facilitate the development of the Caribbean Basin economies. The act provides the countries with duty-free access to the U.S. market for most goods.

Caribbean Basin Trade Partnership Act (CBPTA): a free-trade agreement between the United States and Barbados, Belize, Guyana, Haiti, Jamaica, Panama, St. Lucia, and Trinidad and Tobago.

cash flow statement: summarizes the money that is entering and exiting a business; important in assessing the availability of funds.

chargeback or **chargeback allowance:** payment back to the retailer due to reasons such as late deliveries, issues with quality, or below or above the intended order amount; or obtaining compensation from a vendor for violations of the retailer's regulations, as stated in the vendor guidelines.

code of conduct: guidelines governing business conduct and practices for entities in a business relationship.

collection: a group of related products at a designer to contemporary price zone.

company description: a summary of a company's history—how it was founded and by whom, what its products are, and why they are unique.

competitive advantage/edge: when the factors critical for success within the industry permit the brand to outperform its competitors.

competitor-based pricing: a price structure that varies depending on where the competition is priced.

concept board: a visual montage of images, color palette, swatches, textures, and miscellaneous items that inspires creative excitement towards a cohesive product collection.

conditions of sale: arrangements for a sale that are agreed upon by a buyer and seller and may include the net terms, how the goods will be shipped, and so on.

contractor: an independent entity that agrees to furnish a certain number or quantity of goods, material, equipment, personnel, and/or services that meet or exceed stated requirements or specifications, at a mutually agreed upon price and within a specified timeframe.

conversion rate: the ratio of people who take a preferred action.

co-op or **advertising allowance:** a fee, usually shown as a percentage, to help a retailer with the cost of advertising the brand.

core competencies: what a company does best.

corporation: an entity that manages the everyday jobs of a business and is subject to more regulations and tax requirements than a sole proprietorship or a partnership.

cost-based pricing: determining price by adding a profit percentage on top of the cost of manufacturing the product.

cost of goods sold: what the designer/entrepreneur pay to manufacture each product.

cost sheet: used to calculate the total cost of manufacturing a product.

creative statement: communicates the point of origin, the point of view, the color story, fabric selection, texture, silhouette, and the overarching creative intent for the product.

customer-based pricing: pricing based on an understanding of how much the customer will be willing to pay.

demographic segmentation: dividing the market based on the demographics, such as gender, age, household size, income, occupation, and other variables.

direct cost: actual cost to produce the product. This includes materials, trimmings, labor, packaging, and transportation.

direct mail: featuring a variety of new products or specific seasonal trends that are desired by the target market in a printed form that is sent to the consumer, usually via a catalog or a look book.

direct market channel: any conduit that connects the product producer to the end user.

direct selling: the sale of a consumer product or service, person-to-person, that's away from a fixed retail location and marketed through independent sales representatives.

discretionary income: the income left over after spending on personal necessities, such as food, shelter, and clothing.

distribution channel: a path through which goods and services flow from the company to the consumer.

distribution intensity: the availability and the level of saturation of the product in the marketplace in a concentrated geographic area or channel.

distribution management: the logistical routing used to deliver product from the production facility to the point-of-sale. It includes the planning of optimal unit quantities for delivery for a specific channel partner.

domain name: an identification string of characters that enables people to find your site on the web using an address bar.

dumping: exporting goods at prices lower than the home-market prices.

duty-free: goods on which import duty is not charged, usually only on items sold to departing passengers in an airport.

e-commerce: the buying and selling of products and services through an electronic medium.

electronic data interchange (EDI): a real-time online system used by retailers to handle most communications with a vendor, including issuing orders, reorders, and handling returns.

eponymous brand: brands that reflect the name of the person who has inspired, designed, or created the idea, product, or service.

executive summary: outlines the who, what, where, when, how, and why of the marketing plan.

exclusive distribution: a strategy where a company will distribute their products to a single channel partner.

exports: products of local producer sold to other countries.

geographic segmentation: the means of dividing the market into groups according to a specific region.

grading: adding or decreasing inches (or other measurement units such as millimeters) to a specific part of the sample-sized pattern in order to size up or size down.

guaranteed sale: when a retailer does not sell through the product and wants the brand to take it back after a season.

host provider: maintains a connection to the Internet.

import quotas: a quantity control on imported merchandise for a certain period of time.

imports: products of a foreign producer brought into a country.

income statement: also known as the profit and loss statement (P&L) or revenue and expense statement; measures a company's revenues.

indirect costs: all costs that are not part of the direct costs, e.g., advertising and other marketing costs.

indirect market distribution: the function of selling a product or service from business to business, commonly called B2B.

informational site: gives information about the brand, but one is not able to sell product through it.

initial cost estimate: an approximation of what the item might initially cost. During this process, a prototype is created to estimate the initial cost. The initial cost estimate is sometimes referred to as "pre-costing" or "quick costing" in the industry.

inspection: an activity such as measuring, examining, testing or gauging one or more characteristics of a product or service and comparing the results with specified requirements in order to establish whether conformity is achieved for each characteristic.

intellectual property: the original ideas of an individual or a company, which are protected under the Intellectual Property Law.

intensive distribution: a distribution approach that concentrates product into channels for the targeted consumer to encounter the product at maximum capacity without saturation.

Jordan Free Trade Area Agreement: The act expanded the trade relationship between Jordan and the U.S. by reducing barriers for services, providing protection for intellectual property, and requiring effective labor and environmental enforcement.

keystoning: doubling a product's cost to determine the wholesale cost.

landing page: the page that visitors land on when clicking on a link.

limited liability corporation (LLC): has two or more members and partners report their individual share of the earnings and losses.

line: a group of related products at a moderate to budget price zone.

line sheet: a set of documents that communicate key product information to prospective buyers.

manufacturer: an entity that makes goods through a process involving raw materials, components, or assemblies, usually on a large scale, with different operations divided among different workers.

market demand: demand generated from all potential customers for a specific product over a specific period of time.

marketing mix: a combination of marketing tools that are used to satisfy customers and company objectives.

market penetration: the amount of sales or adoption of a product compared to the total theoretical market for that product or service.

market research: the process of gathering, analyzing, and interpreting information about a market, about a product or service to be offered for sale in that market, and about the past, present, and potential customers for the product or service; research into the characteristics, spending habits, location, and needs of your business's target market, the industry as a whole, and the particular competitors you face.

market segmentation: a subset of a market made up of people or organizations with one or more characteristics that cause them to demand similar products and/or services based on qualities of those products, such as price or function.

market share: the percentage of industry or a market's sales generated by a particular company.

masstige: a compound from the words *mass* and *prestige*. The term is used for products aimed at providing luxury to the masses.

m-commerce (mobile commerce): making purchases using a smartphone.

merchandise classification system: alphanumeric codes that provide identity to the product that results in a style number. A merchandise classification system facilitates planning and developing a comprehensive product collection for consumer selection.

merchandising: the combination of having the right product at the right time in the right quantities in the right distribution channel with the right marketing to reach the target consumer.

mission statement: defines the business/brand, and identifies its reason for its existence.

multisensory experience: a holistic combination of sensory information that filters through the five senses: sight, smell, touch, taste, and hearing.

niche development: a focused, targetable product or service that can be created for the intended market.

North American Free Trade Agreement (NAFTA): an agreement reached by the United States, Canada, and Mexico that eliminated a variety of fees to encourage free trade between the countries.

objective: a goal that can be achieved within a set and expected timeframe with resources.

opportunistic entrepreneur: a person with both superior managerial skills and technical knowledge who starts a business.

order form: an actual form used to record the order. It is an imperative document to close a sale.

partnership: when two or more people unite to have ownership of the business.

personal assessment: a questionnaire or other assessment device used to determine one's qualities related to a certain group of characteristics. The personal assessment offered in Table 1.2 measures the reader's entrepreneurial traits.

planograms: visual representation of a store's products or services and are considered a tool for visual merchandising.

press kit (media kit): a comprehensive packet of information in print or electronic form that is created for use by the press.

primary research: research conducted firsthand.

product assortment: a cohesive group of related products distinct from each other.

product development: the synergistic efforts of market and trend research, planning, designing, merchandising, and production processes to create a product for the intended consumer.

product development calendar: a cross-functional view of the entire product development cycle from concept to production on a single system of record.

product life cycle: the amount of time a product is viable to consumers in the marketplace.

prototype: an early sample that is created to test a concept.

psychographic segmentation: examining groups of customers according to their lifestyles by looking at attributes relating to personality, values, attitudes, or interests.

purchase invoice: a document used for billing items purchased in a transaction.

purchase orders (PO): buyer-generated documents that authorize a purchase transaction.

qualitative research: identifies useful information through market analysis.

quality assurance: ensuring quality product free of defects, poor workmanship, or color shading problems: all activities that seek to guarantee the quality of work.

quantitative research: looks for ways to quantify information using numbers.

retailers: sell product directly to target consumers.

sale price: what the retailer will sell the merchandise for.

sales projections (sales forecasts): They provide an estimate of a company's prospective sales for a given timeframe.

sales representative: a person who sells the product for the brand for a fee, usually a percentage of the sales.

sample or production sample: a product that is given to the buyer so that he or she may see a product before committing to a purchase; a product prototype.

S corporation: similar to a partnership in which income or losses are passed through to individual tax returns; has the same corporate makeup as a standard corporation.

search engine optimization (SEO): the process of getting traffic from the "free," "organic," "editorial," or "natural" listings on search engines.

secondary research: information taken from other resources.

segmentation variables: examining the market through geographic, demographic, psychographic, affirmative and cognitive, and behavioral segmentation.

selective distribution: to strategically select channel partners to sell products.

service mark: a word, phrase, symbol, design, or a combination of these, that identifies and differentiates the source of a service rather than goods.

slotting fee: a fee that is charged to the brand to house their product in a store.

social-cultural segmentation: examining a social group and its culture.

social media: forms of electronic communication, such as websites for social networking and microblogging (Tumblr, Twitter), through which users create online communities to share information, ideas, personal messages, and other content, such as videos.

social responsibility: is acting with concern and sensitivity and staying aware of the impact of your actions on others, particularly the disadvantaged.

sole proprietorship: the most common form of business organization for entrepreneurs. There is only one owner, which gives the entrepreneur complete freedom to run the business.

strategic sourcing: finding the most cost-effective way to manufacture one's product.

strategy: draws from market research and includes the product mix plan to achieve maximum profit potential.

subchapter S corporation: similar to a partnership in which income or losses are passed through to individual tax returns and has the same corporate makeup as a standard corporation.

swatch card: a single card with multiple fabric pieces mounted on it or a set of individual fabric cards that correlate to the product assortment.

SWOT analysis: an analysis often done to comprehend the **s**trengths, **w**eakness, **o**pportunities, and **t**hreats that lie within the brand.

tactic: the advantageous action to meet the goals of a plan.

tagline: the verbal or written portion of a message that summarizes the main idea in a few memorable words.

target market: the consumers upon whom a product's or brand's marketing is focused.

tariff or duty: tax levied by governments on the value of goods based on freight and insurance of imported products.

tariff-rate quotas: import quota allows a limited quantity of goods into a country at a reduced duty rate during a specified period.

textile headers: free textile sample cuts being manufactured by a mill.

trademark: a word, phrase, symbol, design, or a combination of these elements, that identifies and differentiates the source of the goods.

trade shows: places where producers of products or services sell to retailers or wholesalers.

transshipping: transferring for further transportation from one shipment to another.

trend: a movement or a general direction that something moves determined by observation.

trend research and **trend forecasting:** actionable trade intelligence to improve a brand's product strategy, consumer relations, and sales.

U.S.–Chile Free Trade Agreement (US-CFTA): eliminated tariffs and opens markets, reduced barriers for trade in services, and required effective labor and environmental enforcement.

U.S.–Israel Free Trade Area Agreement: expanded trade and investment between the United States and Israel by reducing barriers and promoting trade transparency.

U.S.–Singapore Free Trade Agreement (Singapore FTA): expanded U.S. market access in goods, services, government procurement, intellectual property, and provided cooperation promoting labor rights and the environment.

vendor: an entity that sells a product or service.

venture capitalist: someone who will invest in the business for a percentage of the ownership.

vision statement: defines the brand's purpose while communicating the value of the brand.

wholesale cost: what the retailer pays to purchase the product.

wholesalers: purchase products from entrepreneur and in turn sell it to other resellers, such as retailers or other wholesalers.

zeitgeist: the spirit of the times.

Index